A PEDAGOGY OF RESPONSIBILITY

Drawing on the theories of author and conservationist Wendell Berry for the field of EcoJustice Education, this book articulates a *pedagogy of responsibility* as a three-pronged approach grounded in the recognition that our planet balances an essential and fragile interdependence between all living creatures. Examining the deep cultural roots of social and ecological problems perpetuated by schools and institutions, Martusewicz identifies practices, relationships, beliefs, and traditions that contribute to healthier communities. She calls for an imaginative re-thinking of education as an ethical process based in a vision of healthy, just, and sustainable communities. Using a critical analytical process, Martusewicz reveals how values of exploitation, mastery, and dispossession of land and people have taken hold in our educational system and communities, and employs Berry's philosophy and wisdom to interrogate and develop a *pedagogy of responsibility* as an antidote to such harmful ideologies, structures, and patterns. Berry's critical work and the author's relatable storytelling challenge taken-for-granted perspectives and open new ways of thinking about teaching for democratic and sustainable communities.

Rebecca A. Martusewicz is Professor of Social Foundations and Community Education in the Department of Teacher Education at Eastern Michigan University, USA.

"Martusewicz's celebrations of Wendell Berry in this book offer us priceless gifts and essential insights for healing all the damages of our destructive era. This book challenges us to put into practice Berry's philosophy of living and learning inside as well as outside the confines of classrooms across the world."

—**Madhu Suri Prakash,** *The Pennsylvania State University,*
USA

"This book is long overdue. Berry is one of the 'greats'; his writings still reverberate throughout all fields of education. This book contextualizes Berry's writings in contemporary yet unsustainable times."

—**Amy Cutter-Mackenzie,** *Southern Cross University,*
Australia

"This volume invites educators into a conversation with the work of Wendell Berry, one of America's most revered writers on the themes of environment, culture, community, place, and what it means to be responsibly alive in the world. With careful attention to Berry's novels, essays, and poems, Martusewicz shows how Berry's work can inspire us to re-imagine our place in the world and to inhabit our roles as educators more responsibly."

—**David A. Greenwood,** *Lakehead University,*
Canada

A PEDAGOGY OF RESPONSIBILITY

Wendell Berry for EcoJustice Education

Rebecca A. Martusewicz

NEW YORK AND LONDON

First published 2019
by Routledge
711 Third Avenue, New York, NY 10017

and by Routledge
2 Park Square, Milton Park, Abingdon, Oxon OX14 4RN

Routledge is an imprint of the Taylor & Francis Group, an informa business

© 2019 Taylor & Francis

The right of Rebecca A. Martusewicz to be identified as the author of this work has been asserted by her in accordance with sections 77 and 78 of the Copyright, Designs and Patents Act 1988.

All rights reserved. No part of this book may be reprinted or reproduced or utilised in any form or by any electronic, mechanical, or other means, now known or hereafter invented, including photocopying and recording, or in any information storage or retrieval system, without permission in writing from the publishers.

Trademark notice: Product or corporate names may be trademarks or registered trademarks, and are used only for identification and explanation without intent to infringe.

Library of Congress Cataloging in Publication Data
A catalog record for this title has been requested

ISBN: 978-1-138-96155-5 (hbk)
ISBN: 978-1-138-96156-2 (pbk)
ISBN: 978-1-315-65972-5 (ebk)

Typeset in Bembo
by Taylor & Francis Books

For Gary

CONTENTS

Acknowledgements		*viii*
Preface		*x*
1	Introduction: Toward a Pedagogy of Responsibility	1
2	Neoliberalism and the Dis-membering of Community *With Gary Schnakenberg*	23
3	The Bonds of Love	43
4	Settler Colonialism and *The Unsettling of America*	67
5	Degraded Bodies, Degraded Earth	96
6	STEM Education and the Miracle of Life *With Katy Adams*	117
7	Health as Holism *With Kristi Wilson*	136
8	Re-membering "the Room of Love"	154
9	What is Education For?	169
Index		*177*

ACKNOWLEDGEMENTS

This book has been a long time in the making and many people have contributed to its possibility. Chet Bowers was the first to introduce me to Berry's work and it remained an important resource for both of us during the years we worked closely together. My friend Madhu Suri Prakash was also very influential. Our conversations about Berry began from the first day we met and have never abated. She teases me about our mutual love affair with his writing. Another dear friend, Jeff Edmundson and I collaborated over several years to develop what a pedagogy of responsibility could mean within the EcoJustice framework, and I am especially grateful to him for our work together on Berry's contributions to that concept.

A whole slew of my students have been introduced to Berry because of that initial offering from Chet, and they have been among the strongest advocates for my decision to pull together my thinking about, and love for, Berry's ideas: John Lupinacci, Kristi Wilson, Nigora Erkaeva, Monica Shields, Erin Stanley, Cristal Nicols, and Fabayo Manzira all took a course with me that focused specifically on Berry's fiction, essays, and poetry as sources of educational philosophy. That was a fun semester! For Erin Stanley it turned into a Master's thesis. For Kristi Wilson it turned into a dissertation. Monica Shields worked side by side with me, researching secondary sources and thinking through ideas in the early stages. John Mullen came to this project a bit later but also helped with gathering together and combing through Berry's huge oeuvre to trace the patterned ideas that have been brought to bear in this book. For John it will also culminate in a dissertation. Katy Adams stepped up in the last few months to take on the STEM chapter, despite some initial reservations about Berry's critique of science. I am most grateful for her courage and persistence in writing that chapter under not a small amount of pressure. And, Agnes Krynski has read and edited several chapters for me. Her suggestions have made a huge difference in refining this work.

Eastern Michigan University offered me a semester-long research fellowship that got the ball rolling back in the winter of 2015. And, in the fall of that year I was awarded a sabbatical and a Fulbright fellowship that took me to the University of Tampere in Finland where I had the pleasure to teach and write about Berry, under the influence of a wonderful cadre of colleagues and friends: Veli-Matti Värri, Raisa Foster, Jussi Mäkelä, Jani Pulkki, Olli-Jukka Jokisaari, Vesa Jaaksi, Antii Saari, Taina Repo, Merja Kuisma, and Marikki Arnkil. Ongoing conversations in Telakka and beyond over all sorts of ideas—love, care, competition, posthumanism, embodiment, dialogue, recognition, ethics, neoliberalism, art, phenomenology—have surely found their way into these chapters. Along with the Finns, Derek Rasmussen, my Canadian Buddhist meditation teacher, activist, friend, and collaborator has opened many interesting connections for me between Berry's notion of settling and unsettling and other land-based cultural traditions. Not to mention what I have learned about the four immeasureables as a foundation for EcoJustice. I look forward to those connections and this friendship deepening.

Just a couple months before leaving for Finland, I made my way to Northern Kentucky, to spend a summer afternoon at Lanes Landing Farm, talking with Wendell and Tanya Berry. We sat on their porch and three hours flew by in a heartbeat. I am most grateful for their warm welcome, and lively conversation. I learned a lot from both of them that day and from a series of letters from Wendell responding to my questions that followed. What a gift.

Naomi Silverman stewarded this book from the get go, and as always was a stalwart supporter. I would never have jumped into such a complex project if she had not urged me forward. I am forever thankful for her editorial advice and friendship. I was sad and worried when she announced her retirement, but her replacement has been a godsend as well. I thank Karen Adler and Emmalee Ortega for their patience and kind support as I struggled over some difficult bumps in the last push to completion.

Finally, there is no way to measure the love and encouragement that comes day by day from my family. Beckie and Ben, life has become so much richer, so filled with laughter and amazing discoveries with you two in it. Sweet Pea, Olive, Lady Bug, and Leona you are my daily dose of wiggly joy and sunshine. And Gary, well, there just aren't words. Besides the invaluable scholarly contributions you've made throughout this manuscript, you teach me love every day. This book would not have been written without you.

PREFACE

The primary goal of this book is to explore the influence of author/conservationist Wendell Berry for the field of EcoJustice Education, and to expose educators to his insights as they contribute to the foundations of what Jeff Edmundson and I have referred to in previous work as a "pedagogy of responsibility" (Martusewicz & Edmundson, 2005; Edmundson & Martusewicz, 2013; Martusewicz, Edmundson & Lupinacci, 2015). In spite of the proclaimed prophetic influence of his work on many interrelated fields of study concerned with environmental sustainability (Moyers and Company, 2013), Wendell Berry's importance as an *educational philosopher* has never been addressed in a full-length book. The chapters that follow seek to remedy that by bringing his ideas directly to bear on what we could mean by "a pedagogy of responsibility" as this approach grows out of, and contributes to, EcoJustice Education.

EcoJustice Education is a three-pronged approach that: 1) examines the deep cultural roots of intersecting social and ecological problems, especially as these are perpetuated within educational and other institutions; 2) identifies those practices, relationships, beliefs, and traditions that contribute to healthier communities, human and more than human; and 3) calls for the development of imagination, especially a rethinking of the purposes of education generated from a vision of healthy, just, and sustainable communities. Pedagogies of responsibility emphasize both the critical analytic processes that expose harmful ideologies, structures and patterns, and the qualities contributing to the sorts of responsibility and values (many of these ancient) needed to restore the planet and our communities to healthy balance.

This book is designed as a companion text for the book *EcoJustice Education: Toward Diverse, Democratic and Sustainable Communities* (Martusewicz et al., 2015), not in terms of chapter by chapter pairings but rather through the primary ideas presented. Themes of responsibility, leadership, community membership, friendship, "settler colonialism," racism, human supremacy, consumerism/commodification, scientism, democracy, and agrarianism are brought to bear on education for just and sustainable communities. Thus, it is a book that will be of interest to teachers, teacher educators, philosophers of education, place-based and sustainability educators, and anyone with an interest in Berry's work. For those who are familiar with his often sharp disapproval of institutionalized education—both K-12 and universities—the approach presented here will be of no surprise. I draw directly on Berry's critique of professionalism, expert knowledge and the institutions that support those, while digging into the aspects of his work that are directly about the kinds of educational relationships and outcomes that we need, making a clear distinction in my discussion of the difference between schooling and education. That is a difference that Berry does not always tend to, at least not directly.

As I hope to make clear with Berry's help, pedagogies of responsibility develop competencies needed to engage local practices of care, along with the critical capacities needed to recognize and interrupt our complicity in the exploitive processes at the root of many contemporary social and ecological problems. I discovered Wendell Berry just as I was beginning to wake up to those problems, ten years into my life as an academic. In many ways, his stories, essays and poetry brought me back to myself.

When I was a child, my family lived just a couple miles from my grandfather's dairy farm. My siblings and I grew up free to roam the fields, woodlands, and streams between our house and that farm. While I was young, I lived with a kind of constant heart ache for the indifference most of the people around me seemed to carry for the other creatures—plants, animals, forests, swamps—in our lives. Not my mother, not my grandfather, but others who liked to tease me that the dead creature by the roadside was "just a woodchuck," or the wetland being filled in by big box stores or a new highway was "just a swamp." By the time I was an adolescent I had learned to carefully guard that sensitivity. One day, as a now-tenured professor browsing in a bookstore in Portland, Oregon, I bought a little book of essays by Berry entitled *Another Turn of the Crank* (1995). Reading that book was like coming home.

Little by little, developing confidence in that little girl's sensibilities, I began to speak, to write and to teach from her voice and memories. I began to tell stories about what I had learned as a child. With other scholars, Berry's ideas—both sharp critique and loving embrace—began to inform my memories and my developing understanding of what education could mean if engaged from the principles he lays out, and ultimately what sorts of communities we might create. And while I was raised a spiritual agnostic, I found that I relate deeply with much of his interpretation of Christian Gospels, or at least their most earthly elements. I continue to be moved by Berry's close reading of those ideas, even in my secular skepticism. As Jeff Edmundson and I began to talk and read together, Berry's novels, poetry and essays put in conversation with many others began to inform

xii Preface

our approach to EcoJustice Education, helping us to articulate both a cultural ecological analysis and a vision of the sorts of commitments and communities that education should seek to create. I decided to write this book in order to pay homage to that little girl and her heart, and to draw together all I had learned from Berry to say something more about education. This book is the result.

Chapter Outline

Nine chapters have emerged in the five years it has taken to develop this book. Obviously there is no way to be comprehensive in terms of Berry's huge oeuvre, but I have worked to focus on insights, questions and problems that seem particularly important to education presently. Each chapter can be read as a stand-alone essay but readers will also find a thread of intersecting ideas that runs through the book. The primary themes and ideas have been chosen out of Berry's principles, points of advocacy and analysis in particular as they inform EcoJustice Education and guide a pedagogy of responsibility. Berry is a consummate storyteller, and so I weave his fictional characters in and out of my analysis, along with poetry and his beautiful, often heart-rending prose. Gently chastising me for having written what he considered to be an "ugly word" in a letter I had sent him, he wrote back of the importance of writing that tries to be beautiful. Imagine the experience of being so challenged by Wendell Berry! That comment added months to this project! Still, I have persisted, and one way or another, this collection of essays is the result.

Chapter 1, Introduction: Toward a Pedagogy of Responsibility, provides a brief biography of Wendell Berry and introduces the influence of his work on the field of EcoJustice Education, in particular for developing a pedagogy of responsibility. I introduce in broad strokes the three primary strands—democracy, agriculture and Christianity—that have guided his commitments, and the associated principles that appear throughout his work. I outline his principles of the Great Economy, which emphasize that we are all members of a diverse living order (whether we know it or not), and as such we are responsible for ensuring that our work within it does not cause harm but rather helps it to flourish. We are small within that order and essentially ignorant in the face of its complexity; that is, we will never know or control its mysteries fully, and our illusion that we are somehow outside it has disastrous results. I argue for an understanding of education for eco-ethical becoming that is based on these principles.

Chapter 2, Neoliberalism and the Dis-membering of Community, co-authored with Gary Schnakenberg, examines the emergence of the dominant (for now, anyway) paradigm defining the "little economy," which stands in contrast to the Great Economy and represents what most would simply refer to as "the economy." This chapter traces the antecedents and emergence of the "free-market fundamentalism" of neoliberalism in the 1970s, and identifies several characteristics that have particularly pernicious effects on local communities. It introduces two characters that appear in several of Berry's fictional works, Troy Chatham and Andy Catlett, as a means of illustrating different approaches to being in the world when that world is increasingly reduced to the operations of an abstracted "market" and quantifiable results on balance sheets. The chapter concludes by pointing to the wisdom of love in "the work of local cultures" (Berry, 2010a, p. 139) as the essential antidote to the violence of industrialism and neoliberal politics.

Chapter 3, The Bonds of Love, takes up this idea, tracing connections between Berry's analysis of the necessary relationship between earth, body, mind and spirit for healthy communities, and the work of eco-feminists and materialist feminists who draw similar conclusions. Contrasting this vision to Berry's critique of modern industrial life, the chapter explores what the purposes and definition of education ought to be in order to achieve this vision of healthy communities in a crisis-ridden global context. Berry offers a powerful critique of modern industrial assumptions that naturalize hyper-separated, hierarchized relationships and subjectivities degrading to both body and earth. He offers a metaphysics that is defined by our unavoidable embodiment within a complex living system. Just as microscopic living organisms create the soil in a recursive and generative process of living, reproducing, eating and dying, humans are joined inextricably to the soil as we eat from it to live and reproduce, and return to it in death. For Berry, it is mutuality and affection—love—that joins us together in bonds of protection and care needed to sustain life. Here, Berry's analysis is read in conversation with feminist critiques of modernist perspectives that exclude the recognition of our embedded embodied existence in favor of a dominating rationalism that encloses life-generating relationships. If a conception of love as connection and care is indeed at the heart of the very possibility of life, then education must be about shaping our relationships and productive capacities toward those ways of being that recognize our embodied dependencies on the well-being and intrinsic intelligence of all creatures.

Chapters 4 and 5 dispel claims that Berry's focus on the land and agriculture is a sign of his disinterest in questions of racial oppression or in taking responsibility for a fundamental "erasure" of Indigenous peoples' existence and claims to the land. To the contrary, Berry's particular ideas relative to these complex issues offer important contributions to EcoJustice scholars' insistence that we begin with a deep analysis of how we have been created as subjects of these logics of domination ravaging our communities. For Berry, racism is a primary wound to our humanity for both those who have "painted themselves white" (Coates, 2015, p. 151) and those who have been inferiorized by those very claims, and suffer the violence of degradation. Education must include our work to identify the roots of these harmful assumptions, and to recognize our capacities for love and connection across these divides as a matter of necessary healing. In Settler Colonialism and *The Unsettling of America* (Chapter 4), I review a range of settler colonialism theorists to interrogate processes of degradation, dispossession, and disavowal that continue to rationalize the removal and ideological erasure of Indigenous people from their ancestral land and the consciousness of the dominant white culture. Using that lens, I examine what Berry calls a fundamental "unsettling" required by the growth of an extractive and greedy political and economic system at the heart of European contact and plunder of the North American continent and the planet itself.

In Chapter 5, Degraded Bodies, Degraded Earth, I read Berry's self-reflective essay, *The Hidden Wound* (2010b) on the legacy of slavery within his own family history, and his analysis of intersecting violence to the human body and spirit as well as to the land via racism. Central to Berry's analysis of racism is his recognition of the degradation of land via work that is seen as beneath those who would name themselves white. This compounding of degradations is traced north to industrial Detroit via the Great Migration, and into Detroit's "50-year Rebellion" (Kurashige, 2015). And finally, Berry's own agrarian values are found in the once abandoned lots and parks, where a growing Black Community Food Security Network is reclaiming the land and the Black body as sites of self-determination and love.

Chapter 6, STEM Education and the Miracle of Life, co-authored with Katy Adams, takes seriously recent critiques of the STEM agenda as philosophically grounded in the rationalist, mechanistic, anthropocentric, and individualistic discourses that reinforce global market measures of success. Wendell Berry's eloquent prose builds the case for an alternative vision of success, success rooted in how our personal use of the world contributes to its health and therefore our own, a world where we recognize the infinite not as an "enormous quantity" but rather a cycle that renews (Berry, 1996, p. 88). Three ideas are essential to Berry's argument: (1) Human perspective on the world is limited; science is a human endeavor, therefore science cannot lead to absolute knowledge. (2) Success lies not in progress or our ability to control through technology, but in our capacity to respond appropriately to the real complexities of life in a way that nurtures both natural and human communities. (3) Meaningful knowledge is situated and arises through relationships of affection and action, not the abstract acquisition of more and still more information. Berry's belief in the nature of learning as a holistic endeavor that cannot divorce body from place without injury (Berry, 2000, 1996) invites closer investigation of how people actually teach, learn, and use STEM for healthy communities.

Chapter 7, Health as Holism, co-authored with Kristi Wilson takes this argument into the world of nursing education. The dominant definition of *health* is constructed within socioeconomic, political, cultural, and ecological contexts that affect how personnel in the medical and nursing fields practice. For the most part, practicing nurses and nurse educators define health as the absence of illness; thus their practice is caught in a web of individualism and the neoliberal penchant for efficiencies, mechanization, and profit. They do not recognize the essential connection between our bodies and the earth (Berry, 1996), nor do they recognize that health is created within those complex body/earth relationships. In contrast to the dominant paradigm perspectives of health in nursing and medicine, Berry argues for a definition that emanates from an essential interdependence among all creatures with the earth. As examined in other chapters, Berry makes clear that one cannot be healthy unless one is whole. To be whole is to be aware of the connection of our bodies to other beings that make up existence on this planet (1996). Grounded in Berry's vision of health as holism, this chapter offers a critique of the current healthcare education system by detailing a case study of seven nurse educator/scholars whose work exemplifies aspects of this broad ecological vision. Drawing from their contributions to an alternative vision of health and education, this chapter outlines several courses that would be a necessary start in reforming nursing education toward a more holistic and sustainable vision.

Chapter 8, Re-membering "the Room of Love" takes Berry's critique of neoliberalism home to my childhood town in Northern New York. There by my dying mother's bedside, I remember the membership, the essential teaching and learning, the love that made me who I am today. I let wash over me the sadness of a dying town and the regret of my own leaving as one small thread in its systematic unraveling. I argue for such a painful confrontation as essential to our awakening from the nightmare that has already destroyed so much, and that will be slowed only by love among a membership committed to the flourishing of a place, only by an education that can renew the room of love.

Again emphasizing the wisdom of love, Chapter 9, What is Education For?, summarizes the primary aspects of a pedagogy of responsibility developed in the other chapters, focusing on principles emphasized throughout Berry's work, and the resulting particularities of character as they define and shape membership in community. As a primary challenge that I pose to my own students, I discuss the question, what is education for? Not, what kind of schools or curriculum should we have: Not what is "good teaching?" Rather what are we aiming to accomplish when we set ourselves to the tasks that we define as education? What sorts of skills, attitudes, virtues are we hoping to develop in the young people that we send out into the world? And, what do we expect them to do with those skills and qualities of character? Berry writes that the ecological crisis is a crisis of character, and the crisis of character is a cultural crisis. Recognizing this we see that we are also talking about a crisis of education. This chapter addresses what a pedagogy of responsibility requires as we face these crises.

Contributing Authors

Finally, I have had the benefit of good scholarly help with three of these chapters. Gary Schnakenberg, a human geographer who uses political ecology as a guiding framework, co-authored Chapter 2, Neoliberalism and the Dis-membering of Community. Katy Adams, a science educator who is also the Director of Education at the Ann Arbor Ecology Center, wrote the bulk of Chapter 6, STEM Education and the Miracle of Life. And, Kristi Wilson, a Nurse Practitioner and educator, co-authored Chapter 7, Health as Holism. Each has encountered Berry's work in friendship with me, and have been moved in their own diverse ways to think through his influences. They all stepped up to take on these chapters in the last few months before the manuscript was submitted, adding pressure to their already busy lives. The book would not be the same without them, and neither would I.

References

Berry, W. (1995). *Another turn of the crank*. Washington, DC: Counterpoint.

Berry, W. (1996). *The unsettling of America: Culture and agriculture*. San Francisco, CA: Sierra Club Books.

Berry, W. (2000). *Life is a miracle: An essay against modern superstition*. Washington, DC: Counterpoint.

Berry, W. (2010a). *What matters: Economics for a renewed commonwealth*. Berkeley, CA: Counterpoint.

Berry, W. (2010b). *The hidden wound*. Berkeley, CA: Counterpoint.

Coates, T. (2015). *Between the world and me*. New York, NY: Spiegel & Grau.

Edmundson, J., & Martusewicz, R. (2013). "Putting our lives in order": Wendell Berry, ecoJustice, and a pedagogy of responsibility. In A. Kulnieks, K. Young & D. Longboat (Eds.), *Contemporary studies in environmental and indigenous pedagogies: A curricula of stories and place*. Rotterdam, Netherlands: Sense Publishers.

Kurashige, S. (2015). *The 50-year rebellion*. Oakland, CA: University of California Press.

Martusewicz, R. A., & Edmundson, J. (2005). Social foundations as pedagogies of responsibility and eco-ethical commitment. In D. Butin (Ed.), *Teaching context: A primer for the social foundations of education classroom* (pp. 71–92). Mahwah, NJ: Lawrence Erlbaum Publishers.

Martusewicz, R. A., Edmundson, J., & Lupinacci, J. (2015). *EcoJustice education. Toward diverse, democratic and sustainable communities*. New York, NY: Routledge.

Moyers and Company (2013). *Wendell Berry: Poet and prophet*. Mannes Production Inc. and Schumann Media Center. Retrieved on February 28, 2018 from http://billmoyers.com/segment/wendell-berry-on-his-hopes-for-humanity/

1

INTRODUCTION: TOWARD A PEDAGOGY OF RESPONSIBILITY

> *The Arrival*
> Like a tide it comes in,
> wave after wave of foliage and fruit,
> The nurtured and the wild,
> out of the light to this shore.
> In its extravagance we shape
> the strenuous outline of enough.
> *(Wendell Berry, 1984)*

We are living within a vastly beautiful, diverse, and dangerous world, a sensual, dynamic, "extravagant" world where interactions and connections, cycles and transformations continue to give us a bounty of possibility for life, even while the bling of our consumerist habits blind us to that truth. Those habits—the addiction to buying more and more things, the individualism that produces our greedy consumption, the belief in Eurocentric superiority over the rest of the world, and the inherent "progress" of ever-expanding technologies—are produced within a colonizing industrial legacy that has brought us to great peril. All across this planet, living communities—human and more-than-human—are displaced or destroyed by shortsightedness, greed, and violence. And yet, every day we witness acts of kindness and care on large and small scales. And though it seems to be more and more attenuated, we know at least on some level the connective power of care and affection; we know how to put aside selfish wants in favor of kindness, empathy, compassion, and joy. How do we strengthen those desires for affection and care, those connective ways of being that are at the heart of happiness and collective well-being? How do we identify and challenge the processes and forces that ignore our responsibility to "the strenuous outline of enough"?

Wendell Berry, a Kentucky farmer, poet, novelist, and conservationist, has spent the last 50 years writing between the poles of abundance and restraint, grief and love. In a personal letter to me, he proclaims himself "old-fashioned," a "traditionalist" who prefers to emphasize concepts of forgiveness, kindness, mercy, and affection over rationalist notions of justice that lead us down the path of retribution and a reproduction of hierarchized structures of violence. His life-long study of the historical roots and erosion of virtues, dispositions, and practices that protect the communities and living systems we depend upon trace the roots of our cultural history and our own psyches as saturated with both exploitation and care.

> The terms exploitation and nurture ... describe a division not only between persons but within persons. We are all to some extent, the products of an exploitive society, and it would be foolish and self-defeating to pretend that we do not bear its stamp ... the standard of the exploiter is efficiency; the standard of the nurturer is care. (Berry, 1996, p. 7)

While industrial societies have been built largely on practices and beliefs that define love and care as weak or secondary, often associated with what women do (Martusewicz & Johnson, 2016), I argue with Berry that the relationships, skills and attitudes creating care, affection and mutuality are our most important sources of strength. Throughout this book, using Berry's stories, poems and essays as primary sources of wisdom, my contributors and I examine how values of exploitation, mastery, and dispossession of land and people have become dominant modes of being in an extractive economic and politically subservient system. Berry challenges the inevitability of these systems by arguing for the identification, cultivation and internalization of ways of being based on primary intangible virtues—gratitude, humility, faith, kindness, forbearance. Relationships built on these intangibles have, he tells us, important tangible effects that mitigate against the violence of selfish individualism, hyper consumerism, and the brutality of profit driven market fundamentalism. But these virtues do not simply appear on their own. They must be part of a community's commitments and desires for itself, and thus part of intentional and strategic educational processes that actively engage the imagination toward responsibility and the creation of a robust and sustainable alternative. We name this approach EcoJustice Education.

EcoJustice Education

The two basic strands that define the theoretical and pedagogical tasks of this work are: 1) the development of a critical analysis of the cultural foundations of the ecological and social crises we face globally; 2) a recognition and identification of the existing and ancient relationships, attitudes, beliefs and practices needed for mutual caretaking of each other and the planet, in short, an ethics for

Introduction: Toward a Pedagogy of Responsibility **3**

a sustainable future within the limited carrying capacity of the ecosystems in which we live (Martusewicz, Edmundson & Lupinacci, 2015).

The first strand includes a willingness to examine the complexities of Western industrial culture, as it has developed historically via a set of hierarchized modernist assumptions, deeply imbedded discourses that rationalize specific economic and social policies, as well as day-to-day interactions and psychological conditions that define our sense of the world and our lives together (Martusewicz et al., 2015; Bowers, 1993, 1997, 2012; Martusewicz & Johnson, 2016; Lupinacci & Happel, 2015). EcoJustice Education asks students and teachers to examine the ways a powerful group of historically created assumptions, formed, internalized and exchanged as "regimes of truth" (Foucault, 1980, p. 31), come together to create, rationalize, and maintain these patterns of belief and behavior. Discourses are a closely woven tapestry of exchanged and internalized meanings that are constructed through language and all sorts of other symbolic systems passed on inter-generationally via our institutions and relationships. They have a deeply embedded history in space and time, and function to create and recreate organizing ideas (conceptual maps) via metaphor as a kind of glue for any culture.

Our imaginations—the ways we think, how we see the world and ourselves in it—are scripted according to multiple lines of discursive logic. Thus, our abilities to see differently, to imagine who we are or might be in the world are limited by defined subject positions—by race, class, gender, geography, ability, sexuality and so on—in a logic that rationalizes possession of property and mastery of people and other creatures. Further, we "moderns" believe so fully in our superior knowledge, technology, economic and financial systems that we insist on it being spread to others across the world, whether through religion, capitalism, schooling or a combination of these. As Berry puts it:

> … We have lived by the assumption that what was good for us would be good for the world. And this has been based on the even flimsier assumption that we could know with any certainty what was good even for us. We have fulfilled the danger of this by making our personal pride and greed the standard of our behavior toward the world—to the incalculable disadvantage of the world and every living thing in it. And now, perhaps very close to too late, our great error has become clear. It is not only our own creativity—our own capacity for life—that is stifled by our arrogant assumption; *the creation itself is stifled.* (Berry, 2012a, p. 220; emphasis added)

In this part of the work, we insist that if we are to address the crises sweeping the planet and destroying our local communities, we must examine our own capture in the assumptions, ideologies, practices and institutions that create these problems. We must understand that we ourselves are shaped by, and thus complicit in, these processes. Thus, we must examine our own mindsets, and work to shift our relationships, behaviors and the metaphors we use to construct their meaning.

4 Introduction: Toward a Pedagogy of Responsibility

This is not a matter of assigning blame; it is, rather, a matter of understanding how the complex symbolic processes of culture work on us, and thus of accepting the responsibility to change ourselves and the systems and relationships by which we live.

The second strand of EcoJustice Education asks us to reclaim and revitalize the cultural and environmental "commons," particularly those practices, relations, traditions and beliefs that support mutual aid among humans and between humans and the more-than-human world. In this strand, we work to identify practices in our own day-to-day lives, as well as traditional practices among diverse cultures across the world that are specifically aimed at caretaking, however demeaned they are in our modernist conceptions (Martusewicz & Johnson, 2016; Bowers & Martusewicz, 2006; Bowers, 2012; Esteva & Prakash, 1998). This includes the ideas about who we are in relation to the more-than-human world and what we ought to learn from other creatures if we are to survive. Intersecting with the first strand, it requires that we interrupt those logics of domination, which privilege and prioritize one thing at the expense of another and correspondingly degrade the necessary work of caretaking, which is essential for the flourishing of life.

As I have continued to read and think about the particular influences of Berry's work on this field, a third important strand emerged, also intersecting with the first two in important ways. This third strand requires that we learn to imagine the places where we dwell, what is needed in those places, what is demanded of us by those communities and the living world with whom we share this planet. As educators, we keep at the forefront of our work the question: What is education for? Whom should we be serving, and towards what end? Our questions, as Berry puts it, should lead us to a kindly and orderly world where creation can flourish. To imagine our role in creating healthy communities is to take responsibility, to actively and carefully respond to the needs expressed in the singularity of a particular place.

> For humans to have a responsible relationship to the world, they must imagine their places in it. To have a place, to live and belong to a place, to live from a place without destroying it, we must imagine it. By imagination we see it illuminated by its own unique character and by our love for it. By imagination, we recognize with sympathy the fellow members, human and nonhuman, with whom we share our place. (Berry, 2012b, p. 14)

This third strand circulates through the preceding two as a double responsibility: to *recognize* the damages that we are perpetuating, understanding our complicity, and to *identify* the good: those practices, values, and relationships within the living world around us that exist as gifts to our communities. "Imagination is a particularizing and a local force, native to the ground underfoot" and "placing the world

Introduction: Toward a Pedagogy of Responsibility **5**

and its creatures within a context of sanctity in which their worth is absolute and incalculable" (Berry, 2010b, p. 32).

Pedagogies of Responsibility

As we approach the tasks required by each of these intersecting strands in the EcoJustice framework, we bring specific questions that seek to expose and articulate the particular responsibilities we have as members of this industrial culture. Who are we and how have we been shaped by the primary assumptions organizing our society? What mistakes have we made and continue to make that are rationalized by those assumptions? To whom are we ethically responsible? And as part of this last question: What is to be conserved in our traditions, practices, relationships and beliefs that could help us to contribute to the protection and care of a living planet, and what should be changed? That is, what do we need to learn about ourselves, our places and the larger context in order to live well together (Bowers, 2001, 2006; Martusewicz & Edmundson, 2005)?

From these specific questions, an ethic of responsibility and care emerges that impacts our understanding of teaching and learning. A "pedagogy of responsibility" was first coined by Jeff Edmundson (2003) to distinguish this approach from other critical pedagogies that focus on "transformation" or "liberation" but often leave unexamined our relationship and unavoidable interdependence with the more-than-human world. Perspectives in critical pedagogy often overlook what we and other diverse cultures already know that could help us protect those important ecological and community relationships, edging, instead, toward what Derek Rasmussen (2005) identifies as "a rescuer mentality." Our point is that many of the cultures purported to be in need of liberation or transformation by those who are supposedly "in the know" are already organized by rich cultural traditions and practices that understand what it means to be whole within the patterns of the natural world and larger cosmos. Identifying the skills, values and relationships that continue to exist in our own culture and day-to-day lives, albeit in severely attenuated ways, is an important piece of the EcoJustice approach.

Berry teaches us to look carefully at what works to create healthy living systems in our particular biospheres, regions and communities, reminding us that humans are a small but important part of that complex diverse world. Further, we see the task of transformation to be necessarily directed at *ourselves* as the members of modern cultures complicit in the systems and thus perpetrating these disasters and oppressions. And this means all of us, those benefitting and those being exploited, which is a mixed bag, for we are all multiple subjects of its representational and material processes. Our desires, assumptions, hopes, and imaginations are shaped and reshaped there.

EcoJustice Education and pedagogies of responsibility begin from the necessity to acknowledge the vast diversity creating both living systems and human cultures. We recognize the ways relationships are, in every way, generative processes.

6 Introduction: Toward a Pedagogy of Responsibility

That is, when different elements in the world—biological, geological, or cultural—come into contact with each other, they create differences that make a difference (Bateson, 1972). As Martusewicz et al. (2015) put it

> Diversity is the condition of difference created when there is a relationship between one thing or idea and anything else. When there is a relationship there is also a space of difference between the two things. And that space is very important when it comes to defining what anything means or what its value is in comparison to anything else. ... In this sense, difference isn't really a thing, or an object, but rather a creative, or generative condition created because of relationships among things. ... Relationships are key to both democracy and sustainability. (p. 26)

As such, we also accept the responsibility of *discerning together* how to live in mutually supportive ways, even when those ways may not be clear or self-evident. This willingness to make ethical choices even in the face of all sorts of differences and uncertainty is at the heart of what it means to become educated (Martusewicz & Edmundson, 2005; Martusewicz, 2001). With Berry, we see this as requiring attention to our local places and communities first, aiming our work there specifically, even as we work to analyze the larger globalizing economic, political and cultural forces impinging on us and other creatures.

Thus, we begin from a position that defines education as a concept distinct from, although at times present in, schooling. While we work toward schooling that could contain these possibilities, education should be understood as a process that explicitly requires us to become ethical agents of healthy communities, and is therefore not necessarily located in institutionalized settings, or even formally named "education." Our ethical choices—decisions made about what constitutes the "good" in our lives with and for others—are made as we bear witness to and respond in appropriate ways to both grief and joy, despair and flourishing. These are specific, sometimes paradoxical responsibilities that must be engaged in relations of teaching and learning wherever they take place.

Learning to acknowledge within our own bodies and souls the suffering of others and to use that particular corporal and spiritual experience to propel us into active expressions of mutuality and care is a necessary component of nurturing healthy relationships. Similarly, learning to embrace and rejoice in the happiness of others, allowing joy to bubble up as we witness their happiness and success helps to create the bonds of membership, a sense of belonging and mutuality that is necessary to life. Buddhists name this aspect of love "sympathetic joy."

As we will lay out in the chapters that follow, these capacities—given shape by the development of specific skills and dispositions, practices and commitments—are what guide a pedagogy of responsibility. Berry insists that we will not address the problems that we face until we address the culture that we live in and

Introduction: Toward a Pedagogy of Responsibility **7**

contribute to. And this is our commitment as EcoJustice educators too. Our work must be about examining ourselves as deeply implicated members of our society's symbolic, material and psychological processes. Creating the sort of community members needed to challenge the problems we face must be intentional, focused and sustained political and ethical work. Educators, no matter what context they work in, whether formal or informal, need to understand how to create the proper conditions—the relationships and the lessons—to encourage our students to examine their unconscious patterns of belief and behavior as the means toward healthier, more responsible ways of living on this planet.

Further, as part of a challenge to ingrained patterns of violence, teachers and their students will need to embrace specific sensibilities related to care and restraint, humility and kindness, to imagine what it could mean to live by these and to help others to live by them. Berry is clear throughout his writing that human beings have specific responsibilities guided by fundamental principles required by life on this planet.

Berry as a Philosopher of Education

With this book, we bring Wendell Berry to the fore as an important educational philosopher, a thinker who insists that we understand our necessary immersion in complex and diverse living systems and thus our necessary embodied connections to the land and to each other. Berry's critique of organizations created outside such a recognition—science, the medical professions, universities and schools, for example—helps us to make important distinctions between schooling as an institution created within the political and economic interests of the corporate controlled state, and education as a much broader set of relations and capacities that must be oriented toward learning from and protecting living systems as the source and sustenance of our own survival.

To make a claim for Berry as an important educational philosopher reminds me of a statement he makes in his preface to *The Way of Ignorance*

> Some people who have written about my essays have honored me by supposing that I am a philosopher or a scholar. I am neither. I have no talent for the abstract thought of philosophers and not much interest in it. My reading in philosophy is scant and unskilled. And though I have been a constant reader for most of my life, I have never read systematically. I own a fair number of useful books, but I don't live near a good library, and I am in no sense a researcher. (Berry, 2005, p. x)

This understanding of philosophy that Berry uses to differentiate his own work is actually the meaning or the original intent of the word, *philosophia*, as the love of wisdom. Perhaps it would be more accurate to turn this phrase around, as Luce Irigaray (2002) has argued, to *the wisdom of love*. This turn of phrase seems closer

8 Introduction: Toward a Pedagogy of Responsibility

to Berry's specific approach and commitments: "In my essays I have meant to speak for myself and nobody else. The work that I feel best about I have done as an amateur: *for love*" (Berry, 2005, p. x). Extending this further, he writes:

> But in my essays especially I have been motivated also by fear of our violence to one another and to the world, and by hope that we might do better. If I had not been so reasonably afraid, my essays at least would have been much different and many fewer. (Berry, 2005, p. x)

This double sensibility between violence and love draws us to his work and a definition of education as requiring an ethical struggle toward well-being.

With me, the contributors to this book join a small cadre of educational scholars who have recognized Berry as "a genuinely radical thinker," as Madhu Prakash (1994) writes, a scholar who challenges the dominant certainties of our modern institutions and instead "teaches us to live and learn on the human scale as communal beings, virtuous and ecologically literate" (p. 136) Similarly in line with our own interpretations, Paul Theobald and Dale Snauwaert (1993) recognize Berry's important critique of schooling as fundamentally supporting social and ecological exploitation, and his advocacy for a vision of education as leading to virtues unifying nature and community life. "Knowledge" in Berry's conception is "fundamentally experiential, imaginative relational and interactive with nature" (Theobald & Snauwaert, 1993, p. 3; see also Snauwaert, 1990). Further, as Jane Schreck argues in her dissertation (1990), Berry's philosophy "centers on love as the best animator of learning: love among those teaching and learning, love for what can be learned, and love of how such learning can be applied in a beloved place on earth" (p. x).

This love is set against a culture of violence, in particular an economic system bent on creating tragedy. Henderson and Hursh (2014) examine Berry's contributions to a critique of modern economic ideologies and structures. In particular, they expose the implications of neoliberalism for educational practices and policies as these impact social and ecological well-being in our communities drawing directly from Berry's work. "Wendell Berry … challenges neoliberalism's privileging of monetary values over all others, and the individual over relationships" (p. 175). Throughout his work Berry exposes "a creeping scientism at the expense of other, more local and embodied ways of knowing" (p. 177) which Henderson and Hursh recognize as linked to the ways national educational policies depend on conceptions of efficiency, "scientific evidence and progress to warrant a program of narrowly prescribed educational reforms" (p. 177).

While Henderson and Hursh focus primarily on K-12 education, others have focused on higher education (Baker & Bilbro, 2017; Bonzo & Stevens, 2008; Bouma-Prediger & Walsh, 2004), on what universities ought to focus on if we are to move toward more sustainable ways. I have been affirmed and informed by all of this work, as have my colleagues contributing to this book. The reader will

Introduction: Toward a Pedagogy of Responsibility **9**

see the themes raised by these and many other scholars woven into the conversation that we undertake here to think through Berry's deeply poignant insights contributing to a philosophy of education.

A Brief Biography: "Kentucky was my fate"

Wendell Berry was born in 1937, and grew up in Port Royal, (Henry County) Kentucky on a farm not far from where he lives today. His father was a lawyer who also farmed, and his grandparents were Depression Era farmers, so Wendell and his brother, John, learned what it meant to love the land through hard work and care from an early age. Writing of his father, a lawyer whose own father and grandfather were farmers and who, in spite of his profession, never turned from "an indissoluble devotion to the life of the earth ... to the intricacy and beauty of the lives of things," Berry remembers important lessons offered when he was a boy:

> ... he not only kept me within the reach and influence of my native and ancestral ground, he gave me every encouragement up to and including insistence, to learn everything I could about it. He talked and contrived endlessly that I should understand the land not as a commodity, an inert fact to be taken for granted, but as an ultimate value, enduring and alive, useful and beautiful and mysterious and formidable and comforting, beneficent and terribly demanding, worthy of the best of a man's attention and care. (Berry, 2010a, p. 72)

Berry's childhood was spent roaming his grandfather's fields and woodland, where ultimately his soul was rooted. He spent his high school years at a military boarding school, but never lost a sense of deep belonging and longing for his childhood home. Revealing a deeply placed love and imagination that would animate his novels and poetry in particular, he recalls:

> ... when I was away at school, I could comfort myself by recalling in intricate detail the fields I had worked and played in, and hunted over, and ridden through on horseback—and that were richly associated in my mind with people and stories. I could recall even the casual locations of certain small rocks. I could recall the look of a hundred different kinds of daylight on all those places, the look of animals grazing over them, the postures and attitudes and movements of the men who worked in them ... I had come to be aware of it as one is aware of one's own body ... (Berry, 2012a, pp. 193–194)

Pursuing his love of writing, he went on to the University of Kentucky where he earned BA and MA degrees (1956, 1957) in English Literature. In 1957, he

10 Introduction: Toward a Pedagogy of Responsibility

married his UK classmate Tanya Amyx and moved with her to study with renowned novelist Wallace Stegner at Stanford University. Stegner's deep love of the Western landscape, and his understanding of the kinds of losses endured at the hands of expansionist capitalism was a perfect fit for Berry's own sensibilities, and so Wendell began to write about life in Henry County, Kentucky, publishing his first novel, *Nathan Coulter* in 1960. Awarded a Guggenheim Foundation Fellowship in 1961, he lived with Tanya and their first child in Italy and France for a year and then moved to New York City to take a teaching position at New York University. Berry describes those years as representing a more general cultural milieu where "cosmopolitanism," leaving home, and becoming ensconced in urban life were the credentials of a successful literary life. In his own words:

> ... hadn't I achieved what had become one of the most traditional goals of American writers? I had reached the greatest city in the nation; I had a good job; I was meeting other writers and talking with them and learning from them. I had reason to hope that I might take a still larger part in the literary life of that place. (Berry, 2012a, p. 195)

But, as he goes on to say, he "had not escaped Kentucky" (p. 195). His own literary work, his essays, novels and poetry were already being set in his Kentucky homeplace, examining the demise of rural agricultural life. His deep love of the place, his worry for it, all he had learned as a boy about the soil, the woods, the animals (wild and domesticated), the running of the farms, the relationships with generations of people who had toiled on that particular land, all this and more was working through him. His own writing began to disrupt the whole idea that success or happiness or well-being could be found in the literary world of the city, and in 1962, the Berry family moved back to Kentucky.

Amidst great disappointment and disavowal from colleagues in New York, Berry took a position in the English department at the University of Kentucky (Bonzo & Stevens, 2008). By 1965, he and Tanya made the decision to move with their two children back to Henry County, buying a farm in need of attention on a hillside near the banks of the Kentucky River, and joining six previous generations in Berry's family to care for this land.

In a beautiful autobiographical essay, called "A Native Hill" (2012a), he reflects on this decision to come home. In this essay, he and his dog take us on a walk up the hill upon which his farm is nestled, and as he walks he recounts the history of this land, the mistakes made that have damaged the soil, the reclaiming of old tobacco fields by the surrounding woods, hollows, and streams. This early essay, written in the late 1960s, reads as a map of the influences of the people and the place on the next 50 years of his life and work. We see emerge here the questions that would shape the rest of his life's work and that reflect the very character of the man. These are questions that we too embrace as essential articulations of

Introduction: Toward a Pedagogy of Responsibility **11**

responsibility in the act of becoming educated as an attached, careful member of a place.

> When I have thought of the welfare of the earth, the problems of its health and preservation, the care of its life, I have had this place before me, the part representing the whole more vividly and accurately, making clearer and more pressing demands, than any idea of the whole. When I have thought of kindness or cruelty, weariness or exuberance, devotion or betrayal, carelessness or care, doggedness or awkwardness or grace, I had in my mind's eye the men and women of this place, their faces and gestures and movements ... every day I am confronted by the question of what inheritance I will leave. What do I have that I am using up. (Berry 2012a, pp. 194–195)

And further on in the same essay:

> ... I have at last arrived at the candor necessary to stand on this part of the earth that is so full of my own history and so much damaged by it and ask: What is this place? What is in it? What is its nature? How should men [sic] live in it? What must I do? ... the questions are more important than the answers. They are a part of the necessary enactment of humility, teaching a man what his importance is, what his responsibility is, and what his place is, both on the earth and in the order of things. (p. 223)
>
> The presence of the creation here makes this a holy place, and it is as a pilgrim that I have come. It is the creation that has attracted me, its perfect interfusion of life and design. I have made myself its follower and its apprentice. (Berry, 2012a, p. 226)

From this place and their commitments to it, Tanya and Wendell Berry raised their children, both of whom now live nearby and continue their family legacy as caretakers of the land. For the last 50 years, they have raised sheep on their hillside, used Percheron draft horses to plow and plant fields, grown vegetables in a kitchen garden, and created together a legacy.

We have heard Berry scoffed at for what some academics see as nostalgia for a time gone by, but this is a critical error in interpretation. Berry is not asking us to return to some romantic version of the past (an impossibility); he acknowledges the deeds of his own people on the land, on the people enslaved to work it, and on those who came before his ancestors as steeped in violence. He is deeply ashamed and pained by that history as we will explore further in Chapters 4 and 5 (see, in particular, Berry, 1996, 2010a).

> I am forever being crept up on and newly startled by the realization that my people established themselves here by killing or driving out the original

12 Introduction: Toward a Pedagogy of Responsibility

> possessors, by the awareness that people were once bought and sold here by my people, by the sense of the violence they have done to their own kind and to each other and to the earth, by the evidence of their persistent failure to serve either the place or their own community in it. I am forced, against all my hopes and inclinations, to regard the history of my people here as the progress of the doom of what I value most in the world: the life and health of the earth, the peacefulness of human communities and households. (Berry, 2012a, p. 200)

With this reflection, Berry admonishes us to struggle against the cultural amnesia that erases from our minds and hearts the violence done to establish our lives in our particular places. He lets such recognition creep up on him, settle in, and push him to consider all that has been lost to expansionist capitalism, and what it requires of us now as we identify and work to remedy the damages done to soil, forests, people and creatures by extraction and dispossession. I will have more to say about the ways settler colonialism works to degrade and dispossess Indigenous peoples in North America across the world in Chapter 4.

Berry has put himself to the task of righting wrongs by educating himself about the history of this land, its people, and its creatures, to become, as he says, its apprentice. He asks us to use that wisdom to imagine what could be possible, what we must learn to look for if we are to stop the demise of our communities, what our deepest commitments must be to the people, the land and other species with whom we share this planet. While there is nothing simple in the practice of love and responsibility, if we abandon the relationships, attractions, and affections that create these as the most practical forms of wisdom, there will be no hope for sustaining life on this planet. Serious business, then, without a doubt, but a commitment that this book takes on by learning through the lessons Berry offers us.

Agrarianism, Democracy, and Christianity

In an essay called "Is Life a Miracle?" Berry lays out the general scholarly landscape and inheritances defining his life's work:

> My resources are the things in my cultural inheritance that I have recognized as my own and have tried to live up to: agrarianism, democracy, and Christianity. I believe:
> 1. That good farming and good forestry are fundamental goods, for those who do the work and for those for whom the work is done.
> 2. That it is wrong for people to be excluded from decisions that affect their lives.
> 3. That everything that exists is a divine gift, which places us in a position of extreme danger, solvable only by love for everything that exists including our enemies. (Berry, 2003, pp. 181–182)

Introduction: Toward a Pedagogy of Responsibility   **13**

This book is about the ways his commitments to these lines of influence help us to define our own work as EcoJustice educators. While the book is not about agrarianism directly, we understand Berry's attention in this area to be fundamentally about ecological principles, what we ought to mean by "economy" as the essential work of provisioning a household and community, and what values are needed by communities if we are to achieve a healthy and sustainable life. For Berry, the farm is primarily defined by relationships that if operating within a certain principled order will result in balance, care, and well-being not only for humans, but for the other creatures inhabiting a place as well. In his attention to his own place, we learn about Berry's fidelity to embodied work done well, work that leads to providing for basic needs. He focuses our attention on the sanctity of the body inseparable from the mind or the soul employed with skill to create "enough"—what humans need to live well with other humans and other creatures without abusing the carrying capacity of the land. His views about democracy ground the concept of membership woven through the narrative of his novels in particular, but also the way he defines justice in communitarian terms. For Berry, decisions should be made by those most affected, and community membership must include other living communities and creatures for whom those decisions matter as well. And his reliance on the teachings of Christianity, especially the Gospels, offer what he sees as primary lessons about the values needed to live an orderly life within Creation. His interpretations and questions about these teachings bring him solidly back to the necessity to care for the soil and each other as gifts and as the basis of a spiritually and earthly whole. Indeed, for Berry, while he acknowledges that his questions and these principles are religious, he insists that they are of, and for, the earth. He writes,

> … my questions do not aspire beyond the earth. They aspire *toward* it and *into* it. Perhaps they aspire *through* it. They are religious because they are asked at the limit of what I know, they acknowledge mystery and honor its presence in the creation; they are spoken in reverence for the order and grace that I see and that I trust beyond my power to see. (Berry, 2012a, p. 224)

This sensibility runs through everything he writes. And, while I do not identify as a Christian, I do connect strongly with this recognition of the sacred nature of earthly creation and our responsibilities as humans to it.

Berry's stories, his poems, and his critical essays, all written from this Henry County place, revolve around what it would mean to take these ways of relating seriously as primary guidance for how we should live together in our particular cultural and biological landscapes. Therefore, when we identify these practices, we are aiming at specific forms of teaching and learning embedded in a love of place, in a deep understanding of what the land and its creatures require of us, what it means to make important decisions together, and why our extractive

14 Introduction: Toward a Pedagogy of Responsibility

economic, political and social systems are altogether deadly. Each chapter in this book expands on particular elements of this task. While it is in no way comprehensive, I hope that it will give some indication of the important influence Berry has had on the requirements of a pedagogy of responsibility.

The Kingdom of God as the Great Economy

Berry's work always begins from a powerful faith in the absolute integrity of the living creatures with whom we share this planet, and their productive, transformative connections with each other and with us. This is the living world—both material and incorporeal—made of actual living bodies and their non-material relations in time and space. For Berry there can be no division between the corporeal material of the living earth and what we call spirit, for both are creative of life's wheel of becoming.

Yet in this industrial culture we are taught to think and behave as if the world is outside of us and made of *resources* put there for our own use or entertainment. The institutions, behaviors, desires, and habits created within our taken for granted structures of extraction and selfish accumulation are organized by the drive to master, possess, and use others for our own selfish gains. For industrial systems and its members, the value of any creature, human or otherwise (in particular those whose being is inferiorized), is in our ability to be transformed into profit. And yet, other ways of being in relations of exchange exist and have existed for a long time; these other ways attended carefully by Berry beckon us toward life affirming possibilities for our communities.

In an essay entitled "Two Economies" first published in 1988, Berry describes a set of principles at the heart of all living relations, challenging those beliefs, practices and values that currently guide dominant industrialized human economies. He names the system within which these principles operate, the Kingdom of God, then goes on to offer a more general concept, the Great Economy, in order to acknowledge its general lessons within other cultural and religious frameworks. His aim is to teach his readers what is required of us as humans interacting with a complex and vulnerable living world, what our mistakes have been in our construction of what he calls "the little economy" (our human economy), and what our responsibilities ought to be in correcting those mistakes. The principles that he names offer important guidelines for what a responsible and responsive life must attend to, what it means to become educated within relationships defined by an eco-ethical consciousness and its corresponding commitments. I offer them here and we return to them throughout this book.

The first principle is that the Great Economy includes everything and every relationship on the planet Earth and in the universe. We are all members of this extravagant and mysterious system whether we understand it or not, or whether we desire to be in it or not. Thus, "the fall of every sparrow is a significant event" (Berry, 2010a, p. 116). To be human is to be a creature within this given Creation, not separate or superior, but in it and of it. Everything we do or know is produced within, and a product of, this complex generative system.

The second principle is that there is an order to this set of relationships, and we are part of that order, again whether we know it or not, which means that we have certain responsibilities which must be respected. As Burley Coulter, one of the characters in his Port William stories says, "It's not who's in it and who ain't, but who knows it and who don't" (Berry, 2004, p. 97). "Knowing it" means that we take our places in it with our particular capacities not as a matter of control or possession, but rather developing relationships that nourish it and help us all to flourish.

The third principle is that we can never know finally all the complexity that this order entails. We will always be limited in what we can know simply by virtue of being human in a complex and ever-changing world; indeed, as Berry puts it, we must accept that we are essentially *ignorant* even as we work hard to understand what our places in the world require of us. "The way of ignorance" means accepting that there will always be mysteries beyond our reach. Accepting this requires a certain amount of humility while we seek to define and develop our particular abilities. "The order," he says, "is both greater and more intricate than we can know" (Berry, 2010a, p. 116). This raises a certain unavoidable paradox that defines both ethics and education: while we must seek what it means to live a good life with others, we will never fully know the answer in any final way. We must seek with our questions and offer ourselves to the world, but there will always be more questions as soon as we believe them to be answered.

The fourth principle states that while we cannot know it fully, if we presume to be outside this complex order, or if we endeavor to control it for our own ends only, we do so at our own peril. As Gregory Bateson (2000) put it in *Steps to an Ecology of Mind*: "Lack of systemic wisdom is always punished" (p. 240). Any creature that imagines itself outside of this system of intelligence and order will wreak havoc upon it and thus upon itself. Again, if we believe we are the ones who know and thus see ourselves as superior to all other life forms, our arrogance will be our own undoing. On the other hand, recognizing ourselves to be members of an order much larger than ourselves, we will act with the requisite care and humility.

Finally, the fifth principle recognizes that we can never be certain about "forever," the time we have left as a species, or that this Great Economy of the Earth has in the cosmos, and yet we must continue to work to secure a balanced life in the present for ourselves and the earth's living systems. This fifth principle reminds us that the regenerative nature of creation must be nurtured, protected as our fundamental responsibility. Pleasure, satisfaction and happiness are most valuable in work aimed at the protection and nurture of the lives and relationships that create places and communities. No matter what the future holds, we cannot fully know it, and we must accept our responsibility to the places and people where we live now. That responsibility includes a willingness to identify and challenge those systemic forces that impinge upon the well-being of those places as a part of the love that we develop for them.

16 Introduction: Toward a Pedagogy of Responsibility

Recognizing the ethical, ontological and epistemological implications of these principles requires that we imagine who we ought to be in relation to other living creatures and to each other. Living within the Great Economy, humans are required to organize ourselves in order to acquire what we need to live well together. Like other creatures, we must eat, shelter ourselves, reproduce, care for each other, and so on. And as such we will create, as we have created throughout history, our own particular and diverse ways of producing and exchanging the goods and services needed to live. Everything humans need to live is sourced here, in the Great Economy, and understanding this means that we must learn to take care of those relationships, even while recognizing that we will never know enough. We are, as Wes Jackson implores us to remember, land-based creatures (Berry, Jackson, & Berry, 2016), and to the degree that we do not acknowledge that, we put everything, ourselves included, in peril. Understanding this requires us to honor the gift of life provided by the earth. It requires that we create a little human economy that is in proper relation to the Great Economy.

This question of *use* invariably introduces an important ethical requirement if we recognize the principles of the Great Economy laid out above.

> If we believed that the existence of the world is rooted in mystery and in sanctity, then we would have a different economy. It would still be an economy of use, necessarily, but it would be an economy also of return. The economy would have to accommodate the need to be worthy of the gifts we receive and use, and this would involve a return of propitiation, praise, gratitude, responsibility, good use, good care, and a proper regard for future generations. (Berry, 2003, pp. 146–147)

A human economy will be a good economy, or a "considerate economy" as Berry puts it, if it fits harmoniously within the Great Economy, if it protects it and nurtures it as the very source of its own possibility. It "must correspond to the Great Economy; in certain important ways, *it must be an analogue* of the Great Economy" (Berry 2010a, p. 120, emphasis added).

And yet, living in such a consumerist and profit-oriented culture, we tend not to notice the Great Economy at all. Instead, we assume that our scientific and technological creativity is what is most important for our survival and continued success as a dominant civilization. With Berry, we are concerned about what is destroyed when our human economy overlooks or ignores the gifts offered by the Great Economy. This critique is developed directly out of embracing the intangible virtues and values that Berry helps us to articulate.

> Once we acknowledge the existence of the Great Economy, … we are astonished and frightened to see how much modern enterprise is the work of hubris, occurring outside the human boundary established by ancient tradition. The industrial economy is based on invasion and pillage of the Great Economy. (Berry, 2010a, p. 126)

Introduction: Toward a Pedagogy of Responsibility   17

As the late Australian ecofeminist Val Plumwood (1993, 2002) argued, in modern industrial cultures we learn to homogenize and background those complex ecological processes as "nature," something separate, "out there," and thus either invisible or simply not important enough to think much about except as resources to be commodified and used. When discourses of human supremacy are put together with mechanistic ways of thinking—the idea that "nature is like a machine"—we find systematic violence that treats living creatures as commodities, rivers, lakes and oceans as dumping grounds and drains for toxic industrial and domestic waste, and forests valued in measures of board feet called timber. Such practices desecrate the sanctity of our land, our water, and the other creatures that inhabit these regions, and, in the process, we inflict a deep wound upon our own humanity.

Linking human supremacist world views with other intersecting discourses is a central task of EcoJustice Education. Anthropocentrism, or the idea of human-centered attitudes, beliefs and practices has been central to that analysis. In a conversation at his farm one summer afternoon, Berry brought me up short as I began to articulate this critique using the concept of anthropocentrism. Providing a different take, he argued that all species are "centric" beings; that is, all species work toward their own specific survivability and regeneration, including humans, and this is right and good, a part of the world's order. We humans will never be sparrow-centric, or snake-centric, or dog-centric, or possum-centric, or dragonfly-centric. We are humans with faculties for self-reflectivity and rational decision-making that include the capacity for massive mistakes in relation to the Great Economy, and yet deep love and care for other living creatures as well.

The key for Berry is that we understand the world as created by a complex, mysterious and sacred *diversity of life*. Each species has its own purpose and integrity, each individual creature its own need, and trajectory. We must thus accept with humility our own particular role in maintaining the "wheel of life," even while we cannot finally know all its ins and outs. We must recognize our fundamental ignorance, according to Berry, a position that ultimately confronts human supremacy as the right to dominate (Berry, 2016, 2005). As I hope to make clear throughout this book, there is a difference between humble forms of human centeredness and arrogant forms that lead to violence. Again, attending to the principles of the Great Economy, learning to recognize ourselves as fundamentally limited creatures is key to creating more careful, caring relationships that could begin to help heal the wounds of our industrial economy.

Education for Eco-Ethical Becoming

Remember back to the poem I shared at the start of this chapter: "… wave after wave of foliage and fruit" and "the strenuous outline of enough." How do we teach and learn within the limits of our planetary existence and humanness, even as we honor the extravagant beauty, power, and gift that is life on earth? This

18 Introduction: Toward a Pedagogy of Responsibility

book explores this question beginning from a definition of education as a set of relationships committed to developing ethical responses to the world first and foremost, not as a final project, but as an ongoing process of becoming. The practices that guide those relationships, which we name pedagogies of responsibility, are shaped by our acknowledgment of and commitment to the principles of the Great Economy. Value, Berry insists, can only be found in the Great Economy—in the patterns, and productivity, and transformative processes of what we call "nature," but that includes us, our bodies and minds and our capacities for creative and conserving work. Everything that we need to create the good community is sourced in these complex generative relationships. "A good human economy," Berry tells us,

> would recognize at the same time that it was dealing all along with materials and powers *that it did not make*. It did not make trees, and it did not make the intelligence and talents of the human workers. What humans have added at every step is artificial, made by art, and though the value of art is critical to human life, it is a secondary value. (Berry, 2010a, p. 122; emphasis added)

Our craft as educators is to pass on these principles, to ask our students to address the specifics of how we could live by them in our specific places. How do we make our lives within the necessary principles of the Great Economy, recognizing both the limits of our capacities to know it in any final way, and the limits imposed by the natural order of diverse living systems? How do we translate those principles into virtues and character traits practicable by individuals to guide us in creating mutually caring relationships with others, and practical contributions as members of living communities?

As we develop throughout the rest of the book, Berry's answer is love, not as some simple romantic notion, but rather as it is enacted in the forms of devotion and responsibility required by the principles of the Great Economy, that is by life on Earth. Pedagogies of responsibility are characterized by three irreducible aspects: first, they are *constructed* out of the confluences of place, creaturehood, and community; second, they are *enacted* through imagination, sympathy and affection; and third, their *purpose*, as its name suggests, is the promotion of responsibility characterized by forbearance, humility, and care.[1] These aspects, of course, require that, as we enact imagination and move toward responsible action, we begin to see what has gone wrong, what cultural, political and economic forces, relations and assumptions are wreaking havoc on places, creatures, and communities across the world, and what we should do about it.

There is an important tension between what I call eco-ethical becoming and the need to learn to stay home, to become caretakers of a particular place and its creatures. Becoming is part of a specifically generative and affirmative process that is necessarily creative of all sorts of possibilities. When it is engaged as part of a strictly ethical project, as a means of taking care of ourselves, each other and the

Introduction: Toward a Pedagogy of Responsibility **19**

land, a set of limits is presented that are defined locally. Thus, eco-ethical becoming is not a universalizing process; it is tuned to place, while attentive to larger contexts and forces affecting those places, specifically the creatures who share those places.

So, we ask with Berry as our guide, what sorts of knowledge are needed by members of communities in the specific ecological and cultural localities where they dwell? What sorts of economic relationships would be appropriate in those places? What would decision-making practices look like if the principles of the Great Economy guided their responsibilities to each other and the earth? With our students we are learning to ask, what does a good human economy in a healthy, that is whole, community look like? What does it require of us? In short, what is education for?

To be so committed does not mean that we must rely only on institutions to do the teaching, and certainly not the government to tell us how to do it, or where, or when. Indeed, as Berry adamantly insists throughout his work, and as we will discuss throughout this book, institutions created by the state to support a globalizing extractive economic system are often the worst places to imagine such possibilities. And yet, schools are where our children and their teachers are for hours each day ten months of the year or more. Thus, as teacher educators, we are faced with a critical opportunity and responsibility.

We honor the teachers in schools or universities who, in spite of the political and curricular limitations they are constrained by, engage such responsibility with their students and in their day-to-day lives. We work with educators across the US, Canada, Finland, Jamaica, Australia, Central Asia and other places who, in a variety of contexts, are seriously committed to challenging the industrial complexes and supporting ideologies currently destroying our communities. We will tell their stories here as often as possible. But we also acknowledge that teachers everywhere are under tremendous pressure to do as state mandates connected to corporate interests bid them to do. The more schools and universities are controlled by market fundamentalism and associated neoliberal political processes, the more teachers are pressed to perform for those interests over the interests of the commonwealth. EcoJustice Education offers a way out of that dilemma and toward a strong community of support.

We choose love in the form of active collective responsibility and meaningful work as an antidote for despair and exhaustion. Let us find strength in the gift of Creation and in the recognition that the economic and political systems we have now are disastrous for all life. We offer this book as a commitment to engage with others in this essential care for the planet as our only home. Let our work together, our pedagogical relationships and ethical commitments be the light we need to guide us out of darkness, a source of courage and hope to those going forward.

> It is hard to have hope. It is harder as you grow old,
> for hope must not depend on feeling good
> and there is the dream of loneliness at absolute midnight.

You also have withdrawn belief in the present reality
of the future, which surely will surprise us,
and hope is harder when it cannot come by prediction
any more than by wishing. But stop dithering.
The young ask the old to hope. What will you tell them?
Tell them at least what you say to yourself.
Because we have not made our lives to fit
our places, the forests are ruined, the fields eroded,
the streams polluted, the mountains, overturned. Hope
then to belong to your place by your own knowledge
of what it is that no other place is, and by
your caring for it, as you care for no other place, this
knowledge cannot be taken from you by power or by wealth.
It will stop your ears to the powerful when they ask
for your faith, and to the wealthy when they ask for your land
and your work. Be still and listen to the voices that belong
to the stream banks and the trees and the open fields.
Find your hope, then, on the ground under your feet.
Your hope of Heaven, let it rest on the ground underfoot.
The world is no better than its places. Its places at last
are no better than their people while their people
continue in them. When the people make
dark the light within them, the world darkens.

(Wendell Berry, 2010b, pp. 91–93)

Note

1 Here I acknowledge the contributions of John Mullen to this particular wording and to this chapter more generally as he read and commented on several drafts.

References

Baker, J., & Bilbro, J. (2017). *Wendell Berry and higher education: Cultivating virtues of place.* Lexington, KY: University Press of Kentucky.

Bateson, G. (1972). *Steps toward an ecology of mind (University of Chicago Press edition).* Chicago, IL: University of Chicago Press.

Berry, W. (1984). *Collected poems, 1957–1982.* New York, NY: North Point Press.

Berry, W. (1996). *The unsettling of America: Culture and agriculture.* San Francisco, CA: Sierra Books.

Berry, W. (2003). *Citizenship papers.* Washington, DC: Shoemaker & Hoard.

Berry, W. (2004). *Hannah Coulter.* Washington, DC: Shoemaker and Hoard.

Berry, W. (2005). *The way of ignorance.* Berkeley, CA: Counterpoint.

Berry, W. (2010a). *Imagination in place.* Berkeley, CA: Counterpoint.

Berry, W. (2010b). Sabbaths 2007, VI. In *Leavings: Poems* (pp. 91–93). Berkeley, CA: Counterpoint.

Berry, W. (2012a). *The long-legged house: Essays*. Berkeley, CA: Counterpoint.

Berry, W. (2012b). *It all turns on affection: The Jefferson Lecture and other essays*. Berkeley, CA: Counterpoint.

Berry, W. (2016). *A small porch: Sabbath poems, 2014*. Berkeley, CA: Counterpoint.

Berry, W., Jackson, W., & Berry, M. (2016). Wendell Berry, Wes Jackson and Mary Berry in Conversation. Schumacher Center for New Economics. Retrieved on March 32018 from www.centerforneweconomics.org/e-newsletters/wendell-berry-wes-jackson-mary-berry-conversation

Bonzo, J. M., & Stevens, M. R. (2008). *Wendell Berry and the cultivation of life: A reader's guide*. Grand Rapids, MI: Brazos Press.

Bouma-Prediger, S., & Walsh, B. (2004). Education for homelessness or homemaking? The Christian college in a postmodern culture. *Journal of Education and Christian Belief*, 8 (1): 53–70.

Bowers, C. A. (1993). *Education, cultural myths and the ecological crisis: Toward deep changes*. Albany, NY: State University of New York Press.

Bowers, C. A. (1997). *The culture of denial: Why the environmental movement needs a strategy for reforming universities*. Albany, NY: State University of New York Press.

Bowers, C. A. (2001). *Educating for eco-justice and community*. Athens, GA: University of Georgia Press.

Bowers, C. A. (2006). *Revitalizing the commons: Cultural and educational sites of resistance and affirmation*. Lanham, MD: Lexington Books.

Bowers, C. A. (2012). *The way forward: Educational reforms that focus on the cultural commons and the linguistic roots of the ecological/cultural crises*. Eugene, OR: Eco-Justice Press.

Bowers, C. A., & Martusewicz, R. A. (2006). Revitalizing the commons of the African-American communities in Detroit. In C. A. Bowers, *Revitalizing the commons: Cultural and educational sites of resistance and affirmation* (pp. 47–84). London, UK: Rowman and Littlefield.

Edmundson, J. (2003). Translating theory into practice: Investigations toward the design of a model for a cultural-ecological teacher education program. *Dissertation Abstracts International: Section A. Humanities and Social Sciences*, 64(10): 1164.

Esteva, G., & Prakash, M. S. (1998). *Grassroots postmodernism: Remaking the soil of cultures*. London, UK: Zed Books.

Foucault, M. (1980). *Power/knowledge*. New York, NY: Pantheon books.

Henderson, J., & Hursh, D. (2014). Economics and education for human flourishing: Wendell Berry and the oikonomic alternative to neoliberalism. *Educational Studies: A Journal of the American Educational Studies Association*, 50: 167–186.

Irigaray, L. (2002). *The way of love*. London, UK: Continuum.

Lupinacci, J., & Happel, A. (2015). Recognize, resist and reconstitute: An ecocritical conceptual framework. *The SoHo Journal: Educational Foundations and Social Justice Education*, 1(1): 45–61.

Martusewicz, R. A. (2001). *Seeking passage: Post-Structuralism, pedagogy, ethics*. New York, NY: Teaches College Press.

Martusewicz, R. A., & Edmundson, J. (2005). Social foundations as pedagogies of responsibility and eco-ethical commitment. In D. Butin (Ed.), *Teaching context: A primer for the social foundations of education classroom* (pp. 71–92). Mahwah, NJ: Lawrence Erlbaum Publishers.

22 Introduction: Toward a Pedagogy of Responsibility

Martusewicz, R., & Johnson, L. (2016). EcoJustice education. In I. Van der Tuin (Ed.), *MacMillan Interdisciplinary Handbooks: Gender, v2: Nature* (pp. 57–71). New York, NY: MacMillan.

Martusewicz, R. A., Edmundson, J., & Lupinacci, J. (2015). *EcoJustice Education: Toward diverse, democratic and sustainable communities.* New York, NY: Routledge.

Plumwood, V. (1993). *Feminism and the mastery of nature.* New York, NY: Routledge.

Plumwood, V. (2002). *Environmental culture: The ecological crisis of reason.* New York, NY: Routledge.

Prakash, M. S. (1994). What are people for? Wendell Berry on education, ecology, and culture. *Educational Theory*, 44(2): 135–157.

Rasmussen, D. (2005). Cease to do evil, then learn to do good (A pedagogy for the oppressor). In C. A. Bowers & F. Apffel-Marglin (Eds.), *Rethinking Freire: Globalization and the environmental crisis* (pp. 115–132). Mahwah, NJ: Lawrence Erlbaum Associates.

Snauwaert, D. (1990). Wendell Berry, liberalism, and democratic theory: Implications for the rural school. *Peabody Journal of Education*, 67(4): 118–130.

Theobald, P., & Snauwaert, D. T. (1993). The educational philosophy of Wendell Berry. *Holistic Education Review*, 6(3): 37–43.

2

NEOLIBERALISM AND THE DIS-MEMBERING OF COMMUNITY

With Gary Schnakenberg

> When Mattie inherited her parents' estate, she used the moneys from the estate and the sale of the property in town to clear the Keith place of the inheritance taxes and outstanding debts. And then here is what Troy could have done. He could have made it safe in Mattie's keeping. He could have seen that, safe in her keeping, it would have made both of them safe for the rest of their lives. If he had to keep on in his debt-driven plunge toward whatever grandeur he thought would satisfy him, then he could have left her and her inheritance clear of it. But that is not what he did. He followed the ways of "business," not of farming or family or marriage. When the apple fell from the tree at last, he was there waiting, with his own hands cupped to receive it. (Berry, 2000a, p. 337)

In the novel *Jayber Crow* (2000a), Berry employs the character of Troy Chatham to illustrate the changes that took place in American agriculture in the decades after the Second World War. Unlike his traditionally-minded father-in-law Athey Keith, Troy is enthusiastic about undertaking a more "modern" approach to farming his land, which includes utilizing new technologies such as chemical fertilizer and maximizing acreage under production. This in turn requires the purchase of new and/or more equipment on credit, necessitating greater production to pay back loans and interest, which can only be accomplished through the purchase or rental of more land from other farmers, requiring even more loans. For Troy, taking on this type of financial risk was part of the "new" farming (in addition to the normal farmers' risks of weather, price fluctuations, and pest outbreaks); he tells Athey, "you've got to spend money to make money" (p. 185).

After Athey's death, Troy not only maximizes production on his own farm, but continues to expand operations by renting acreage on other farms. He sees himself as engaging in the *business* of farming; not "just a farmer," but someone

24 Neoliberalism and the Dis-membering of Community

with the status of a businessman. The business of farming is primarily about *volume*, and "Troy's one aim was to be at work with the greatest available power in the greatest possible field. During the sixties, with Athey gone and [his mother-in-law] Della out of the way, and Mattie [his wife, Athey and Della's daughter] resigned or unable to resist, he began tearing out fences, plowing through waterways, bulldozing groves of trees. He didn't want anything in his way" (p. 271). His mantra was "modernize, mechanize, specialize, grow" (p. 270). When older farmers wonder how, when losing money or just breaking even on growing corn, the solution was to grow more corn, Troy replies with metrics well-known to economists: efficiency, economies of scale, and volume (p. 278). When some balk at borrowing money in such circumstances, Troy's answer is, "Debt is just an ordinary business practice ... I never expect to be out of debt again in my life. If you've got anything paid for, borrow against it. *Use* it. Never let a quarter's worth of equity stand idle" (p. 279). After Della dies, Mattie inherits her parents' farm, and Troy persuades her to mortgage it for a high-tech dairying operation and for economic leverage to buy more land.

Troy is blind to the impacts of this approach on his community and neighbors (or even his own family), as more farming families leave the land and he becomes increasingly estranged from his wife and children in his relentless pursuit of the grandeur of size and the idea of "becoming somebody." Eventually the debt catches up; the price of land drops, and with the loss of equity he is forced to sell the timber on the "Nest Egg," a fifty-acre piece of untouched and forested land beloved by his wife (and Jayber Crow, Mattie's friend and the protagonist of this novel) in order to raise cash. It is denuded as Mattie lays dying of cancer in hospital.

This thread running through the novel describes a transitional period in American agriculture, from the "get big or get out of farming" advice and abandonment of government agricultural price supports by Eisenhower's Secretary of Agriculture Ezra Taft Benson (Sherow, 2007; Williams & Carter, 2011, p. 152) to his Nixon-era counterpart (and former Benson assistant) Earl Butz's similar exhortations to "get bigger, get better, or get out" and "adapt or die, resist and perish." (Risser, 1976; Berry, 1996; Davidson, 2003; Lehrer, 2010; Williams & Carter, 2011; Carlisle, 2015). Berry's response to Butz, written in 1982 as the Preface to the Second Edition of his book, *The Unsettling of America* (1996), could not be clearer:

> Then Secretary of Agriculture Earl L. Butz issued the most optimistic, the mostly widely obeyed, and the worst advice ever given to farmers: that they should plow "fencerow to fencerow." (p. vii)

That the situation was not good—for farms or farmers or rural communities or nature or the general public—was even then evident to an experienced observer who would turn aside from the preconceptions of "agribusiness" and look at the marks of deterioration that were plainly visible. And now, almost a decade later,

Neoliberalism and the Dis-membering of Community 25

it is evident to everyone that, at least for farmers and rural communities the situation is catastrophic: "Farmers are losing their farms, some are killing themselves, some in the madness of despair are killing other people, and rural economy and rural life are gravely stricken." (p. vii)

While *Jayber Crow* was published in 2000, the temporal setting for Troy Chatham's ruinous actions runs from the 1950s through the 1970s. Here as in other works of fiction, Berry employs his characters and their circumstances to not only describe historical issues involving rural communities and the broader society, but, using local language to imagine the quality and effects of relationships among people in a particular place, as commentary on issues and conditions facing communities around the world.

In *The Art of Loading Brush* (2017), Berry offers a comprehensive list of the agrarian values from which his own understanding of a viable local economy and decent community arises. Readers will no doubt begin to recognize the articulation of similar or related principles woven through other chapters as well as in what follows. We include his list here as a kind of foundation from which to understand Berry's critical analysis of the development and enactment of specific ideas in the policies guiding our current globalized industrial economy. As we lay out in some detail below, these particular policies began to show up after World War II in various sectors, and have now come to dominate both the US and global economic and political landscape, especially since the 1970s. As Troy's story indicates, Berry is especially concerned with the ways agrarian principles have been tossed aside in favor of a view of profit-based progress and wealth accumulation devastating to both human and ecological communities across the planet.

Berry is careful to offer the caveat that what he names as "agrarian" describes "a person of a kind," but the traits "…do not describe a perfect human being" (2017, p. 9). Rather, we see this list as a description of the ways particular virtues might be enacted in people's day-to-day choices and commitments. Our work to define and practice pedagogies of responsibility is precisely aimed at developing the internalized qualities needed for dignified life within diverse, democratic and sustainable communities. A person characterized as agrarian, would possess, according to Berry:

1. An elated, loving interest in the use and care of the land, and in all the details of the good husbandry of plants and animals.
2. An informed and conscientious submission to nature, or to Nature, and her laws of conservation, frugality, fullness or completeness, and diversity.
3. The wish, the felt need, to have and to belong to a place of one's own as the only secure source of sustenance and independence. (The freed slaves who pled for "forty acres and a mule" were more urgently and practically agrarian than the "Twelve Southerners" [a reference to a work that Berry was criticized for praising]).

26 Neoliberalism and the Dis-membering of Community

4. From that to a persuasion in favor of economic democracy, a preference for *enough* over *too much*.
5. Fear and contempt of waste of every kind and its ultimate consequence in land exhaustion. Waste is understood as human folly, an insult to nature, a sin against the given world and its life.
6. From that to a preference for saving rather than spending as the basis of the economy of a household or a government.
7. An assumption of the need for a subsistence or household economy, so as to live so far as possible *from* one's place.
8. An acknowledged need for neighbors and a willingness to *be* a neighbor. This comes from proof by experience that no person or family or place can live alone.
9. A living sense of the need for continuity of family and community life in place, which is to say the need for the survival of local culture and thus of the safekeeping of local memory and local nature.
10. Respect for work and (as self-respect) for good work. This implies an understanding of one's life's work as a vocation and a privilege, as opposed to a "job" and a vacation.
11. A lively suspicion of anything new. This contradicts the ethos of consumerism and the cult of celebrity. It is not inherently cranky or unreasonable. (Berry, 2017, pp. 8–9)

For some readers of Berry, his emphasis on these values makes him "old fashioned" and out of touch with reality. But, whose reality? Instead, we see Berry steadfastly exposing the development of a particular "reality" that is leading to the demise of life on this planet, and articulating, even demanding, a way of being—ancient in its broad and diverse outlines—that is respectful of living beings in their particular places. While recognizing a much longer history of violence in an exploitive industrial system, this chapter takes a close look at what exactly has led to the specific ideological, economic and political shifts we've seen beginning in the 1950s, accelerating in the 1970s and becoming crystallized as inevitable by the 1980s.

As the 1970s unfolded, a specific economic-political ideology was being developed, antecedents of which appeared especially in US agricultural policies in the 1950s as Berry's story of Troy reveals. This ideology, now known as neoliberalism, continues as of this writing to be the predominant way of thinking in nearly every state around the globe, defining the character of economic exchange, political policy, and many other types of relationships. In this dominant role, it continues to have deleterious effects on (but certainly not limited to) rural communities, both in the United States and around the world.

This chapter examines the history of the development of neoliberalism, in particular as it has disrupted communities across this country and beyond. We will be particularly interested in the ways that Berry responds to the destructive effects of its primary principles, especially its focus on individualism as inherent in human nature, the development of economies of scale supported by financialization and energized by merciless competition, the expanding use of technology, and their consequential impacts on land and people.

We introduce another of Berry's characters, Andy Catlett, whose life he traces through several short stories and a novella to illustrate the ways agrarian principles might be learned and lived. The men and women in these Port William stories express a collection of character traits important to Berry's philosophy of education and his critique of institutions. Andy, as we will see, is a farmer as well, and a neighbor to the Chathams, but he has chosen a very different path than Troy, born of a particular education received primarily from his parents, grandparents, their hired hands, and neighbors. Even as he struggles, his character and life story resist the outcomes of the system to which Troy Chatham is captive. We begin with a discussion of that system and its ideological foundations.

Political and Economic Foundations of Neoliberalism

Although the term has earlier origins, *neoliberalism* gained prominence in the 1980s as the dominant paradigm in Western capitalism, and therefore served as the basis for a set of influential organizing characteristics for society as a whole. In the original and now largely forgotten meaning of the term as it emerged in interwar Germany, Boas & Gans-Morse (2009) described the "Freiburg School" theorists as having "placed humanistic values on par with economic efficiency" (p. 149) and derided their *laissez-faire* contemporaries such as Ludwig von Mises as "paleoliberals" due to their blind free-market faith. As will be described below, the ideology of neoliberalism as it has come to be conceived and applied took on a meaning diametrically opposed to that applied by the Freiburg School thinkers.

Classical "liberalism" was a political philosophy influential in the nineteenth century (but included relations in the economic sphere) that rejected the hereditary and monarchical power dominant in past eras in favor of a "forward-looking" emphasis on individual rights and liberty. Its foundations rest on the work of John Locke and is associated not only with the economist Adam Smith but also "utilitarian" philosophers such as Jeremy Bentham and John Stuart Mill who were concerned with "achieving the greatest good for the greatest number." On the other hand, "neoliberalism" is primarily economic in focus, but also includes ideas about the proper role of the state in facilitating this economic activity.

Broadly speaking, neoliberalism based on political philosophies and economic theories of von Mises and his student Friedrich Hayek, Milton Friedman, and others set forth a fundamentalist free-market approach as the only path to promote economic growth and efficiency, spur technological progress, and achieve optimal income distribution, thereby maximizing social well-being. Any active intervention, or even participation, by government would inevitably worsen economic performance and fail to bring about the aforementioned social benefits, no matter how well-intentioned (Kotz, 2015, p. 12).

Although often framed (especially by opponents) as some monolithic entity, like capitalism itself, neoliberalism is a complex assemblage with a number of features. The following section will provide some historical context for the emergence and rise of neoliberalism, as well as expand upon the broad strokes above regarding neoliberalism's characteristics.

Origins of Neoliberalism

As most high school students could readily explain, capitalism is based on the idea of profit (surplus value). From the origins of industrialization in the English Midlands in the second half of the 1700s through the late nineteenth and early twentieth century emergence of the "Robber Barons," the Trusts, Standard Oil, the auto industry, and the like, few regulations existed on how these profits were made, and those regulations that came along did so in a rather piecemeal fashion. However, beginning in the immediate post-World War II era and extending through the late 1970s, states and corporations broadly followed the prescriptions of British economist John Maynard Keynes to one degree or another. The first half of the twentieth century saw a series of shocks—the Bolshevik Revolution of 1917, the Great Depression and labor unrest of the 1930s, and the economic mobilization for World War II. These shocks led large businesses in the US to support classic Keynesian policies. In other words, they by-and-large supported the notion that government should take an active part in promoting economic growth, maximizing employment, delivering social benefits, adjusting interest rates to reduce the peaks and valleys of the business cycle, following progressive tax policies, running deficits when necessary, and so on (Harvey, 2005; Kotz, 2015). Kotz (2015) refers to these decades after the war's conclusion as the era of "regulated capitalism" (p. 6).

By the 1970s, however, a shift was underway resulting from several intersecting factors that, in sum, presented business, and large business in particular, with a crisis. After peaking in the mid-1960s, corporate profit *rates* (as a percent of revenues beyond all costs, not actual profit *amounts*) began falling from the late 1960s due to a combination of import competition from Japan and Western Europe, the collapse of fixed exchange rates of the Bretton Woods system, expansion of the welfare state and associated taxation (e.g., the EPA, OSHA, Food Stamps, Medicare), "stagflation," and the first oil crisis of 1973 (Harvey, 2005, pp. 12–13; Kotz, 2015, pp. 63–67). This crisis led to an abandonment of the broadly regulatory philosophy that marked capitalism of this period. The story of two different associations of business leaders is illustrative of this change.

In the 1940s, leaders of several large businesses organized the Committee for Economic Development (CED) "as a private, non-profit, non-political association" (McQuaid, 1982, p. 115). The CED Board grew from just over a dozen at the group's founding in 1942 to 43 in 1948, representing "almost a who's who of US big businesses" (Kotz, 2015, pp. 53–54). The organization advocated "collective bargaining ..., Keynesian policies to regulate the business cycle, and government provision of social welfare programs" (Kotz, 2015, p. 54). By the 1970s, the voice of US business and industry had become instead the Business Roundtable, founded in 1972, which unlike the CED, acted as a lobbying arm to halt the expansion of regulation and defeat bills that would increase the costs of doing business and generally promoting the transformation towards the neoliberal restructuring project (Kotz, 2015; Drutman, 2015).

Although initial markers of neoliberalism appeared in the administration of Democratic President Jimmy Carter, with the undoing of a somewhat progressive tax reform bill and advancing de-regulation of the economy, neoliberalist policies were championed and expanded significantly by UK Prime Minister Margaret Thatcher and US President Ronald Reagan after their elections in 1979 and 1980, respectively (Harvey, 2005; Kotz, 2015), and came to be closely associated with them. After the fall of the Berlin Wall in late 1989 and the weakening and eventual dissolution of the Soviet Union over the next two years, neoliberal free-market capitalism was triumphant, leading to (rather premature) declarations of the "end of history" (Fukuyama, 1989, 1992).

Characteristics of Neoliberalism

Although it was stated earlier in this chapter that neoliberalism as a set of practices is not monolithic, it nonetheless exhibits some fairly consistent internal elements or principles. Chief among these is a near-fetishization of the abstracted, generalized "market," which according to early proponents of neoliberalism "trumps all because it comprehends all" (Mullen, 2016, p. 9). The market is unassailable, according to Mirowski (2009, quoted in Mullen, 2016): "The market ... can always provide solutions seemingly caused by the market in the first place ... Any problem, economic or otherwise, has a market solution, given sufficient ingenuity" (p. 439). This principle leads directly to another: the rejection of almost any regulation of, or even role in, economic activity by the government as a violation of this fundamentalist laissez-faire free-market approach. Government interference in business via regulations is defined as an impediment to political freedom; "freedom," accordingly, is the supposed outgrowth of this unfettered economic activity to the point that neoliberalism came to be framed as the "exclusive guarantor of freedom" (Harvey, 2005, p. 40). The only legitimate role of government in this ideological system is to enforce law and order to protect private property.

These "primary" characteristics of neoliberal ideologies result in several "secondary" characteristics when put into practice. Three secondary characteristics are particularly relevant: financialization, maximization, and individualism. As we'll see further on, these characteristics are addressed by Berry's fiction as well as his essays, as they erode a more orderly and kind, if less technologically "advanced" way of life.

Financialization

As pointed out above, neoliberal deregulation of the financial sector resulted in the invention of new speculative investment tools that yielded spectacular profits—at least for awhile—for those who could take advantage of them. In the era of "regulated capitalism" (Kotz, 2015), the financial sector's function was primarily to lend capital to the productive sector; in the neoliberal era, it was increasingly oriented towards highly speculative and risky profit-generating activities worldwide, divorced from any lending functions to the productive sector (p. 107, see also Kotz, 2008).

The financial sector continued to increase its role in the US economy into the current century, reaching 8.3 percent of GDP in 2006, compared to 4.9 percent in 1980 and 2.8 percent in 1950 (Greenwood & Scharfstein, 2013). Landy (2013) pointed out that total compensation of financial intermediaries (profits, wages, salaries, and bonuses) as a fraction of GDP reached an all-time high, totaling around 9 percent at the time of his writing.

Emphasis on finance within an economy exacerbates inequality. In the US, the share of national income held by the top 10 percent peaked in the 1920s at just below 50 percent before dropping into a narrow range between 30 and 35 percent from the mid-1940s to around 1980, when it trended steeply upward, again reaching 45–50 percent in the 2000s (with one downward blip to about 43 percent during the Great Recession), and touching 50 percent in 2010 (Piketty, 2017, p. 31). The greater the percentage of national income from the financial sector, the lower the percentage of national income from wages and salaries; by extension, when return on capital investment is high, inherited wealth grows faster than wealth resulting from output of labor.

> Under such conditions, it is almost inevitable that inherited wealth will dominate wealth amassed from a lifetime's labor by a wide margin, and the concentration of capital will attain extremely high levels—levels potentially incompatible with the meritocratic values and principles of social justice fundamental to modern democratic societies. (Piketty, 2017, p. 34)

For agricultural communities, the growth of the financial sector has had severe effects. Perhaps most significantly, the global banking and finance sector—not at the scale of the local community bank, many of which have disappeared through consolidation—became inserted, to a new degree, into rural/agricultural life. Historically, high levels of debt had been anathema to farmers given the range of hazards and risks they face (for example, unfavorable weather and crop failures) and an antipathy to urban elites in business and government "back East" (Slaybaugh, 1996; Pollan, 2006); farms had traditionally maximized use of on-farm resources and kept their use of credit to a minimum (Sage, 2012).

For actual farmers, as well as Berry's fictional Troy Chatham, the need for credit went hand-in-hand with the requirements of the productionist imperative reflected in agricultural policies beginning in the 1950s. The exhortation to produce more required more land under production, usually through putting marginal land under cultivation (with attendant ecological impacts) as well as purchasing more land, in conjunction with using "modern, technological methods." Sage (2012) describes this process of intensification as altering the balance of the mixed family farming system:

> [F]armers were expected to borrow money to buy machinery and use credit by banks to purchase inputs. Gradually the financial institutions have become an integral part of the new agri-food system, providing a source of credit for new rounds of investment against the collateral of agricultural land. It is in this context that the coercion and enforcement used on farmers to ensure adoption of new practices and technologies now seems especially stark. What was once a largely self-sufficient unit, forming part of a local or regional mosaic of food producers, has now become encircled by creditors, input suppliers, knowledge providers, and those voracious industrial and commercial operators downstream … [while] farmers' share of the value of a basket of food items fell from 47 percent in 1988 to 36 percent in 2007, a decline of one-fifth in real terms. (pp. 36–37)

Maximization

The period of neoliberalism's rise coincides with a wave of globalization of economic activity. The rise of neoliberalism was a necessary element within the process of economic globalization in two important ways. First, the erosion of governments' abilities to regulate economic activity and the championing of the "free market" that characterizes neoliberalism led to the growth of transnational companies and the concomitant growth in global production chains, and associated "footloose" character. Rather than remaining grounded in a particular place, companies could seek new locations for various aspects of their operations based on tax benefits, attractive labor costs (or, "low wages"), lax environmental regulations, and the like. Those actors who were in a position to take advantage of globalization did so, which led to strong competitive pressure across businesses to reduce costs and lower prices further to ensure profitability (Kotz, 2002).

32 Neoliberalism and the Dis-membering of Community

Second, and coming from this, only large and highly capitalized entities are able to achieve the economies of scale that drive costs down and improve the "efficiency" required for continued growth, the Grail of capitalism (Binswanger, 2009; Kuepper, 2017). At low prices, volume is necessary for profitability. The results are "productionist" approaches to economic activity, and ongoing consolidation/acquisition/expansion in order to become large enough to reach the threshold volume.

Thus, the "maximization" effect of neoliberalism produces effects on communities at multiple scales. On the global scale, it acts as a catalyst for the current wave of globalization, which disrupts local businesses and livelihoods, introduces new types of industrial activity and associated environmental problems (in locations where environmental safeguards are lax or absent), and is a driver of rural-to-urban migration across the Global South (Davis, 2006; Grau & Aide, 2008). At the scale of the community in the rural United States, it is responsible for the decline of local businesses and boarding up of Main Streets and the sale of land by smaller farmers who cannot break even to "agribusiness operators" who can achieve the efficiencies, unit costs, and production levels necessary to be profitable (and are large enough to receive subsidies not available to smaller farm operators). Competition driven by aims to have the lowest production costs in a globalized agro-economy requires standardized crop varieties with fast maturation rates, and erodes local knowledge as well as bio- and cultural diversity (Sage, 2012).

Troy's drive to acquire more, his dream of "farming big," and his relentless pursuit of being a businessman, all reflect not only the agricultural policies of the post-World War II United States, but also of the pervasive ideology of neoliberalism as it manifested in the personal choices of farmers being wooed by its promises of success and upward mobility. Troy is after becoming a big man in the Port William community where "getting big" —in spite of the huge risks involved—means disposing of the degrading mantle of "hick" or "hillbilly." To "maximize" his prowess in the game, he goes deeper and deeper into debt, buying bigger machinery, putting more land under production without rest, using chemical inputs, and eschewing as backward all the traditional practices his father-in-law, Athey had used to sustain a living on that land.

"Maximization"/globalization runs contrary to Berry's (1990) insistence of our need to act at the "scale of our competence" (p. 200). The "global" is not a scale of effective action; we must act to "care for each of the planet's millions of human and natural neighborhoods, each of its millions of small pieces and parcels of land, each one of which is in some precious way different from all the others" (Berry, 1990, p. 200). We have the ability to care well for only our households, neighborhoods, and small parcels of land. This is, as Henderson and Hursh (2014) point out, Berry's plea for "oikonomics," an economy of the household and homemaking. For Berry, a sensible economy is one that recognizes that true value is only found in the living relations of Creation, or what we introduced as

Neoliberalism and the Dis-membering of Community 33

the principles of the Great Economy in Chapter 1. This means that the forms of exchange, use, production, and consumption will be engaged with an understanding of limits, both of human understanding of the complexities of the larger living world and its mysteries, and the limits demanded by that order itself. It thus requires the cooperation and mutuality among the membership of one's local place, its people and its creatures.

Individualism

A powerful and pervasive element making up the fabric of American mythology is a particular take on the concept of individualism. With antecedents in anti-monarchical Lockean liberalism of the late seventeenth century and the revolutionary rejection of the *ancien régime* in late eighteenth-century France (reflected in *The Rights of Man and the Citizen*), "individualism" in the widely-used sense today emerged only in the nineteenth century: the word does not appear in Samuel Johnson's famous 1755 *Dictionary of the English Language* (Eagleton-Pierce, 2016). American individualism combines elements of New England Puritanism, the Jeffersonian ideal of the "yeoman farmer," the freedom from Britain won in the War of Independence, the writings of Franklin, Emerson, and Whitman along with the rejection of ideas associated with "coastal elites" (Anderson, 1971; Lukes, 1973; Barlow, 2013). This American strain of individualism eschewed behaving as expected based on one's "station" in life and was closely linked to the experience of, and opportunities presented by (at least for white settlers), the American frontier (Turner, 1893; Fevre, 2016). Perhaps surprisingly, the ideology of individualism gained traction in the late 1960s and early 1970s as an outgrowth of social movements connected to civil rights, feminism, human rights, and greater demands for "self-actualization" instead of being defined by others as part of a monolithic group or the "liberation" of the individual from the conforming strictures of society (Eagleton-Pierce, 2016).

The timing mentioned above is instructive, overlapping as it does with the development and emergence of neoliberal ideologies, expansion of which were no doubt aided by this thread of individualism. Neoliberalism promotes the notion of self-reliance, personal responsibility, individual choice and discourages social solidarity and collective action, working to limit the "sites and spaces of the social toward which we can be said to bear a moral responsibility" (Popke & Torres, 2013, p. 213; see also Harvey, 2005). In a similar vein, Miller and Rose (2008) point out that within neoliberalism, the notion of the individual is less derived "from membership of a collective body than an individual whose citizenship is active. This citizenship is to be manifested ... in the energetic pursuit of personal fulfilment ..." (p. 82).

This aggressive self-reliance, rarely practiced to the extent it is mythologized, became especially associated with the inhabitants of rural areas such as ranchers

34 Neoliberalism and the Dis-membering of Community

and farmers who were spatially and philosophically far removed from the corrupting influence of "the city" and therefore closer to the purity of the American ideal. Miller and Rose's (2008) use of the notion of "membership" in the preceding paragraph invokes Berry's frequent employment of the concept. The type individualism championed by neoliberalism is rootless and disconnected, running counter to the needs and interests of rural communities, and even individual farmers and their families.

Further, neoliberalism's emphasis on the individual had the effect of "individualizing" risk; if farmers weren't making it, the fault lay with them as individuals and their actions or inactions, rather than with structural inequalities and the operation of a distant globalized economy (Gray & Lawrence, 2001; Cheshire & Lawrence, 2005). While self-reliance in many ways has indeed long been a part of rural identity (note number three on Berry's list of agrarian characteristics, see p. 26), the rise of neoliberal ideologies separated it from other long-standing elements of agricultural life, such as cooperation (Cheshire & Lawrence, 2005), or in Berry's language, neighborliness, and made selfish accumulation a primary attribute of both rural and urban life.

Berry traces these changes, emphasizing the drastic reduction of small farms across the country, the extraction of profits from the communities in which they were generated as agriculture became industrialized and part of a globalized economy, serving anonymous and distant commodity and financial markets that have no regard for, or even recognition of, limits. Larger and larger landholders needing larger and larger machines became the only ones able to maintain operations on the land.

We read across Berry's work his acute despair over the demise of rural communities, the destruction of the soil and forests, the mechanization and commodification of everything, even the animals themselves once cared for and treated with dignity in traditional husbandry practices key to small farms everywhere. Berry bears witness to the dissolution of relationships once built on trust, respect and mutual dependence, especially around neighborliness and good work. He decries the turning over of traditional land-based knowledge to "experts" and scientist–specialists in universities and policy-making organizations who promote this decline of sensible subsistence-based land stewardship in favor of efficiencies, profit, and the idea that we are somehow perfecting the species with our ever-expanding technology. "We should abandon the idea that this world and our human life in it can be brought by science to some sort of mechanical perfection or predictability" (Berry 2000b, p. 135).

While Berry does not completely eschew science, he insists that the wisdom most needed is that held in common with those who have attended to life in a particular place over many generations, developing the practices and knowledge needed by those places, and thus learning to flourish there. This is never a matter of individual autonomy, but rather of deeply cultivated relationships of care and nurture. It is a matter of understanding our absolute dependencies with other

Neoliberalism and the Dis-membering of Community **35**

creatures on the gift that preserves the cycle of life, and the violence of those systems—economic, cultural, and psychological and educational—that ignore it.

"Nothing Living Lives Alone"[1]

Andy Catlett is an old man. Looking back over his life, he is troubled. Not that this state of mind is anything new; he knows, has known most of his life, what has been lost. He is witness to the abuse and dismemberment of his community.

> It was a country that he and his people had known how to use and abuse but not how to preserve. In the coal counties, east and west they were strip mining without respect for the past or mercy to the future, and the reign of an compunctionless national economy was established everywhere. Andy began to foresee a time when everything in the country would be market-able and everything would be sold, when not one freestanding man or woman would remain. (Berry, 2008, p. 79)

Ruminating on a broken fence (Berry, 2017), or rather a mess made by those who he had begrudgingly hired to fix it, and his declining ability to either fix it himself or clean up the mess, he is remembering. He has been a writer (a jour-nalist) and a farmer all his adult life, having left to go to college and returned to claim his place in the membership of Port William. As such, he has spent most of his life moving back and forth across boundaries between the hills and hollows, fields and forests of his rural homeland and the excitement and exuberance of cities, between a world—now mostly gone—of neighborly countenance and another of rationalized greed and exploitation. He is thinking back to a moment when, in his own mind and out of his own mouth, these two worlds collided (2008). An embarrassing moment, perhaps, but telling too. It happened not long after losing his right hand (he still thinks of it as giving his hand) to a machine on the farm, an accident that left him enraged and grieving for months. On this particular day, he was at a conference, "The Future of the American Food System." Finding a seat in the back of the auditorium, the rage, fear, and frus-tration of his dismemberment was still in his throat. Soon it would be inflamed. He had been invited to this conference for his reputation as someone who might offer "the other side" of the story of agriculture. He remembers now with returning anger, the words of the government official who opened the conference:

> "When I was a boy," the high official said, "45 percent of our people were on the farm. Now we have reduced that to about 4 percent. Millions of people have been released from farmwork to make automobiles and TV sets and plumbing fixtures—in other words, to make this the greatest industrial

nation the world has ever seen. Millions of people have been freed from groveling in the earth so that they can now pursue the finer things in life."

"And the 4 percent left on the farm live better than the 45 percent ever hoped to live. This 4 percent we may think of as the permanent staff of this great food production machine that is the farms and fields of America."

"... Let me tell you something. This is economics we're talking about. And the basic law of economics is: Adapt or die ... This is the way a dynamic free market economy works. This is the American system." (Berry, 2008, p. 9)

A string of other experts followed, citing statistics for inputs and outputs, proclaiming a 500 percent increase in the tonnage of fertilizer used on American farms since 1950, increases in tractor horsepower and decreases in human work hours, and a precipitous drop in farm populations from 23 million to 7.8 million (2008, p. 13). Andy recalls his eyes drooping and his head dropping as he dozed off, then waking suddenly: "He felt like a sentinel on watch, a mourner at a wake, aggrieved, endangered, and falling asleep" (2008, p. 14).

Soon, it's his turn to take the lectern. He is introduced, and stands before the audience. "Instead of the text of the speech he had prepared, he spread on the rostrum the notes he had made on the speeches preceding his."

"... No one who has spoken this morning has worked a day on an actual farm in 20 years, and the reason for that is that none of the speakers wants to work on a farm or be a farmer. The real interest of this meeting is in the academic careerism and the politics and the business of agriculture, and I daresay that most people here, like the first speaker, are proud to have escaped the life and work of farmers, whom they do not admire."

"... I don't believe it is well understood how influence flows from enclosures like this to the fields and farms and farmers themselves. ... The 15 million people who have left the farms since 1950 left because of damage. There was pain in the departure, not shown in any of the figures we have seen. Not felt in this room. And the pain and the damage began a long time before 1950 ..." (2008, pp. 18–19)

He had gone on to tell them a story about a nearly disastrous financial loss his grandparents had suffered due to the capricious nature of financial policies farmers were forced to live with. And finally this:

"I say damn your systems and your numbers and your ideas. I speak for Dorie Catlett and Marce Catlett. I speak for Mat and Margaret Feltner, for Jack Beechum, for Jarratt and Burley Coulter, for Nathan Coulter and Hannah, for Danny and Lyda Branch, for Marin and Arthur Rowanberry, for Elton and Mary and Jack Penn." (2008, p. 20)

Neoliberalism and the Dis-membering of Community   37

With that naming of the membership—a critical remembering—he was left "empty, shaking, wet with sweat" (p. 20). And then he had left. In the next two days, in his bed in an empty hotel room and on the streets of San Francisco, one after another, the membership came to him in memories and stories from times long past and recent, with traces of stories in other stories. And finally, the order of loving care restored to him, he had come home to Flora, his children and their life in Port William.

So, here he is today, more memories coming to him: the days spent as a young boy on his grandparents' farms, running free across the fields and woodlots, fishing or swimming, or learning at the side of the hired hands, or his uncles and their neighbors. He remembers weekends on the Feltner farm, his grandpa picking him up in the horse-drawn wagon as he stepped off the bus (2006), and an afternoon spent climbing a tree—many trees—and getting nearly lost high in the canopy as he followed a young squirrel, mesmerized by its beauty. And oh! His grandmothers' scolding when he returned too late to do his chores (2011). He remembers raising chicks to sell, learning "the old ways" with that same grandmother.

> Out the door he can see the red sky in the west. And he loves it there in the quiet with her, doing what has been done forever. "I hope we always do it forever," he says. She looks down at him, and smiles, and then suddenly pulls his head against her. "Oh my boy, how far away will you be sometime, remembering this." (2008, p. 47)

He remembers his neighbors' help the summer after his accident.

> When his first crop of alfalfa was ready to harvest in mid-May, they came to help him—Nathan and Danny and Jack, and Martin and Arthur Rowanberry. Or rather, they came to harvest his hay ..., his embarrassed, "I don't know how to thank you" and Nathan's grin as he grabbed his right arm and gave it a tug, "Help *us!*". (2008, pp. 31–32; emphasis in original)

And now, he's old and he needs to clean up a mess. Nearly all of them are gone. He feels the weight of their loss, and another wave of angry embarrassment as he realizes his mistake of not supervising the crew of arrogant young men who had "fixed" his fence, ignoring his careful instructions. He can't bear to ask his son, so he has called another young man from town. Just home from college, Austin has worked for Andy before; he's happy to come. He arrives and now they set to work loading brush in a wagon pulled by Andy's two gelding percherons. The young man tosses a branch into the wagon, and a lesson begins: "the art of loading brush" (2017).

Andy said

38 Neoliberalism and the Dis-membering of Community

> "Austin, my good boy, damn it, wait a minute. We ain't going to make a mess to clean up a mess again ..." "... come and pick up that branch you just threw on and turn it over so it takes up less room. Now snug the butt up against the headboard of the wagon. ... That's right ... that's the way we do it. We pick up every piece and look at it and put it on the load in the place where it belongs ... that's the way we shape the load." (2017, p. 254)

Andy thinks to himself that "maybe in the passing on of his ghostly knowledge he was doing his duty to Austin" (p. 255). And he muses to himself that he is giving his own life a restart by teaching this boy something of what he has been taught.

> "My dear Austin, my good boy, ... if you don't have people, whose hands can make order of whatever they pick up, you're going to be shit out of luck. And, in my opinion, if the art of loading brush dies out, the art of making music finally will die out. You tell your professors when you go back, that you met an old provincial man, a leftover, who told you: No high culture without low culture, and when low culture is the scarcest *it* is the highest. Tell 'em that. And then tell me what they say." (2017, p. 256)

Finally, they use their load of brush to help divert water that was creating a gully, probably begun from unwise

> plowing and cropping of the slopes ... Austin stepped with the happiness of his young strength into the work ... they had undone the bad work of the fencers. Maybe they had helped a little the healing of the hurt world. And he was proud of the boy. (2017, p. 257)

Conclusion

> ... the industrial economy, from agriculture to war, is by far the most violent the world has ever known, and we are all complicit in its violence. Our prevalent ways of using our land—land use plus industrial technology, minus care—produce commodities highly profitable to corporations at the unaccounted cost of massive waste and destruction. ... Because these ways are so immensely profitable, their political and scientific defenders are accredited by wealth and power, hence by respected listeners. Advocates for kinder ways are mostly unheard. (Berry, 2015, p. 98)

Berry recognizes that his lifelong advocacy for "low culture"—care of the land, the protection and nurturing of neighborliness, of humility and kindness as a way of life has fallen on mostly deaf ears. Andy misses "the membership" as it was held together by those values. As the younger generation grows up to be encouraged to leave in order to pursue "success," the thread of love, nurtured by

Neoliberalism and the Dis-membering of Community **39**

a specific kind of education, is cut. His remembering is about the long line of teachers that held the community together over generations, the lessons, knowledge and values passed down in stories. In memory, he recognizes that over his life he has made many friends who were allies and teachers. Through Andy, Berry names these friends in the fictional characters in the life of Port William, but also in real life people from his own experience (2017). And while some of these are scientists and academics, Berry is without a doubt suspicious of a university education that is, he says, mostly about teaching us to leave home to become part of the ever-expanding global economy. In resistance to this, Berry poses the intergenerational passing down of wisdom—the wisdom of love—from one generation to the next, even while he proclaims the particular failures of his own people. Speaking once again through Andy Catlett he says

> Their failure ... had certainly been economic, for they had wasted or destroyed much of the natural wealth they had possessed at the beginning ... Before their failure was economic, it had been cultural. They had destroyed so much, partly no doubt in ignorance, but mostly for want of a cultural imperative to save it. (2017, p. 202)

One of the most important imperatives of a pedagogy of responsibility is to take up this challenge: to both expose the deeply violent systems—discursive, ideological, economic, institutional—produced by industrial culture, and to identify the ways of being, the practices and principles that could, even in small ways (but hopefully in bigger ways too), heal this damaged world. Healing will not happen in isolation: "nothing living lives alone" (2011). It can only happen if we recognize our interwovenness, the absolute unavoidable nature of our immersion in the complex weave of life. Neoliberal policies, and the old modernist ideas from which they spring, are fundamentally about fragmentation, disconnection, and extraction for short term individual benefit. Reducing everything to privatized market forces pulls apart relationships of trust and generosity that communities depend upon, in the name of efficiency and progress.

Such an organization of human economic and political life cannot go on long without destroying everything, including the people behind its disastrous policies. So what do we do as we face those disasters? Our shorthand answer, and the answer that Berry has spent his life trying to detail, is that we have to learn what it means to love, what it means to engage an "order of loving care" that attends to what maintains life itself.

This is what Andy Catlett is trying to pass on to young Austin: that there is a reason to attend responsibly to work done well, in caring orderly practices on the land and in our day-to-day relationships that help others, even in something as seemingly innocuous as loading brush. Good work that offers help where needed contributes to the drawing together of membership in a community. Learning to

40 Neoliberalism and the Dis-membering of Community

be responsible is about learning particular virtues: kindness, humility, forbearance, gratitude, generosity, as the stuff, the internalized "tools" of a particular way of being in the world. In traditional land-based communities, such as Berry describes, these qualities, while intangible, are often learned through the passing down of stories that share both what worked in particular situations, and what went badly wrong. The stories form a thread of intergenerational memory, lessons that hold the members of a community in an embrace of security, care, and love. This is Berry's message as Andy Catlett wanders the city remembering the membership via long ago stories. He is remembering his community and healing himself from the deep wounds of increasing fragmentation.

Without an education that helps to develop these virtues, and encouraged instead by appetites for selfishness, competition, and accumulation (what capitalism teaches us is our true nature as humans), we will remain responsible for (further) suffering, including our own. A pedagogy of responsibility asks us to name those tendencies that violate life and wound us all, deeply rooted in our cultural practices, political and economic systems, institutions, and psyches. And, it asks us to identify what it means to come awake to the embrace of the world's living tapestry, and to the bonds of love necessary to cycles of life itself, to imagine the possibilities that come alive in those bonds. As Hannah Coulter says to Andy, "By whose love, Andy Catlett, do we love this world and ourselves and one another? Do you think we invented it ourselves? I ask with confidence, for I know, you know we didn't" (Berry, 2010, p. 159).

Note

1 This section is a composite created via our imaginations from several works of fiction by Berry where Andy Catlett is the central character. These include *Andy Catlett: Early Travels* (2006), *Remembering: A Novel* (2008), "Nothing Living Lives Alone" (2011), *The Art of Loading Brush* (2017), and "The Order of Loving Care", a chapter in *The Art of Loading Brush* (2017). We have indicated where we are drawing directly from Berry's text, and where we are paraphrasing directly from the stories. Other connective narrative comes from our imaginations, with apologies (and gratitude) to Wendell Berry.

References

Anderson, Q. (1971). *The imperial self.* New York, NY: Alfred A. Knopf.

Barlow, A. (2013). *The cult of individualism: A history of an enduring American myth.* Santa Barbara, CA: Praeger.

Berry, W. (1990). Word and flesh. In *What are people for? Essays by Wendell Berry* (pp. 197–203). Berkeley, CA: Counterpoint.

Berry, W. (1996). *The unsettling of America: Culture and agriculture.* San Francisco, CA: Sierra Club Books.

Berry, W. (2000a). *Jayber Crow: A novel.* New York: Counterpoint.

Berry, W. (2000b). *Life is a miracle: An essay against modern superstition.* Washington, DC: Counterpoint.

Berry, W. (2006). *Andy Catlett: Early travels*. Emeryville, CA: Shoemaker and Hoard.

Berry, W. (2008). *Remembering: A novel*. Berkeley, CA: Counterpoint.

Berry, W. (2010). *Hannah Coulter: A novel*. Washington, DC: Shoemaker and Hoard.

Berry, W. (2011). Nothing living lives alone. *The Threepenny Review* (Spring): 10–13.

Berry, W. (2015). *Our only world: Ten essays*. Berkeley, CA: Counterpoint.

Berry, W. (2017). *The art of loading brush: New agrarian writings*. Berkeley, CA: Counterpoint.

Binswanger, M. (2009). Is there a growth imperative in capitalist economies? A circular flow perspective. *Journal of Post-Keynesian Economics*, 31(4): 707–727.

Boas, T. C., & Gans-Morse, J. (2009). Neoliberalism: From new liberal philosophy to anti-liberal slogan. *Studies in Comparative International Development*, 44(2): 137–161.

Carlisle, L. (2015). *Lentil underground: Renegade farmers and the future of food in America*. New York, NY: Avery.

Cheshire, L., & Lawrence, G. (2005). Neoliberalism, individualisation, and community: Regional restructuring in Australia. *Social Identities*, 11(5): 435–445.

Davidson, O. G. (2003). Decline and denial. In R. O. Davies, D. R. Pichaske, & J. A. Amato (Eds.), *A place called home: Writings on the midwestern small town*. St. Paul, MN: Minnesota Historical Society Press.

Davis, M. (2006). *Planet of slums*. London: Verso.

Drutman, L. (2015). How corporate lobbyists conquered American democracy. *The Atlantic*. Retrieved from www.theatlantic.com/business/archive/2015/04/how-corpora te-lobbyists-conquered-american-democracy/390822/

Eagleton-Pierce, M. (2016). On individualism in the neoliberal period. Paper presented at Political Studies Association Annual International Conference, Brighton (UK), March 21–23.

Fevre, R. (2016). *Individualism and inequality: The future of work and politics*. Cheltenham, UK and Northampton, MA: Edward Elgar.

Fukuyama, F. (1989). The end of history? *The National Interest*, 16: 3–18.

Fukuyama, F. (1992). *The end of history and the last man*. New York, NY: Simon and Schuster.

Grau, H. R., & Aide, M. (2008). Globalization and land-use transition in Latin America. *Ecology and Society*, 13(2): 16. Retrieved from www.ecologyandsociety.org/vol13/iss2/a rt16/

Gray, I., & Lawrence, G. (2001). *A future for regional Australia: Escaping global misfortune*. Cambridge: Cambridge University Press.

Greenwood, R., & Scharfstein, D. (2013). The growth of finance. *Journal of Economic Perspectives*, 27(2): 3–28.

Harvey, D. (2005). *A brief history of neoliberalism*. New York, NY: Oxford University Press.

Henderson, J. A., & Hursh, D. W. (2014). Economics and education for human flourishing: Wendell Berry and the oikonomic alternative to neoliberalism. *Educational Studies, A Journal of the American Educational Studies Association*, 50(2): 167–186.

Kotz, D. (2002). Globalization and neoliberalism. *Rethinking Marxism*, 12(2) (Summer): 64–79.

Kotz, D. (2008). Contradictions of economic growth in the neoliberal era: Accumulation and crisis in the contemporary U.S. economy. *Review of Radical Political Economics*, 40(2) (Spring): 174–188.

Kotz, D. (2015). *The rise and fall of neoliberal capitalism*. Cambridge, MA: Harvard University Press.

Kuepper, J. (2017). Globalization and its impact on economic growth: How globalization affects international investors. The Balance: International investing. Retrieved from www.thebalance.com/globalization-and-its-impact-on-economic-growth-1978843

Landy, B. (2013). Graph: How the financial sector consumed America's economic growth. Commentary, February 25. The Century Foundation. Retrieved from https://tcf.org/content/commentary/graph-how-the-financial-sector-consumed-americas-economic-growth/

Lehrer, N. (2010). *U.S. farm bills and policy reforms: Ideological conflicts over world trade, renewable energy, and sustainable agriculture*. Amherst, NY: Cambria Press.

Lukes, S. (1973). *Individualism*. Oxford: Basil Blackwell.

McQuaid, K. (1982). *Big business and presidential power: From FDR to Reagan*. New York: William Morris & Co.

Miller, P., & Rose, N. (2008). *Governing the present*. Malden, MA: Polity Press.

Mirowski, P. (2009). Defining neoliberalism. In P. Mirowski, & D. Plehwe (Eds.), *The Road from Mont Pelerin: The making of the neoliberal thought collective* (pp. 417–455). Cambridge, MA: Harvard University Press.

Mullen, J. (2016). On being like a fox: Wendell Berry on neoliberalism and education. Paper presented at the American Educational Studies Association Annual Conference, Seattle, WA, November 2–6.

Piketty, T. (2017). *Capital in the twenty-first century* (A. Goldhammer, Trans.). Cambridge, MA & London: Belknap Press of Harvard University Press.

Pollan, M. (2006). *The omnivore's dilemma: A natural history of four meals*. New York: Penguin.

Popke, J., & Torres, R. M. (2013). Neoliberalization, transnational migration, and economic subjectivity in Veracruz. *Annals of the Association of American Geographers*, 103(1): 211–229.

Risser, J. (1976). Why they love Earl Butz. *New York Times*. Retrieved from www.nytimes.com/1976/06/13/archives/why-they-love-earl-butz-prosperous-farmers-see-him-as-the-greatest.html

Sage, C. (2012). *Environment and food*. New York, NY: Routledge.

Sherow, J. E. (2007). *The grasslands of the United States: An environmental history*. Santa Barbara, CA: ABC-CLIO.

Slaybaugh, D. (1996). *William I. Meyers and the modernization of American agriculture*. Ames, IA: Iowa State University Press.

Turner, F. J. (1893). The significance of the frontier in American history (Excerpts). Retrieved from http://nationalhumanitiescenter.org/pds/gilded/empire/text1/turner.pdf

Williams, E. M., & Carter, S. J. (2011). *The A-Z encyclopedia of food controversies and the law: Volume I A-P*. Santa Barbara, CA: Greenwood.

3

THE BONDS OF LOVE

This chapter looks at our unavoidable embeddedness in a complex, rich and diverse material reality comprised of the myriad incorporeal relations that are earthly existence itself, and the role of responsibility and affection, of restraint and humility in creating healthy human communities within that generative context. What do we need to understand about earth, about ethics and about education in order to live well together? And what does love have to do with an answer to that question?

As discussed in Chapter 1, I begin an approach to education from the premise that ethics must be understood as our ability to suffer in the face of others' suffering and to respond in caring ways, as we also embrace the capacity for joy, in particular others' joy. That is, ethics—our desire for "good" in the world—is pursued relationally as we engage with a whole range of others, and must be linked directly to empathy, care, joy and responsibility. Given this understanding of ethics, education should be understood as the development of one's ability and desire to work toward collective well-being—to open our hearts by asking again and again to whom and to what we are ethically responsible.

I take seriously here the idea that ethics and thus education requires a recognition that our bodies are an important aspect of this mixture, that we are in the world sensually as a part of our conscious and unconscious existence which includes our reasoning capacity. There is no "reason" outside our affective experiences, and these together are always experienced in relationship to others. Further, eros, as an embodied, physical experience of love, is a connective sensual force that can awaken us to the sorts of relationships needed to protect life. And as I develop below, our body is comprised of, and is in relation to, many bodies as it all forms a pulsing, cyclical and sacred system of living and dying, joy and grief. Nothing happens—no ideas, no creation, no

44 The Bonds of Love

birth, no death—outside a multitude of generative relationships, or as Buddhists put it, nothing comes into existence outside its relationship to something else.

Considering these essential relations, this chapter reads Berry's work—especially his essay "The Body and the Earth" from *The Unsettling of America* (1996)—in conversation with Gregory Bateson and a range of ecofeminist and post-humanist feminist philosophers to explore what the purpose of education must be as we recognize our erotic embodied immersion within a complex system of life that is this earth. What interferes, and what could it mean to define education within the necessary bonds of love?

Walking in the Forest

Let me begin with a story from my own life, something to ground the thinking I'm going to do here about love, the body, and the earth. It's a simple enough tale about budding friendship and a walk in the woods.

I was living in Finland in the fall of 2015, and this particular day in September was a gorgeous blue-sky day. Taina, a woman I had recently met, invited me to go mushroom hunting in Kauppi, a city-managed forest bordering Tampere. I had been struggling to get this essay started, and was frankly reticent to let that struggle go. But, I was also lonely and needing a break. So I agreed. We met at Tammelantori, a busy open market, the oldest still operating in Tampere, and spent the first half hour or so just wandering through the lines of tables arranged with all sorts of stuff from knitted woolens and rag rugs to used books, pots and pans and other household things, fresh vegetables, flowers, and berries. The place was alive with chatter and laughter, people moving about talking with each other exchanging goods and greetings. Taina pulled me into a set of busy connections with the people of this city, into a local exchange process ancient in its relational patterns and bursting with lively dependencies, old patterns of craft knowledge and food-ways, mixing together with the stuff of a modern consumer society. I talked with a woman about dogs, and another about books. Taina's basket was filled with potatoes, berries, a pretty jar. It all touched me: the scene and the conversations among people. I could feel myself relaxing, warmth spreading through my chest and limbs.

Soon we were walking through city neighborhoods to Kauppi. Tampere maintains and protects forestland, used for foraging and recreation by city residents, and home to a rich diversity of plants, old growth trees, as well as small mammals and rare birds. We walked under big old spruces and firs, wandering along wildlife paths searching, talking, pausing in the quiet. Passing an old woman picking the last of the season's blueberries, Taina called out a greeting. Showing me this plant or that, she shared how she had learned much and forgotten more about the life of the forest from her mother. She told me stories. How when she was just six years old her uncle took her mushroom hunting

The Bonds of Love   45

because, he said, she would understand its meanings and importance. How she cross-country skied these trails as a girl in school. The hours melted into the soles of our feet and blew through our hair. We inhaled deeply, lifting our faces to the sky, the breath of the forest entering our lungs and our blood in another ancient exchange, this one millions of years old, direct evidence of the materiality of the world entering our bodies and helping to create a bond of friendship between us. Taina pointed to a glade where sunlight was making the mosses glow: "It's really beautiful, isn't it?" We smiled. My heart got full, and affection grew for this place and for this woman in this place.

But why start here, with a walk in the woods? I am not so foolish as to believe that one walk between two women is enough to address the serious problems that we face, or that all we need to do is go to the woods on some Thoreauian quest. Still, that day two women engaged with something enormous and powerful, much more complex than either of us could possibly know, beyond the materiality of the forest or our bodies, and yet we felt it; it seeped into our pores, and danced on our skin, rippled out in laughter. It towered above us, and scurried underfoot, and waved in the breeze. I learned a little about some of its members from Taina whose family had lived and learned and loved in this place over many generations. This is a holy place for her, and I knew it was so in my own way too, in a way that these words can't quite touch.

And yet, these words, this storytelling, are effects of that time and place too, a sort of sense-making mediation of the forest's procreant capacities: forest to body to words to yet unknown possibilities, a moving network of biological and cultural relations, that are also more than the biology or the culture. As David Abram (2010) writes, "To make sense, is to release the body from the constraints imposed by our outworn ways of speaking, and hence to renew and rejuvenate one's felt awareness of the world. It is to make the senses wake up to where they are" (p. 265). Of course, what I learned that day is that for Taina and her family, there is a generations-old awareness of where they are, expressed in stories and knowledge and specific practices, spiraling back around to the presence of the forest again and again, protecting it, and feeding them body and soul. That was an important piece of the joy experienced that day, hearing about that intimate connection, Taina's sense of satisfaction and peace (even without finding many mushrooms!) and feeling the forests' gifts myself.

Relationality: The Body and the Earth

As members of modern industrial societies, we move around in a vastly diverse set of living relations, mostly unaware of their specific generative processes, or their necessity to our existence. We are touched all day long by an active sensuality, living effects of the world around us, but we have been schooled, indeed our culture has created itself to imagine that we are outside all of it. We learn to ignore or even demean our embodied experiences, to define sensuality as either a

46 The Bonds of Love

figment of our imagination or as irrational "romantic" nonsense, soft or feminine perceptions in a world demanding rational efficiencies, measurement, control and profitability. The economic and cultural system that we've inherited operates every day to abstract mind from body, humans from nature. "Knowing" is controlling and using this "outside" for our own purposes without limits.

In truth, we are bodies made of other bodies engaging in a world of still more bodies. As Berry puts it, "While we live, our bodies are moving particles of the earth, joined inextricably both to the soil and to the bodies of other living creatures" (Berry, 1996, p. 97). The active world of living beings continues to create and engage us (even as we are unaware), imploring us through its power and its beauty to wake up to our errors, to feel with our sentient bodies, our hearts and minds its reality and our responsibilities to it as to ourselves. For Berry, while this reality is material, Creation is holy, whole, and demanding of our care.

In short, we are constantly being compelled toward love without recognizing it. And we don't recognize it because we have been taught that love is inferior to reason as a way of being and that the world is other, there for us to use as needs or wants be. But is such a position "reasonable" if it leads to violence and destruction? What should we mean by reason or the mind? And is love really its opposite?

Thinking back to that day with Taina, I'm reminded of a short passage from Berry's novel, *Hannah Coulter* (2004): Hannah, an old woman, walks a well-worn path in a forest on her farm. She reflects on the importance of the forest and a stream running through it to the life that she and her husband Nathan shared with their neighbors, their children and this land itself, to what she calls "the membership." Walking along she hears the voices of the forest and the stream, and as her memories intersect with its stories, she knows a deep and abiding love for this place and its creatures:

> ... you listen and you realize it is talking absolutely to itself. If our place has a voice, this is it. And it is not talking to you. You can't understand a thing it is saying. You walk up and stand beside it, loving it, and you know it doesn't care whether you love it or not. The stream and the woods don't care if you love them. The place doesn't care if you love it. But for your own sake you had better love it. For the sake of all else you love, you had better love it. (Berry, 2004, p. 85)

Wendell Berry has spent the last 50 plus years writing to emphasize the need for love created out of, and within, living processes and against the rationalist arrogance that puts these processes at peril. In his poetry, his novels and his prose he has set for himself the task of expressing with words what he knows will not be pinned down, never fully captured. In his essay, "The Body and the Earth" (1996), Berry lays out a detailed description of the intricate interconnections and dependencies between the body (all bodies) and the earth. The mind or spirit, he tells us echoing Gregory Bateson's *Steps To an Ecology of Mind* (1972), cannot be separated out of these connections though we imagine it as an autonomous capacity of the individual brain. Such an epistemological error lies at the very foundation of a whole series of violent relationships and processes, now fueling both economic and thus educational assumptions and processes.

We are the inheritors of an institutional, ideological, and psychological system that naturalizes a whole series of hierarchized relationships that essentialize the power of the human mind to control and possess the world. From Plato's ideal forms to Kant's love affair with the Copernican revolution, and Descartes "I think therefore ...," we are taught to idealize the human mind or soul over a bodily, earthly existence, and the spiritual over the material, assuming a natural hierarchized division. Reason/Emotion, Mind/Body, Man/Woman, Human/Animal: against the folly and harms of this imagined set of divisions, Berry implores us to consider the "network of mutual dependencies among body, soul (or mind, or spirit), community and world," (1996, p. 110), all susceptible to and conductors of each other's influence. "... this is a network by which each part is connected to every other part ... The influences go backward and forward, up and down, round and round, compounding and branching as they go" (p. 110).

The health of a community, any community, is always created when the specific communicating and connective relationships of a particular place—the sun, the plants, animals, micro-organisms, stream, forest and humans within a particular climatic bioregion for example—are working together. The condition of "health" entails the particular patterns or order of interaction of the particular bodies in any system toward mutual well-being, that is, toward *living on* in a way that does not allow any particular creature to exceed the limits of the system. This is quite complex of course; there is no one fixed or predictable model or set of patterns for what "working together" means, and yet there is, Berry insists, order in the system. And for our part, it must be an "order of loving care" that we work toward (Berry, 2017).

To be clear, "health" is beyond full human comprehension or control though we must be responsible for our parts in it, which means putting ourselves to the always-contradictory task of learning while knowing we'll never know enough. To understand this is to recognize and honor the power and ultimately the mystery of life itself. It is also to understand that we will need a particularly humble and yet discerning approach to teaching and learning, as we will be discussing throughout this book.

Berry's work explores a metaphysics that is defined by our unavoidable embodiment within a complex living system of relationships that will always be beyond us even as we are made by it. His is not a vision of some idealistic utopic place. Over and over he reminds us that to understand such an embodied and spiritual reality is to recognize the unavoidable relation between life and death, joy and grief. It requires struggle within ourselves as individuals and collectively to find the proper order in our communities with no ultimate end possible. This

48 The Bonds of Love

includes recognizing and accepting that we are part of the "wildness" of creation even as we create our domestic orders that imagine we could do without it.

> ... the most dangerous tendency in modern society, now rapidly emerging as a scientific industrial ambition, is the tendency toward encapsulation of human order—the severance, once and for all, of the umbilical cord fastening us to the wilderness of the Creation. The threat is not only in the totalitarian desire for absolute control. It lies in the willingness to ignore an essential paradox: the natural forces that so threaten us are the same forces that preserve and renew us. (1996, p. 130)

The forest, he tells us, must accompany the farm, not as a woodlot for potential profit, but rather as a sacred place where creation is allowed to flourish on its own terms, and as a place of instruction, as well as a place of contemplation and peace. Further, "the wild" exists on the farm itself, among the cultivated rows and in the margins between the fields. Such is the importance of the margins, he tells us, as a source difference, renewal, growth, and survival. "That is what agricultural fertility is: the survival of natural process in the human order. To learn to preserve the fertility of the farm we must study the forest" (Berry 1996, p. 130).

Berry refers to this vast living order most often in his work as the Creation or the Kingdom of God (as discussed in Chapter 1), belying a lifelong study of Biblical scripture in which he finds important ancient guidance on these matters. His reading most often reveals a clear earthbound, creaturely, and ecological commitment and sensibility, and a clear critique of notions and practices of "mastery."

> ... the Creation is bounteous and mysterious and humanity is only part of it—not its equal, much less its master. ... Creation provides a place for humans but it is greater than humanity and within it even great men are small. Such humility is the consequence of an accurate insight, ecological in its bearing, not a pious deference to "spiritual value." (1996, p. 98)

Perhaps especially in his poetry or his interpretation of other poets, I read Berry working in reverence of the insistent becoming of life in specific places among specific creatures: this "great coherence" or, as he quotes in the poetry of Katherine Raines (Berry, 2010), "the Presence" of Being that flows into creatures and also "overflows its boundaries." That is, it is a presence that is always becoming more than itself, and more than we can know, a generative materiality that is also not material at all, that won't be understood finally by our words or our ambitions, but is nonetheless, essential to our own existence.

While interpretive of Christian gospel, Berry's work does not arise from an abstracted religiosity. His Kingdom of God is not above or separate from the earth in any transcendental sense. He is grappling with what life means, how it

The Bonds of Love   49

comes to be, while recognizing that he/we can never fully know. His spirituality is rigorously grounded in the soil and in the mysteries that flow through the real, the material. His is a materialism that does not exile the spiritual or separate earth from mind; it is rather an expression of earthbound faith that burns through his words and the way he has chosen to live as husband, father, farmer, conservationist, and poet.

> I have been groping for connections—that I think are indissoluble, though obscured by modern ambitions—between the spirit and the body, the body and other bodies, the body and the earth. If these connections do necessarily exist as I believe they do, then it is impossible for material order to exist side by side with spiritual disorder, or vice versa, and impossible for one to thrive long at the expense of the other; it is impossible ultimately, to preserve ourselves apart from our willingness to preserve other creatures, or to respect and care for ourselves except as we respect and care for other creatures; and most to the point ... it is impossible to care for each other more or differently than we care for the earth. ... the earth is what we are made of and what we live from. (1996, pp. 122–123)

Berry writes from a faith in the absolute integrity of living creatures, the diverse species with whom we share this planet, and their particular productive, transformative connections with each other in a particular place with us, as well as all that came before us. Life requires death, which produces life. Creatures are born, live, die, and feed other creatures, which live, die and feed still others. This is the sacred process of life on earth. We best understand our part in this recursive process, he tells us, if we are to live on. Or as Hannah tells us we had better love the stream as a part of this larger dynamic presence, if we intend to care for those we love. In a poem from his book *Sabbaths 2013*, he, like Hannah, reflects on his life in its place:

> The old dog with her gray muzzle
> and I with my fringe of white hair
> please ourselves by nearness to the fire
> inside while outside the birds answer their calling to stay alive. We all
> now have fewer days than we had
> yesterday. But it comes to me
> that I know at last how all of us
> are held in the union, the communion, the assembly,
> the great membership of this world's life
> that comprehends its numberless
> becomings and farewells. In the Kingdom of God
> all who ever lived are living.
>
> *(Wendell Berry, 2015a, p. 25)*

50 The Bonds of Love

"The Kingdom of God" Berry tells us further on in this poem, "is life itself"
(Berry 2015a, p. 26), "the great membership of this world's life." For Berry, this
is a comprehensive system of exchange, an economy from which all life, visible
and invisible, ensues. These principles operating in "the Great Economy" are alive
and available to be learned each day if we pay attention and are willing to let go of
the hubris taught by our "enlightenment" history. If we recognize ourselves as
members of this order, we will see that we too are summoned by these principles
to behave in ways that preserve its integrity and with it our existence.

When I read Berry's exploration of, and personal reflection on the ways of Creation,
I hear the wisdom of Gregory Bateson, as well as voices from within a tradition of
ecofeminist ethics, and what is being called "new materialism." So let me move us there
to those voices for a moment, as a means of digging into these principles a bit more.

Bateson's Ecology of Mind

> A Grace: For Gregory Bateson
> I.
> The storied leaves fall through the stories
> of air. Their call is to return. The ground
> gathers them all into its plot, as it gathers
> fallen hands. Autumnal as stories begin.
> they end when their patterns rhyme, in beauty, vernal
> II.
> In rhyme of hand with leaf, time with time,
> we recall what grief forgets, what joy has never
> seen: the chief beauty of the world,
> patterns of patterns. Though deaf, we dance. The music
> that moves us, deaf and blind, is our relief.
> *(Wendell Berry, 1980, p. 36)*

Although the language that these authors use is quite distinct from each other
given the disciplinary traditions being drawn upon (Bateson coming out of, and
drawing on, anthropology, biology and "cybernetics," Berry the humanities
within the Western tradition, including Biblical scripture), they each begin from
the systemic relational nature of life, "its patterns of patterns" and the problems
that occur when limits within this system are ignored or overlooked. As Bateson
tells us, the living world, the very possibility of existence, is created in a recursive
system of relationships among differentiating effects that are creative of everything: sentient, non-sentient, biological, geological, social, psychological, linguistic and everything in-between. Everything created on earth including our ideas,
our attempts to make sense, make art, make knowledge is possible because of our
immersion in these connective patterns or circuits of information within which
move differences that make a difference.

The Bonds of Love   51

For Bateson, this system of relationships that Berry was referring to among body, mind, spirit, and earth constitutes an ecology of Mind and cannot be located in any singular place or organism. Mind is a generative relational process of communication, differentiation, and meaning, linking and creating all. "The world of mental process" Bateson tells us, is the result of "exchanges of information and injunction that occur inside organisms and between organisms and that, in the aggregate, we call *life*."

> In fact, wherever *information—or comparison—*is of the essence of our explanation, *there*, for me is mental process. Information can be defined as a difference that makes a difference. A sensory end organ is a comparator, a device which responds to difference. Of course, the sensory end organ is material, *but it is this responsiveness to difference* that we shall use to distinguish its functioning as "mental." (Bateson & Bateson, 1987, p. 17, emphasis added)

Mind consists of a complex interactive system of communication, reception, and transformation where information interacting with forms, creates relational spaces and differences which then have particular effects, and these travel on to create other differences, effects, and so on in a recursive circuit. The possibility of life for all species is generated and regenerated as a result of these recursive differentiating circuitous relations. The body itself is composed of such information circuits, as are social and ecological systems. And bodies, human societies, and ecological systems all operate together within an even larger cosmological system. Everything is in relation, sending information and differentiating effects to whatever is touched, and those differences make more differences which make more differences and so on. Within these systems there are mechanisms that keep things in balance. To go back to my opening story, Bateson tells us that in a forest, for example,

> Those creatures and plants live together in a combination of competition and mutual dependency, and it is that combination that is the important thing to consider. ... all sorts of interactive balances and dependencies come into play, and it is these processes that have the sort of circuit structure that I have mentioned. ... In a balanced ecological system whose underpinnings are of this nature, it is very clear that any monkeying around with the system is likely to disrupt the equilibrium. (Bateson, 1972, p. 37)

If a particular limit is exceeded in the system, disequilibrium results. For example, if a particular population exceeds a natural balance between population and available food source, "runaway" occurs causing peril in the system itself, in this case the demise of the food source, of others who depend upon it, and eventually

52 The Bonds of Love

of the original population. "Some plant will become a weed, some creatures will be exterminated, and the system as *balanced* system is likely to fall to pieces" (Bateson, 1972, p. 437). The same, he tells us is true of our own bodies within which there is "an uneasy physiological competition and mutual dependency among the organs, tissues, cells and so on." The competition and mutual dependencies function within the aforementioned system of differentiating relationship that Bateson calls Mind.

Mind cannot be separated off from, made exterior to, or superior to the rest of these relationships. It is, in fact, located in the relational spaces created among the myriad elements (bodies) in relationship and making networked information sharing connections in the system. According to new materialist scholars, these networked, creative processes are considered to be a form of agency within the material world but more from them in the next few pages. Bateson, like Berry, is insistent on the limitations that accompany our humanness: our attempts to make sense, to say something about these connections and effects in the material world, will always be limited by our need to *represent* it, our use of language, or some other representational form. While language itself works along these same lines of differentiation, there will always be a gap or what I've called "a limit space" (Martusewicz, 2001, 2016) between the material world (with us in it), and our attempts to say something about it. The representational maps we make are not the territory we wish to "know." Or, as Bateson has put it drawing on the now famous line by Joseph Korsybski, "the map is not the territory" (1972). Our words, texts, our discourses are only maps, representations or interpretations of what we see and wish to "know" in the world. In fact, what we call knowledge is maps of maps of maps, never the world itself, though the world is always there informing our interpretations.

This is what Berry means too by the third Principle of the Great Economy: that we humans can never know finally all the complexity that this order entails. Our sense making expressions about the world will never be the world itself. First, there is always a gap between what we say, and what the world actually is; and second, the actual generative process that is constantly in process will always be beyond our ability to capture it with science, or art, or pedagogy. We are in it and of it, although in our arrogance, we too often delude ourselves into believing we are separate subjects, the only "knowers" and as such its masters. And still, even while we may recognize these limits, we must try to make sense of it as we live in it. That is what the order of loving care demands. So, the maps we make and the metaphors we use to do so matter: they can either be dedicated to preserving the diverse and generative creation of living systems as our own life's blood, or exploiting them for selfish purposes that are ultimately deadly. We can work toward care and nurture, or violate the very relationships we need to live.

Life is generated in relationships, where differences are being created in the moving becoming of every instant. When we think about all this, when we begin to recognize the implications of such comprehensive and complex processes, we begin to see that we humans, as every other particular species alive, are small within it. And, though we are touched by it, moved by it, implicated in it, we often forget—or we live by cultural representations that block our knowing—that thought is embodied, and connected sensually and emotionally to many other bodies. Our bodies are the receivers of a vast array of messages that could, if we opened our ethical capacities, our desire, and consciousness remind us that our own actions—our work, our knowledge, our art—have rippling effects, and thus must be chosen with care within limits if we are to survive, if life itself is to survive. So here is a second sense of limitation that both Berry and Bateson agree on: not only are we limited in what we can possibly know as humans about the wider world, but, recognizing this, we must also live with restraint, and with the recognition that the earth itself, even while it is generative beyond our capacity to know it, is a system that relies on limits. And this is where we have, as inheritors of a mechanistic and supremacist cultural system, gone so drastically wrong.

Against Division: Berry and Ecofeminism

Our culture is a powerful meaning system creating structures, institutions, policies, words and ideologies—all abstractions that function in our minds as if they are "reality." And of course, in part, they are real because they have real effects, but our social conventions teach us that we are outside the order established by "other" systems of life. "Wisdom," Bateson says echoing Berry's principles of the Great Economy, is "knowledge of the larger interactive system—that system which if disturbed, is likely to generate exponential curves of change ... [human] conscious purpose is now empowered to upset the balances of body, of society, and of the biological world around us" (1972, p. 439).

Berry, too, offers a powerful critique of the ways we humans have imagined ourselves to be superior to, and thus divided from, the demands of this order. Indeed, we go about our daily lives within imagined divisions, even while we are born of, and only exist in, relationality. Modern industrial patterns of exploitation naturalize hyper-separated, hierarchized relationships. These patterns codify subjectivities—who we identify ourselves to be and who we are defined to be by others—that are degrading to body and earth, to creatures and communities. As he analyzes these intersecting forms of degradation, Berry's work can be read alongside a number of important ecofeminist scholars.

First, dividing the spiritual from the material or natural, and defining the former as what shall be valued while the latter is just so much dead matter, modern thought rationalizes unrestrained use and abuse of "the gift of Creation."

> If we divide reality into two parts, spiritual and material, and hold (as the Bible does *not* hold) that only the spiritual is good or desirable, then our relation to the material Creation becomes arbitrary, having only the quantitative or mercenary value that we have, in fact, and for this reason, assigned

54 The Bonds of Love

to it. Thus, we become the judges and inevitably the destroyers of a world we did not make and that we are bidden to understand as a divine gift. (Berry, 1993, p. 109)

Here we see Berry's conception of holism: the interconnectedness and essential mystery of the world as the "breath of God that is our fundamental bond with one another and with other creatures" (1993, p. 109) and thus, as that which makes the material world sacred. Imagining the sacred to be elsewhere, beyond these relationships, we have given ourselves permission to desecrate the earth.

Such a discursive system devalues and categorizes certain bodies (for example, racialized, gendered or other than human) for certain tasks, set apart from intelligence, from reason, from spirit. For Berry, this fundamental disconnection or division of body and soul, or body and mind, inaugurates "an expanding series of divisions" including reason and emotion, man and woman, civilized and uncivilized, human and nature. Thus, modernist ideological systems make it possible to isolate, degrade, enslave and own other bodies.

To think of the body as separate from the soul or as soulless, either to subvert its appetites or to "free" them, is to make an object of it. As a thing, the body is denied any dimension or rightful presences or claim in the mind. The concerns of the body—all that is comprehended in the term nurture— are thus degraded, denied any respected place among "the higher things" and even among the more exigent practicalities. (1996, p. 113)

"This division among bodies," he tells us, "is first sexual." With this Berry expresses his own version of feminism: the first sexual division, following upon the separation of body and mind comes when nurture is defined as both an inferior activity of the body (already inferiorized), and the exclusive realm of women. Here we begin to get a glimpse of the essential value of work for Berry as the capacity to nurture, and its inferiorization in industrial culture as a central dehumanizing problem:

Women traditionally have performed the most confining—though not necessarily the least dignified—tasks of nurture: housekeeping, the care of young children, food preparation. In the urban-industrial situation the confinement of these traditional tasks divided women more and more from the "important" activities of the new economy. Furthermore, in this situation the traditional nurturing role of men—that of provisioning the household which in an agricultural society had become as constant and as complex as the women's role—became completely abstract: the man's duty to the household came to be simply to provide money. The only remaining task of provisioning—purchasing food—was turned over to women. This determination that nurturing should become the exclusive concern of women served

The Bonds of Love   55

to signify to both sexes that neither nurture nor womanhood was very important. (1996, p. 114)

Berry goes on to analyze the further exploitation of women as agricultural society gave way to advanced capitalism, and abstract, mechanized, and masculine forms of production (off the land) became valued over work with the hands or body. The further away from the body and the earth, the more valued the activity. While white men went to work in an economy off the farm and in the growing cities, white women became consumers and purchasing agents for the middle class household; customers, rather than producers. "She was saddled with work from which much of the skill, hence much of the dignity, had been withdrawn" (p. 114). Further, she was identified exclusively with bodily reproduction, while the abstract and extractive labor of men, their reasoning capacities within an increasingly abstract and mechanized world became of highest value.

All these forms of centric or supremacist thinking—the idea that some are inherently superior to others—wind around and support one another discursively and become internalized, part of our psychic realities, deep down, not even part of our conscious selves necessarily, but operating in powerful ways to silence what might otherwise be important challenges to violence. Success is wealth, rationalized to buy and sell bodies, the power to exclude and to kill. Work by the body—reproductive in its very essence—is demeaned as "feminine" or "base," primitive, irrational. Machines become highly prized for their ability to replace the body, to free us—or some of us—from physical labor defined as degrading. We will have more to say about this as it founded slavery and racism in Chapter 5, Degraded Bodies, Degraded Earth. Racism and the endangerment of the Black body is a direct result of this cultural move to divide and hierarchize.

Perhaps, Berry muses, we have come to this misapprehension of our own embodied reality, our essential connections to other bodies and to the earth, because of a particular historical and scientific misrepresentation of "materiality," leading to a form of economy that can only result in violent effects.

Perhaps it happened because materialists, instead of assigning ultimate value to materiality as would have been reasonable, have abstracted "material" to "mechanical," and thus have removed from it all bodily or creaturely attributes. Or, perhaps the abstracting impulse branched in either of two directions: one toward the mechanical, the other toward the financial, which is to say toward the so-called economy of money as opposed to the actual economy ... of goods. Either way the result is the same: the scientific-industrial culture, founded *nominally* on materialism, arrives at a sort of fundamentalist disdain for material reality. (2015a, p. 7)

Caroline Merchant's early work, *The Death of Nature* (1990), traced how such a mechanistic (and patriarchal) vision of the Earth and cosmos was accomplished

56 The Bonds of Love

during the Scientific Revolution, and it is not difficult to see that these two lines, the mechanistic and the financial, ultimately intertwine with divisive hierarchies that support one another in the most disastrous ways. Locke's assertion of the right (of some) to private property as located within the rational ability to make the land "productive" and the associated human right to accumulate as natural is located exactly here, within a hierarchized structure that made some humans (European colonizers) more worthy of such accumulation than others (the Indigenous people who had dwelt on the land), and all humans naturally superior to "matter."

The late Australian feminist philosopher Val Plumwood (1993, 2002) also traced the development of hyper-separated power/knowledge regimes, and their social and economic institutionalization. Examining the degradation of body and earth from Plato's ideal "forms" to present instrumental rationalism, Plumwood exposes the valorization of a particular regime of rationality with its corresponding weave of centric discourses fundamental to the history of colonization and founding the current globalization of a so-called free market system. Capitalism is built upon the separation of mind from body and earth, relying on a system that naturalizes human supremacism, racism, sexism, and the impoverishment of all aspects of our living world.

> Beyond all its other follies, the global free market shows its rationalist origins and its irrational course in its ecological disembedment [sic], its disregard for the enabling preconditions of human and non-human life. … The failure to recognize the limits arising from other living beings and systems is a product of a monological and deeply human-centered view of humans and nature. (Plumwood, 2002, pp. 24–26)

While Berry would argue with the use of the concept "human-centeredness" as the basis of her critique, Plumwood's overarching recognition of necessary limits ignored by global capitalism's foundations in hierarchized, hyper-rationalist and mechanistic ways of being joins with Berry's concerns. The outcomes of valuing division over relationship—for the land, for human communities, and for other creatures—are devastatingly clear. Our modernist economic disposition is to define ourselves as gods with the right to buy and sell the living creatures of the world, thus determining who lives and who dies. For Berry, this is the folly of a prideful species, one who mistakes his own consciousness for supremacy. Difference from the One is believed to be inherent weakness, a murderous delusion presented as righteousness. Capitalism—our destructive "little economy"—is organized by violence, ordering time into mechanized efficiencies built on the assumption that one can measure and thus control life. Resting on a fundamental misapprehension that "the world and all its creatures are entirely comprehensible, manipulable, and controllable by humans" (Berry, 1996, p. 230), selfish accumulation and profit is thus valued over life itself. Everything becomes an object

The Bonds of Love   57

for the market and the essential generative relationships among bodies at the heart of the earth's living systems are pulled apart, disrupted and degraded, forcing planetary systems to the brink of collapse. Here is the rest of Berry's poem from *Sabbaths 2013* (2015a) begun earlier in this chapter:

> Only we humans, we the poor,
> suffer the ancient mistake, dividing
> the living from the dead, confusing life
> with time. We divide life from death
> for the purpose of killing each other, killing
> ourselves, or we confuse living bodies
> with machines, the truly dead, to increase
> happiness and 'create wealth.' Hell
> fills the difference. The wrens, searching
> the brush for this day's food, rightly
> give not a thought to death, singing,
> as they live and move, the longest song.
> The Kingdom of God is life itself.
>
> *(Wendell Berry, 2015a, p. 26)*

Contrary to a system of thought that partitions and measures everything as a method of control, consumption and profit, Berry is adamant that life, The Kingdom of God, is vital materiality suffused with the spirit of becoming. Whatever its origin (and no matter what our stories of its origin), the earth's material relationality is our life's blood, the origin and ongoing vital mix from which we humans came to be and are afforded the miracle of continuing on. We refuse to embrace this immersion and our careful and loving practices within it at our own peril.

Eco-ethical Becoming and Vitalist Materialism

Calling for an ethics that refuses the dualism between internal and external, mental and material, reason and emotion, materialist feminist Karen Barad (2007) enters the conversation with this:

> … phenomena—whether lizards, electrons or humans—exist only as a result of, and as part of, the world's ongoing activity, its dynamic and contingent differentiation into specific relationalities. "We humans" don't make it so, not by dint of our own will, and not on our own. But through our advances, we participate in bringing forth the world in its specificity, including ourselves. We have to meet the universe half-way, to move toward what may come to be in ways that are accountable for our part in the world's differential becoming. All real living is meeting. And each meeting matters. (p. 353)

58 The Bonds of Love

Barad, with Berry and Bateson, is interested in how matter comes *to matter*, and how it comes to make itself *felt*. Recall my story of the forest at the beginning of this chapter. For Barad, attractions and intra-actions, shifts or transforms of all sorts energize this system including what we do and how matter moves and touches us. She proposes a "relational ontology" in much the same sense as Berry, arguing that agency and action in the system is not only human. These must be understood to be generated as the effects of differentiating processes within material being, not simply possessed by rational humans.

> Eros, desire, life forces run through everything, not only specific body parts or specific kinds of engagements among body parts … Materialism itself is always already a desiring dynamism … energized and energizing … enlivened and enlivening. (Barad, 2012, p. 59)

Barad is not anthropomorphizing the world; she is not imagining a stream or trees to have human intentions or desires. Like Hannah Coulter, she does not assume that the forest loves us, but she does recognize the ways that matter (from atoms to blue whales) moves, creates, and responds. She is interested in the ways that we can be touched by the complex generative processes happening all around us, and further, the possibility in that relational "tissue of life" to produce accountability and responsibility on our part. Ethics, our ability to care, to steward, to nurture is part of this order too.

Because matter is made of relationality, it demands ethical responsibility from us even as we recognize our ongoing and unavoidable failure to reach any final answers about how we should live on this earth. Obviously as Barad, Berry and Bateson make clear, not all intra-actions or interventions will produce life-affirming effects. But, if we take the time to attend carefully, matter in the Great Economy will teach us its principles. If we pay attention to those places where we live over enough time, we may begin to see what preserves the ongoing becoming of things, and what shuts it down unnecessarily, what produces toxic combinations ultimately devastating to creatures and human communities, and what protects water and food sources. We may learn much of how we should conduct ourselves from nature herself if we are patient and observant and careful enough. This is why Berry is so adamant about recognizing how the needs of local communities present themselves within specific bioregions, places that contain specific creaturely activities and needs. Human culture and knowledge should develop in concert with those needs even as they shift and change over time.

Ideological and discursive systems that imagine domination, exploitation and control as natural or as our "God-given right" substitute arrogance for what Creation requires us to recognize, that these becomings within differentiating relationships make up a living world that we are in and of. As Barad says, "Ethics is about mattering, about taking account of the entangled materializations of which we are a part including new configurations, new subjectivities, new possibilities" (Barad, 2012, p. 69).

Jane Bennett comes to this conversation with similar interests in countering a rationalist logic. For Bennett, like Barad, matter is vital, alive, restless, active, always transforming itself and the world for better or worse. It is not that matter holds an ethics unto itself, but the vitality of the material world including our relationships with it and within it, is a vital matter. Much like Bateson and Berry, Bennett draws our attention to the ways in which the world acts upon itself and us in an active becoming. Writing to disrupt "the onto-theological boundaries of life/ matter, human/animal, will/determination, and organic/inorganic ..." (Bennett, 2010, Kindle location 101), she focuses on the ways these processes can "induce in human bodies an aesthetic-affective openness to material vitality" (Kindle location 100) and thus the possibility for care.

Such is the source of an essential ethical turn, a blurring of old binaries and divisions. As Berry puts it,

> the way to respect the body fully is to honor fully its materiality. In saying this, I intend no reduction. ... I believe that the Creation is one continuous fabric comprehending simultaneously what we mean by spirit and what we mean by "matter." (1995, pp. 90–91)

To argue for materiality, as Berry does, is to dispel the mythology of a dualistic body/mind/spirit split, while also exposing an important distinction between what is organic and what is mechanical. This is a division, Berry argues, that we *must* learn: a body is not a machine. Material relationality, the interaction of bodies with other bodies, creatures with other creatures, is the source of life and love in the world. The world of love is born in, and of, material relationality:

> ... the body lives and moves and has its being minute by minute, by an interinvolvement with other bodies and other creatures, living and unliving ... . (Berry, 1995, p. 95)
>
> A body, love insists, is neither a spirit nor a machine. ... It belongs to the world of love, which is a world of living creatures, natural orders and cycles, many small, fragile lights in the dark. (1995, p. 103)

Echoing Berry, another ecofeminist, Susan Griffin speaks of "threads of connection that run everywhere" (1995, p. 153), of the "holiness" of our bodies in relationship with other bodies, and with that which gives us pleasure and life.

> I climb a tree, reach for a plum and eat it ... placing that plum in my mouth I have experienced joy. The fruit of many months of sunlight and earth and water has entered me, becomes me, not only in my stomach, my blood, my cells, but because of what I have learned. The plum has been my lover. And

60 The Bonds of Love

> I have known the plum. Letting the plum into the mind and body, I will always have that taste of sweetness in my memory. But I cannot know this sweetness, the full dimension of it unless I am aware of the holiness of this meeting. (1995, p. 152)

The meeting is holy because of this long line of connections that makes it possible, and for what is still to occur. Recognizing this makes us aware of how delicate and intimate and yes, erotic these connections are. But the tree, she goes on to tell us, and everything that makes the tree possible, does not exist *for* us.

> If I think the plum tree exists only to feed me, I have lost the meaning that is mixed with every pleasure. The tree exists for the sake of its own being. And it is also part of a commons, its fruit the inheritance of bird and animal alike. I must know this to receive the full value of communion. (1995, p. 152)

Everything is in connection, and "within every meeting other meetings occur" (Griffin, 1995, p. 152) so many that we cannot possibly know or name them all. Recognizing this opens us to the eros of the world as we walk through it, and to an ethics that recognizes difference as the result of every inter and intra-action. Love is our mindfulness of the Other as we are touched by an unavoidable difference, and the irreplaceability of relationships of care within the material world as our responsibility to its, and thus our own, survivability.

For these post-humanist feminists, as for Berry, there will be no shift in our social, economic or political landscape or relationships without an affective and thus ethical shift, without feeling an emotional empathetic response, which will inevitably include an erotic embodied, as well as a subjective dimension. The shift must come through our bodies and our hearts via the vital agency of the greater world, thus awakening us to the Presence of life itself in and among us, or as Berry (1996) puts it, to the realization that we are mere particles of the earth and the earth particles of us. Our actions to alleviate suffering, our response-ability, must come from there.

Jane Bennett argues that, "There will be no greening of the economy, no redistribution of wealth, no enforcement of rights without human dispositions, moods, and cultural ensembles hospitable to these effects" (Bennett, 2010, Kindle location 131). What sorts of subjectivities are demanded of us now, as we witness the wreckage that is the result of our erroneous ideological inheritance, and how do we engage the world so as to energize the desire to care as an antidote to our consumerist addictions? What habits of mind, what virtues and related practices are demanded of us now? There is no one simple formula as Wendell Berry knows well, for each locality contains and produces its own particular diversity of relations and inherited damages.We must begin from affection as a force of relational caretaking that pays attention and learns from the local ecosystem what it

The Bonds of Love **61**

needs from us. If we pay attention to what matters as part of our own earthly materialist existence, we will be created differently in such intra-action.

To be hospitable means to open ourselves to the recognition that this greater materiality—this Great Economy—is our home and thus requires a certain intimacy and care, or as Berry insists, affection, kindness and neighborliness that create the bonds of love that protect the membership in one's place. Affection is connection and "involves us entirely" (Berry, 2012, p. 33).

Recognizing that we are part of processes and relations creating a network of life much bigger than, but also a part of us requires an ethics made of reverence, humility, joy and wonder. If we understand that our own and our children's possibility of life is dependent upon recognizing that our membership in a larger order requires restraint and gratitude, limits and balance in a complex living system, we may also awaken to what others—both humans and other species— have to teach us. We may become aware of the ways this larger order—trees, moss, desert, wind, sun, rain, ocean, grasses, birdsong, microorganisms, bears, dogs, peepers and more—touches us erotically, imploring us toward the possibility of love as the desire to be alive and aware in affectionate relationship with others, to care, to protect, and to heal while we too are offered well-being.

We may learn to engage discernment, to try to make decisions with others framed by caution. We may stay put long enough to know something about a place and its creatures, recognizing that we cannot possibly know all we need to know, and this in part because of the constant process of becoming that we are engaged in, and subsumed by, but not as a matter of reducing the other to ourselves. Indeed, to be responsible in a place is to recognize with affection and wonder all that we did not know before, to be constantly surprised and delighted at the otherness of creaturely becoming. That is, that we take a certain amount of pleasure in the vast diversity of what we do not know, that we refuse to allow knowledge to shut out difference. In this sense, ethical relationships are always becoming different than they were before precisely because the world is in a constant state of becoming. Tending "toward infinity rather than totality, [ethics] can never be fixed, frozen, or fully accounted for" (Smith, 2001, p. 184). That sensibility must be the source of humility, but also curiosity and joy at what life gives us.

Considering this exposes the hegemony of autonomy and individualism as an arrogant illusion, and offers up a paradox that we must learn to accept. We humans are part of a pluralistic process of becoming that is constantly "overflowing its forms," (Berry 2010, p. 128) generating effects, mostly unpredictable, and thus uncontainable in any final sense. Accepting this, we must also recognize an obligation to live within *limits* in order (paradoxically) to preserve this very process of unbounded becoming. And, as part of this, we accept that our ethical responses, our questions, our decisions, our knowledge will never be finished and must be embraced as part of this becoming with others, human and more than human. Ethics as Mick Smith (2001) writes (reading Luce Irigaray) is thus always excessive.

62 The Bonds of Love

This paradox is at the heart of all educational encounters. As conscious beings, there will always be another question, another possibility, another gap between what we "know" and what we do not, and between what we can say, and the world itself. We will be caught eternally in the interpretations of interpretations, or differences that make a difference, creating and facing over and over the limits of our epistemological capacities. Even so, as we learn to live ethically with others, we will be asked to think and to choose what is "good" for our families, our community, other creatures, and the world—again and again—as part of our particular becoming. Drawing from his reading of John Lukacs, Berry puts it like this:

> There is no knowledge but human knowledge ... we are therefore inescapably central to our own consciousness ... this is "a statement not of arrogance but of humility. It is yet another recognition of the inevitable limitations of mankind." We are thus isolated within our uniquely human boundaries, which we certainly cannot transcend by means of technological devices. (Berry, 2012, p. 26)

To accept this fate with fidelity and gratitude is what it means to love. It is to be in the bonds of love, an ontological and ethical mandate.

An educational mandate. If we don't *learn and pass on* what it takes to work within these bonds and this becoming, we will suffer the consequences. We *are* suffering the consequences. This is why education as the willingness to engage ethically with the world while recognizing limits is absolutely essential; a matter of character development via encountering and internalizing the virtues of humility, generosity, kindness, and forbearance. Such development happens via relationships of affection for, and acceptance of, the other without attempting to transform or control. Here is Berry again:

> We cannot know the whole truth, which belongs to God alone, but our task nevertheless is to see, to know what is true. And if we offend gravely enough against what we know to be true, as by failing badly enough to deal affectionately and responsibly with our land and our neighbors, truth will retaliate with ugliness, poverty, and disease. The crisis of this line of thought is the realization that we are at once limited and unendingly responsible for what we know and do. (2012, p. 27)

Indigenous peoples around the world know this well. We so called "moderns" better get going.

On Love, Imagination, and Pedagogies of Responsibility

So where do we go from here, from this recognition of our unwitting complicity in a hyper-consumerist system that keeps many of us comfortable ultimately at the expense of our own health, and clearly at the expense of the living relationships we depend on. EcoJustice Education calls upon a pedagogy of responsibility to interrupt such complicity. A pedagogy of responsibility requires that we work with our students to trace the deeply embedded cultural roots of problems that we face, their ideological, political and economic history and effects, to "denaturalize" and disrupt them. To make them visible. This means offering students concepts, narratives and experiences that help shake up the taken for granted or paralyzing inevitability of consumer capitalism. We must also imagine the world, or more specifically the places where we live as they are and as they ought to be. This means staying put long enough to develop an intimate knowledge of a place. Responsibility requires familiarity which is the only way that affection can grow, by knowing our neighbors, and recognizing our dependencies in that place. But it also requires that we work to imagine what we do not yet know. As Berry puts it, "For humans to have a responsible relationship to the world, they must imagine their places in it. To have a place, to live and belong to a place, to live from a place without destroying it, we must imagine it" (2012, p. 14).

With imagination, we also embrace wisdom where we find it in creation:

> Nature (and here we capitalize her name) is the impartial mother of all creatures, unpredictable, never entirely revealed, not my mother or your mother, but nonetheless our mother. If we are observant and respectful of her, she gives good instruction. As Albert Howard, Wes Jackson and others have carefully understood, she can give the right patterns and standards for agriculture. If we ignore or offend her, she enforces her will with punishment. She is always trying to tell us that we are not so superior or independent or alone or autonomous as may think. (2012, p. 27)

Learning from the Huron River

So, with such instruction and imagination in mind, let me share with you a hopeful example of what this might mean in a practical sense. A few years ago, my university commissioned a mural to be created by a well-known Detroit artist, Chazz Miller, with specific conditions. He was to collaborate with a group of primary students in an afterschool Art–Ecology program where they were learning about life on, and with, the Huron River in Ypsilanti, Michigan. The teacher, a former student, asked me to visit early in the process. So, on the first day I had a conversation with those students, before the art project commenced. Standing before them, I asked, "Can a river be our teacher?" There was the briefest of pauses and then hands flew up:

> "Yes!" "No!" "Maybe!"
> "Yes!"

64 The Bonds of Love

"How so?" I asked. "What might a river have to teach us?"
One young girl ventured, "Well, we could learn what lives there, what fish and birds and stuff." How? "We could go there and look."
"What else?"
"We could put our feet in and see what it feels like; if it's warm or cold. What the bottom feels like."
"What would the River be teaching us then?"
"Well, maybe what needs rocky bottoms, or what plants like it warmer or colder …"
Another, "And maybe find out who has used the river."
And another, "We could learn how it's being harmed too!"
"Yeah, the river could tell us how it's been polluted!"
I waited for more.
A young boy, perhaps a second grader, raised his hand tentatively.
"Maybe the river could help us learn how to care for it better. How to be better people."

With this, the project began. They visited the river in the midst of winter; they learned about the history of the people who had lived there from the Potawatomi to the European colonists, to their own families. They learned about the factories that once existed along the shore, what got dumped in the river, and the trains that stopped nearby to carry off the products produced there. They studied their own cultural and economic history, and they studied the biological history of the river, the diversity of animals and plants who now live or once lived there.

And they drew and painted it all. They learned from Chazz how to create shapes that turned into creatures on the page, how to use those sketches to construct a mural, offering ideas for what they wanted to see depicted there, where their own drawings and paintings might fit. It was a lively, often-chaotic several weeks, resulting in a beautiful mural, and 17 very excited proud 7–12 year olds.

Wendell Berry tells us that the communities we need will be those based on imagination and affection. Barad, Bennett and Griffin remind us that such affection is not created in isolation, that it is generated within the constant erotic and generative unfolding of the world itself. That is what I experienced on my walk with Taina, the forest coming to us, touching us sensually and moving us toward friendship, affection, love, not the forest's love for us, but an affirmation of the life of the place and thus, growing affection between us and for that place.

When I asked the students if a river could be a teacher, I did not do so to make a river like a human. What I was asking them to imagine, and what they did imagine, was what they might learn, what messages might be taken in by engaging a relationship of affection and respect with a river. I was inviting them to imagine that relationship, and so to move toward a connection that could

The Bonds of Love **65**

grow toward love and thus toward care. That was the brilliance of their teacher Lisa's use of art as a tool for expressing both critique and well-being, a means toward community healing.

This is where a pedagogy of responsibility begins, with this recognition of the patterns and relations that connect us to the holiness and wholeness of the world which is always in the process of becoming other than itself. We will not build the sorts of relationships we need without recognizing the vital actions of other species and earthly elements around us, or imagining who we ought to be with those elements and creatures. This means that as teachers, we must work to engage the ethical sensibilities of our students, sensually and emotionally and analytically, as an invitation to love the world we live in—"our only world" as Berry (2015b) reminds us. Reason is not the superior opposite of love; it is its helpmate, as is imagination.

Education must be defined by our willingness to engage with the living world in responsive, responsible and creative ways, while recognizing that we will never know enough to finish that project. Art, whether it be painting, sculpture, curriculum or pedagogy, is about recognizing the primary value in the Great Economy, and our capacities to create secondary value that nurtures and protects that value. We must learn that it is in the bonds of affection and care, humility and restraint, kindness and compassion that we will forge healthy enduring communities. That's part of what the kids in this art project learned. They used art, biology, history, and love. To conclude, here is Berry once more:

> Care allows creatures [and people] to escape our explanations into their actual presence and their essential mystery. In taking care of fellow creatures, we acknowledge they are not ours. We acknowledge that they belong to an order and a harmony of which we are ourselves a part. To answer to the perpetual crisis of our presence in this abounding and dangerous world, we have only the perpetual obligation to care. (Berry, 1995, p. 77)

References

Abram, D. (2010). *Becoming animal: An earthly cosmology*. New York, NY: Vintage.

Barad, K. (2007). *Meeting the universe halfway: Quantum physics and the entanglement of matter and meaning*. Durham, NC: Duke University Press.

Barad, K. (2012). Interview with Karen Barad. In R. Dolphijn & I. van der Tuin, *New materialism: Interviews and cartographies* (pp. 48–70). Ann Arbor, MI: Open Humanities Press, University of Michigan Library.

Bateson, G. (1972). *Steps to an Ecology of Mind*. New York, NY: Ballantine Books.

Bateson, G., & Bateson, M. C. (1987). *Angels fear: Toward and epistemology of the sacred*. New York, NY: MacMillan.

Bennett, J. (2010). *Vibrant matter: A political ecology of things*. Durham, NC: Duke University Press.

66 The Bonds of Love

Berry, W. (1980). *A part*. San Francisco, CA: North Point Press.

Berry, W. (1993). *Sex, economy, freedom and community*. New York, NY: Pantheon Books.

Berry, W. (1995). *Another turn of the crank*. Washington, DC: Counterpoint.

Berry, W. (1996). *The unsettling of America*. San Francisco, CA: Sierra Club Books.

Berry, W. (2004). *Hannah Coulter: A novel*. Washington, DC: Shoemaker and Hoard.

Berry, W. (2010). *Imagination in place*. Berkeley, CA: Counterpoint.

Berry, W. (2012). *It all turns on affection: The Jefferson Lecture and other essays*. Berkeley, CA: Counterpoint.

Berry, W. (2015a). *Sabbaths 2013*. Monterey, KY: Larkspur Press.

Berry, W. (2015b). *Our only world: Ten essays*. Berkeley, CA: Counterpoint.

Berry, W. (2017). *The art of loading brush*. Berkeley, CA: Counterpoint.

Griffin, S. (1995). *The eros of everyday life: Essays on Ecology, gender and society*. New York, NY: Doubleday Press.

Martusewicz, R. A. (2001). *Seeking passage: Post-structuralism, pedagogy, ethics*. New York, NY: Teachers College Press.

Martusewicz, R. A. (2016). Reading Bateson and Deleuze on difference: Toward education for eco-ethical consciousness. In W. M. Reynolds & J. A. Webber (Eds.), *Expanding curriculum theory: Dis/positions and lines of flight* (2nd edition) (pp. 62–76). New York, NY: Routledge Press.

Merchant, C. (1990). *The death of nature: Women, ecology and the Scientific Revolution*. San Francisco, CA: Harper San Francisco.

Plumwood, V. (1993). *Feminism and the mastery of reason*. New York, NY: Routledge.

Plumwood, V. (2002). *Environmental culture: The ecological crisis of reason*. New York, NY: Routledge.

Smith, M. (2001). *An ethics of place: Radical ecology, postmodernity, and social theory*. Albany, NY: State University of New York Press.

4

SETTLER COLONIALISM AND *THE UNSETTLING OF AMERICA*

Having been immersed in Wendell Berry's work for several years, I've been talking about his ideas publicly, presenting at conferences, teaching it to our students, using it to support both a fundamental critique of the discourses/beliefs rationalizing the violence inherent in industrial consumer culture, and arguing for the sorts of restraint, humility, responsibility, affection and care that he argues are the only way out of the mess we're in socially and ecologically.

On several occasions, well-known scholars have made comments to me about Berry's work, either questioning what they suspect or worry to be "a certain erasure" in his work of the experiences of Indigenous peoples who were forcibly removed from the land he now farms and writes about, or proclaim that they cannot take his work seriously because he is, in their words, a "white settler colonialist." For example, in a published dialogue among Jeff Edmundson, Richard Kahn, and myself on the influence of Berry on our work, Kahn tells a story of his former North Dakota students' inability to relate any sense of relationship with, or knowledge of, the Sioux tribes that lived or were living in the area, going on to say:

> For the record, I find that this erasure pervades a great deal of the environmental educational and social justice research in education, with such research (no matter how important or well-meaning otherwise) itself arguably constituting a type of settlement. Although I did not have such a tool at my disposal at the time, I have come to understand this problem through the lens of "settler colonialism" (Veracini, 2010). It appears to be as devious and resilient a formation as the global capitalism that is its macro-imperialist shape. I worry deeply about this, both in the context of Berry's own life and work, as well as in the academic reception of such work (Martusewicz, Edmundson & Kahn, 2012, p. 52).

68 Settler Colonialism & *The Unsettling of America*

Richard's comment was provocative for me to say the least. There have been a handful of other such statements or interactions at conferences and in classes by scholars and students who either want to know to what extent Berry has learned from or consulted the Indigenous people in his native Kentucky, or just flat out name him a white settler colonialist whose work therefore is to be considered suspect or simply inexcusable, as is anyone else who draws from it. To prove their point, those making such statements identify Berry as a white male farmer occupying land taken from Indigenous people generations ago and passed on through property laws and inheritance, a neo-agriculturalist arguing arduously for "settling the land." Which of course he is and he does!

At first, I was perplexed by these comments since nothing in my reading of Berry's significant body of work pointed to the sort of erasure that Richard asserted. And yet, had I ever read him with these ideas in mind? How much did I know, after all, about settler colonial studies and its defining claims or tenets? I respect Richard Kahn and others who had made similar comments, so his assertion and worry began to gnaw at me. Serious questions began to take shape: What are the primary analytic claims of settler colonial studies? To what extent does Berry's work take up similar points or analyses to acknowledge the violence of dispossession that removed Indigenous people from the land he and his ancestors have occupied? I had already read his landmark essay and book, *The Unsettling of America* (1996), so I had an idea about this, but I also recognized a unique argument being made in that book that I knew needed to be put into conversation with this larger body of critical work. Was I prepared to discover flaws in Berry's thinking, or more importantly my own?

As a descendant of several generations of settler farmers in Nothern New York, these questions have urged me to explore the emerging field of settler colonialism studies, to reread Wendell Berry's work relative to its primary arguments and to think more carefully about my own work. As Dolores Calderon (2016) writes: "As researchers committed to decolonial research in education, we must be vigilant of the ways we might reproduce capitalist regimes of knowledge which in the United States are organized by an ongoing settler colonial project" (p. 5). This chapter aims to take her admonition seriously.

Degrade, Dispossess, and Disavow

To begin, let me try to define the parameters of settler colonialism as defined by those analyzing its complexities. As indicated by Lorenzo Veracini's theoretical overview, debates and differences within this growing field of study make a clear definition complex and thus somewhat difficult to summarize. However, some important characteristics emerge from this literature. Importantly, settler colonialism is not necessarily characterized by a master–slave relationship with the Indigenous population but rather by the need to dispense with the people living within the desired territory in order to take it for one's own autonomous use. Or, as Walter Hixon writes, it is distinguished by a "logic of elimination" and not exploitation. Veracini (2010) quotes Patrick Wolfe:

> The primary object of settler colonialism is the land itself rather than the surplus value to be derived from mixing native labour with it. Though, in practice, Indigenous labour was indispensible to Europeans, settler colonization is at base a winner-take-all-project whose dominant feature is not exploitation but replacement. The logic of this project, a sustained institutional tendency to eliminate the Indigenous population, informs a range of historical practices that might otherwise appear distinct—invasion is a structure not an event. (Wolfe, quoted in Veracini, 2010, p. 9)

According to this perspective, under settler colonialism, the invaders come to stay, make their homes in the territories they invade, and, in order to do so, must lay claim to the right to domesticate a locality by employing biopolitics in managing domestic domains including the existing population. In general, it involves relationships among three different groups: the colonial settlers, the indigenous people who are colonized; and "a variety of exogenous alterities" (Veracini, 2010, p. 16). This third group includes migrants who are not there to establish or claim membership in a sovereign political order, and those who have not arrived at the place autonomously (enslaved or indentured labor). While analyses of the complexities of settler colonialism continue to be exposed, there is general agreement on the foundational processes that make this historical and ongoing process possible.

First, the settler colonizers (and those wishing to join their ranks) must establish that the Indigenous and exogenous others are inferior Others, subalterns to be legitimately "managed," thus claiming themselves as normative and thus "righteous." This brutal and dehumanizing assertion of white supremacy (Rowe & Tuck, 2017; Bonds & Inwood, 2016; Seawright, 2014) is experienced bodily, psychologically, and geographically by Indigenous people, as well as by the perpetrators (albeit in significantly different ways). An epistemological and ontological narrative defining the Indigenous Others' assumed inherent biological inferiority rationalizes threats of, or actual physical violence intended to control them physically or remove them from the land in order to build self-sustaining states independent of a motherland from which the colonizers arrived (Calderon, 2016).

Drawing from a Lockean definition of humanity relying on the naturalized ownership of property, centuries-long Indigenous dwelling on and use of the land was judged illegitimate due to European assessment of their perceived inability to make it "productive." According to Locke, human superiority—humanness itself—is defined by one's ability and willingness to use the land for profit, to make it produce for its owners, or to offer itself up to human needs and wants.

Ownership of private property is thus seen as a sign of civilization, of rational human behavior and a moral good. Eventually, movement across the "New World" to claim more and more of its resources was asserted simply as God's plan, "Manifest Destiny" for European settlers.

Initially, however, as Nancy Isenberg argues, this land was not necessarily seen as the Eden it is sometimes portrayed to have been. The foundational assertions of European supremacy is accompanied by the perception of the territory of the New World among some as "a giant rubbish heap" in need of transformation via the use of Old World sensibilities (Isenberg, 2016, p. 2) including the labor of the European underclasses. In spite of their lowly class position, these European miscreants would be used to remake the land into the image of productivity required by those seeking to profit from its transformation. And as this historical process unfolds, the Indigenous people are simply defined as unwanted obstacles to progress, part of the wilderness to be cast aside.

For the settler, the assertion of one's God-given right to the land brings forth conflicting, or at least intersecting, subject positions and forms of agency. On the one hand, according to Veracini, the settler is defined by the desire to become, or assert an identity as, indigenous to a place and thus able to lay claim as autonomously situated or rooted there. This desire is created within the narrative of inherent superiority relative to the land and Others defined as degradable. If the Others do not deserve to be there due to an inherent lack, indigeneity of the settlers becomes not just feasible but true and righteous. The land demands it. Sovereignty is thus rational, and the settlers are there to claim the place as a new "home." As Tuck and Yang (2012) point out, homemaking on land where others have been removed in order to claim indigeneity is a primary aspect of the settler colonizers' desire and the internalized ideology of removal.

On the other hand, settler subjectivity brings with it the will and already present (if complicated) subjective characteristics and desires to *Europeanize* the newly acquired locale. That is, the settlers rely on their already attained, mostly invisible (though fluid) European ideologies, and ways of being in the world: their customs and traditions, ontologies, and epistemologies including certainty of the superiority of European ways. These positions facilitate the ideological removal of other ways of being. Armed with such certainty (even while contradicted by the anxieties and fears associated with their relationships with unknown Others), settlers' sense of indigeneity really can only include themselves, since they are the ones chosen to be in, and on, this land. Why would one need to entertain learning from, or relating to, those native to a place if one already believes oneself naturally superior and the land thus rightfully one's own and awaiting the hand of production? These two tendencies—indigenization and Europeanization— create an active rationale for displacement wherein the native cultural ways and relationships with the land are all but erased from view.

Importantly, as Veracini points out, this ongoing co-presence of both the desire for, and perhaps belief in, settler indigenization along with the carried-forward ontology and epistemology of Europeanism means that "a settler society is always a society to come" (2010, p. 78); it cannot come into being precisely because it is based on an epistemological system established elsewhere in relation to other ecological systems, other political and cultural realities. It does not establish itself in relation to the complex features of the land itself, a practice that would take many generations and require a commitment to learn from those established there. The particular skills and values, the knowledge needed to live in the "New World" which could have been learned from the existing peoples have been eschewed from the start precisely because Indigenous people were considered inferior, part of an undeveloped wild landscape. Yet a fantasy of the moral right to the land and the illusion of orderly settlement is kept in place by denying that the violence of displacement ever happened or claiming its rational necessity that needs no further examination.

The unavoidable trauma caused to both the victims and perpetrators of the violence of displacement must be disavowed, sublimated, and covered over by an imaginary of hard working moral people, peacefully settled in an orderly community. As Veracini points out, such disavowal of the violence committed to the people or the land and its creatures (the exploitation of animals for fur, and trees for timber is epic in this history) leads to "stubborn and lingering anxieties over settler legitimacy and belonging" (2010, p. 77). This internalized psychic trauma of settler colonialism is born of an ongoing series of violations:

> In addition to an inevitable original founding violence, one should also emphasize that settler collectives are also escaping from violence. In this context, a "secure future" in a new land is recurrently and dialectically opposed to an "uncertain prospect" in an old one, and a determination to produce a settled political body is routinely expressed in formulations of setter colonial political traditions. (Veracini, 2010, p. 77)

The constant ideological and physical struggles are juxtaposed against the ongoing desire for, and fantasy of, a secure and orderly peace in a new land which never comes. To keep such a fantasy in place, the violence must be either disavowed or legitimated. Thus, the circle of degradation, displacement and disavowal forges the deeply ingrained psychological grooves necessary to extractive capitalism. This is precisely why scholars analyzing settler colonialism insist that the creation and re-creation of this metanarrative is an ongoing process and part of the primary discursive system produced and reproduced by dominant Eurocentric culture and internalized by all of us located in it (Rowe & Tuck, 2017; Calderon, 2016; Tuck & Yang, 2012). A fundamental denial of wrongdoing must be held in place by the constant reassertion of moral superiority and righteousness. It is this internalized logic of domination that blinds the settlers historically and currently to both the demands of a developing exploitive corporate state which needs them to assert its right to wealth and power gleaned from the land that they initially claim, and to the ongoing violence playing out on their own spirits, bodies, and families in the name of civilizational progress and national power.

Veracini goes on to argue that settler colonial phenomena articulate "a recurrent need to disavow" its practices which are discursively "concealed behind other occurrences."

> The settler hides behind the metropolitan colonizer (… "he is not responsible for colonialism" and its excesses), behind the activities of settlers elsewhere, behind the persecuted, the migrant, even the refugee (the settler has suffered elsewhere and "is seeking refuge in a new land"). The settler hides behind his labour and hardship (the settler does not dispossess anyone; he "wrestles with the land to sustain his family"). Most importantly, the peaceful settler hides behind the ethnic cleanser (colonization is an inherently non-violent activity; the settler enters a "new, empty land to start a new life"; indigenous people naturally and inevitably "vanish"; …) Settler Colonialism obscures the conditions of its own production. (Veracini, 2010, p. 14)

To be clear, the analysis that European settlers may have been escaping violence is not to offer an excuse for what they did once in a new territory, but rather to recognize an important structure of violence that is ongoing for Indigenous people currently, without doubt, but also reaching into the lives of the settler generations as well, and to understand the complex subject positions that are at play in this process.

Veracini's analysis of this overarching structural violence is placed in context by Karl Polanyi's now-classic economic history of *The Great Transformation* (2001), analyzing the dislocation of peasant farmers via the systematic installment of enclosures required by the market economy. "Market society" required a new way of thinking, a great transformation of the day-to-day means of making a living. Whereas for thousands of years land and people are deeply intertwined, in Europe a new form of economic exchange came to replace these ancient relations. A partnership between the developing nation state and the organization of abstract and exploitive economic systems makes private ownership of land for the purpose of political and economic power a requirement. Legalized enclosure processes thus moved people off land that they may have occupied and lived from in relatively reciprocal interdependencies for hundreds of years, forcing them into paid (exploited) labor for the new economic system. As Akulukjuk, Erkaeva, Rasmussen & Martusewicz point out:

> This "great" transformation was made possible due to three powerful ideas: converting humans into human rental units; converting land into enclosed, monetized property; and deploying a vast, symbolic, persuasive system called

money to usurp all other value. To these three—labour, land, money—Polanyi added a fourth key fabrication—the invention of hugely fictitious bodies—*corporations*—with the legal standing of humans. (forthcoming)

Capitalism was created via a rationalization of economic relations via legal institutions but also via important shifts in ideological and thus subjective systems as well, even for the people victimized by it. Prior to the transformation, people generally controlled and engaged in markets to serve their communities, but after the shift, the economy (managed via the systematic enactment of exploitive class relations, both ideological and material) began to take on the power to determine people's lives. As Peter Linebaugh (2014) has written, resistance to these enclosures or non-participation was systematically criminalized. "Imprisonment grew with enclosures replacing the old chastisements, like the stocks. A massive prison construction program accompanied the enclosure of agricultural production" (Kindle location 95), creating a whole new population of people considered threats or superfluous to the system. One of the resolutions to the problem of this population was to ship them as "waste" across the Atlantic to the New World as indentured labor. Expanding on Veracini's categorization of settlement population groups, Nancy Isenberg (2016) writes:

> The colonists were a mixed lot. On the bottom of the heap were men and women of the poor and criminal classes. Among these unheroic transplants were roguish highwaymen, mean vagrants, Irish rebels, known whores, and an assortment of convicts shipped to the colonies for the gallows. Not much better were those who filled the ranks of indentured servants, who ranged in class position from lowly street urchins to former artisans burdened with overwhelming debts. They had taken a chance in the colonies, having been impressed into service and then choosing exile over possible incarceration. (p. 13)

These were "expendable people … unloaded from England" (p. 14) whose labor would be used to transform the vast and weedy wilderness into potential riches, or simply be sent away to die in the unknown territories out of the way of imperialist expansionism in Europe. Veracini differentiates such indentured labor and involuntary migrants from an intentional collective who "irrupted" into a specific locale to assert sovereignty (2010, p. 17); the explicit class positions of those sent to do the dirty work of settlement and their desires to overcome their own exploitation cannot be understated. After all, those sent as involuntary indentured labor had much to prove, and this new land was a perfect place to reassert themselves. Imagining that the ancient land-based subjectivities would at least to some extent be motivating desire as they encountered the new territories, even as they began to be reconstituted by this new system, cannot be far from the mark. Along with their specific class-based subjectivities, orientations, and desires,

74 Settler Colonialism & *The Unsettling of America*

there would be shared ideologies across these groups, namely to become part of the eventual "success" of a settler state.

The arrival of European settlers to the Americas must be understood, therefore, as occurring in the midst of this economic (and thus ideological and psychological) transformation. The particularities of their individual desires and motivations are complicated by this history. Veracini's recognition of the contradictory psychological relation to violence and complex subject positions of European settlers who both experienced violence themselves but then also rationalized the removal of the Indigenous people is important to this story. He writes, "As 'settler society' can thus be seen as a fantasy where a perception of a constant struggle is juxtaposed against an ideal of 'peace' that can never be reached, settler projects embrace and reject violence *at the same time*" (2010, p. 77, emphasis in original). Disavowal thus follows on the heels of degradation and dispossession, and back around again, reinforcing the self-identification of moral superiority and reinforcing the sublimation of trauma among the perpetrators.

Wendell Berry also focuses on this structured series of violence which he refers to in a book first published in 1977 as *The Unsettling of America*. He includes in this analysis more recent dislocation of the small farmers (descendants of original settlers) in the development of industrial agriculture which may be why he is identified with settler colonialism. If the comments that I've heard leveled against him draw on these foundational definitions of what constitutes settler colonialism, they should fit somewhere in this description: that Berry disavows or ignores the degradation and violence done to Indigenous people by his own or his ancestral participation in these processes of elimination, and thus "erases" Indigenous people from the very land he farms.

My intention here is to demonstrate something quite to the contrary by reading across a more complicated set of positions and analyses. In many ways, Berry's cultural critique has been focused on exposing this very process of dispossession and displacement. In what follows, I read across Berry's work to ferret out his analyses of these historic processes. While there is no one "go-to" source I can offer where he definitively examines settler colonialism either historically or in its current manifestations, I hope to offer the reader Berry's critical interpretation of both the historical structures (ideological, economic, social) and contemporary effects as both supportive of current scholarship in this field, but also differing in important ways.

"It's Always Been Wayward"

At first, as I worked to understand these perspectives on Berry's thought, I was tempted to simply respond with, "Ah well, you just haven't read enough of Wendell Berry. See *The Unsettling of America*. Period." But of course, the task I've laid out for myself is much more complex than this. I needed to learn more about this history myself and I needed to read more of Berry. I will get back to *The*

Unsettling of America because I think it is an early and very poignant register of the arguments in Berry's work that followed its publication 40 years ago. But I'd rather start my response with a bit of his fiction.

While thinking about these questions, and reading current literature on white settler colonialism, I stumbled upon Berry's short story, "The Wild Birds" (2004). In the story, one of Berry's most amusing and even controversial characters, Burley Coulter, is visiting his lawyer friend Wheeler Catlett. Burley has arrived at Wheeler's office with his nephew Nathan Coulter and Nathan's wife Hannah, declaring that he wants to draw up his will. Wheeler assumes that he wants to pass on the old Coulter place to Nathan and Hannah, but Burley corrects him. He wants to pass his farm on to a young man named Danny Branch, who is his unacknowledged illegitimate son. Wheeler argues with him that this is not how such things are done; property is passed on along legitimate bloodlines. But, as the conversation unfolds we learn that Burley is forcing Wheeler to confront some deep truths about a long history of occupation on this land, as well as his own missed opportunities to do right by Danny's mother and their son. Wheeler, defending the importance of "an orderly handing down" of land and the preserving of sanctioned family connections on it argues hard. He is defending the dead. He is defending what he believes with all his might is morally right: preserving the plans and hopes for the land and the children of those now long gone. But Burley insists that all that is, and has always been "wayward."

> "Wheeler [Burley says]—I lie awake. I've thought this over and over, from one end to the other, and I can't see that the way it has been is in line with what anybody planned or the way anybody thought it ought to be."
>
> [Wheeler:] "But they did plan. They hoped. They started hoping and planning as soon as they got here—way back yonder."
>
> [Burley:] "It missed. Or they did. Partly, they were planning and hoping about what they'd just finished stealing from the ones who had it before, and were already quarreling over themselves. You know it. And partly they were wrong. How could they be right about what hadn't happened? And partly it was wayward." (Berry, 2004, p. 350)

In this brief but poignant exchange Berry expresses a powerful acknowledgment of the violence of dispossession that came with the arrival of European settlement, as well as a sharp critique of the rationalization that accompanied the continued occupation. And, he also acknowledges that much of the destruction resulting was not planned; it was not necessarily done with malevolent intent on the part of those who made the territory their home. When Burley says "partly it was wayward" he means that this original violence puts everything that followed into question. It puts the whole culture into question, including his own actions and the actions of those who preceded all of them, even though those who came before could be known to be good people. He is challenging Wheeler's sense of what is morally right and orderly. He is complicating and challenging the very mindset that came with and perpetrated the dispossession "way back yonder." Wheeler says, "Well, you're talking to an old man too, damn it! But, I still have some plans and hopes, and I still know what would be best for my place!" (Berry, 2004, p. 351). To him that means maintaining a certain tradition associated with inheritance of property, a certain order that he assumes is the best way to protect the land and the community.

And partly he is right, at least to the degree that those who continue on the land have been well prepared to be good "members" and ethical caretakers. But in his speech to his friends is also an important disavowal, and Burley hears it. Burley knows that this "order" is built on a very shaky foundation. And he knows that in spite of that foundational violence, he needs to do what is right for this community and the land that they depend on now in this time, while he is still alive to do it. So here we see in Berry's thinking, a complicated love that arises in almost everything he writes, one that sees clearly a series of horrendous even murderous mistakes and injustices, but simultaneously insists on asking what is our responsibility now, in this moment, to this place, to these creatures and people?

I say "love" here because Berry always returns to the absolute need for caring, responsible relationships as what will heal the deepest of wounds. I say complicated because part of this love requires an indictment on a set of beliefs and practices creating in us a specific kind of cultural character, to use his words, that continues to cause tremendous damage in this country and worldwide. We have inherited, he says, a cultural and ecological crisis that continues to be supported by an individual and collective crisis of character (Berry, 1996). We see him come back to these crises—ecological, social and individual (which is to say educational)—in his poetry, his fiction, and his analytic essays. As we have been arguing from the outset, Berry is a relentless critic of Western industrial culture, and he knows that American colonial history is founded on genocidal violence that removed Indigenous people from the land. But he also offers a different analytic take on the material and ideological structures that affected that dispossession, and ultimately on the definition of "settlement."

The Unsettling of America

The Unsettling of America originally published in 1977 and reissued several times since, is one of Berry's most biting indictments of modern industrial culture. Here Berry lays out an analysis of an overriding historical process of "unsettling" that has been rationalized as civilizational "progress" and growth even as it ravages the living systems of the world. He starts this analysis of the critical damages perpetrated on *both* the land and people (not just dispossession *of* the land *from* the people) with a brief but clear description of the European search for wealth: gold, animal pelts, timber, and land that displaced the native people and continued to displace those who came after.

> Conquests and foundings were incidental to this search—which did not and could not end until the continent was laid open in an orgy of goldseeking in the middle of the last [nineteenth] century. Once the unknown of geography was mapped, the industrial marketplace became the new frontier and we continued, with largely the same motives and with increasing haste and anxiety, to displace ourselves—no longer with unity of direction, like a migrant flock, but *like the refugees from a broken anthill*. In our own time, we have invaded foreign lands and the moon with the high-toned patriotism of the conquistadors, and with the same mixture of fantasy and avarice. (1996, p. 3; emphasis added)

Berry argues that "the greatest 'American revolution' to come to this continent was the coming of a people *who did not look upon the land as a homeland*" (p. 4, emphasis added) but rather were here to pillage it for profit, and leave, or move on to the next territory to do the same. This process, of course, required *unsettling* whatever people stood in its way, and used the bodies of settlers, along with the bodies of both Indigenous and kidnapped Africans—those who came to stay—to help accomplish the taking of the territories to be exploited. Some of these were pushed off their European homelands by European enclosure acts or other legalized means of disruption and degradation, and brought to this continent as indentured laborers with the intention of settling and making homes.

Some—Berry calls them "Stickers"—came with the desire to settle, to connect with and nurture the land, to homestead, and even, as Hixon (2013) writes, worked to establish somewhat ambivalent but nonetheless mutual relationships with the Indigenous peoples. But these tendencies were, as Berry laments, weaker than the forces of exploitation that pushed them here in the first place. Those tendencies were ultimately overthrown or simply ignored as the frontier and the commodification of the land was pushed further and further west removing every barrier in its path. The first to go, of course, would be the Indigenous communities as they, and soon after, the settlers themselves, became "the designated victims of an utterly ruthless, officially sanctioned and subsidized exploitation. The colonists who drove off the Indians came to be intolerably exploited by their imperial governments. And that alien imperialism was thrown off only to be succeeded by a domestic version of the same thing" (Berry, 1996, p. 4).

In this early work, and throughout his subsequent analyses, Berry traces the overriding de-indigenizing demands of capitalism, not without considerable expression of grief over what happened to both the Indigenous people here and the land itself, and not without intense examination of the damaging world view of his own people. It required displacement and a sense of "expendability" and efficiency in the presence of abundance, and a complete disregard and

78 Settler Colonialism & *The Unsettling of America*

degradation of Indigenous values of restraint and protection. "Industrial economics has always believed this: abundance justifies waste. This is one of the dominant superstitions of American history—and of the history of colonialism everywhere. Expendability is also an assumption of the world of efficiency" (Berry, 1995, pp. 103–104).

In order to take possession of, and commodify the land, the living beings taken—the beaver, the trees, the fish, even the soil itself—had to be perceived as just so many exchangeable objects feeding the profit-making machine. Here we see Berry's refusal of anthropocentric assumptions that "exploitation" is primarily a "master-slave" relationship among humans. Instead, he recognizes and even emphasizes that those who came to homestead were operating from a mentality that defined "the land" as an object to be taken and misused, which meant that all the living beings on it were nothing more than objects for sale or consumption. This fundamentally exploitive (and extractive) relationship with the soil and creatures of a place is precisely why those who came needed to manage and ultimately remove the Indigenous populations they encountered, even those with whom they may have made relationships, as Hixon points out. While it may not have required the exploited labor of those people, the processes of colonization certainly did involve the exploitation of other living beings defined simply as commodities.

Berry describes a supremacist episteme and ontology rationalizing selfish individualism, racism, and exploitive anthropocentrism as what was needed to make this successive process of dispossession possible. As discussed earlier, the seizure of land that violently removed Indigenous people was accomplished by Enlightenment rationalization of private property that defined the natives' inferiority as evident in their failure to make it appropriately "productive" (Cronon, 1983; Seawright, 2014). For those who came to settle, success would be defined by first acquiring the land needed to farm (helped along of course by removal policies of the nation state), and later expanding in order to compete within the burgeoning industrial market. And, according to Berry, the only way to avoid victimization in this process has been to "succeed," that is to make it into the class of exploiters, and then to remain so specialized and so "mobile" as to be unconscious of the effects of one's life or livelihood. This escape is, of course, illusory (1996, p. 5). Soon enough, that very market—the source of success—would be determining whether life on that land was possible at all.

In the next century and a half, the descendants of those Europeans who displaced the Indigenous would be removed as well in favor of industrial technologies, and "get big or get out" Federal agricultural policies that have all but destroyed once fertile soil and ecosystems that had nurtured communities here for centuries, as well as the white communities that had settled (see Chapters 2 and 8). "Let me emphasize that I am not talking about an evil that is merely contemporary or 'modern' but one that is as old in America as the white man's presence here" (Berry, 1996, p. 5).

Settler Colonialism & *The Unsettling of America*   79

This is what Burley Coulter knows in his heart has been "wayward" all along: that the settlement of his own community was built upon mis-recognition, wrong-headedness and wrong-doing and whose members now suffer the consequences, not the least of which is blindness to those consequences. This is what we see Berry dealing with in the work that has become a lifetime's oevre, as he tells the story of our suicidal destiny with expanding extractive relationships with the earth, and our refusal to learn from those who came before what we would need to know. He is disgusted by the cultural arrogance that led to such destruction and continues to rationalize it. Echoing Veracini's analysis of the role of imported Europeanization among the settlers, he writes:

> The history of the white man's use of the earth in America is a scandal. The history of his effort to build here what Allen Tate calls "a great culture of European pattern" is a farce. To farm here, as we have done for centuries, as if the land and the climate were European, has been ruinous, ecologically and agriculturally, and no doubt, culturally as well. (Berry, 2010a, p. 105)

Taking this analysis further, Berry recognizes the refusal of white settler society to learn from those who have lived on this continent for centuries before the arrival of Europeans, beginning from their insistence on their own superiority.

> For examples of a whole and indigenous American society, functioning in full meaning and good health within the ecology of this continent, we will have to look back to the cultures of the Indians. That we failed to learn from them how to live in this land is a stupidity—*a racial stupidity*—that will corrode the heart of our society until the day comes, if it ever does, when we do turn back to learn from them. Inheriting the cultural growth of thousands of years, they had a responsible sense of living within the creation—which is to say that they had among much else, an ecological morality—and a complex awareness of the life of their land which we have hardly begun to have. (2010a, p. 107, emphasis added)

Contrary to erasing or disavowing the violence that was and is perpetrated on the lives of Indigenous people, Berry looks deeply into the cultural processes that caused this founding violence, focusing on both the historical development of an exploitive economic system on those who preceded white settlers, and the specific psychological, institutional, and interpersonal effects that continue to degrade contemporary Indigenous people as well as his own people and the land itself. It may be that his wording, "we will have to look back at the culture of the Indians" overlooks the present people who carry such knowledge, in a kind of nod to a noble savage. I cannot say whether he has engaged with contemporary Shawnee elders around these questions in his area of Kentucky, but Berry is a diligent seeker of knowledge around the forms of land use and ecological values

80 Settler Colonialism & *The Unsettling of America*

that he desires to see reclaimed and revitalized. As I'll discuss further on, his agricultural and forestry interests have taken him to visit Indigenous peoples around the world, always with an eye to what practices and traditions still exist that embrace the restorative connections and relationships of earthly care needed urgently. This knowledge he sets against "the exploiters' revolution."

And yet, here he complicates the story again refusing simple "us and them" "victimizers and victims" binaries to think about his own ancestral history.

Against Simple Divisions

As discussed in the Introduction and continues as a recurring theme, one of the most important aspects of his work is his refusal of a simple analytic division between victims and exploiters (or perpetrators) as individual subject positions, actions, or roles. Instead, Berry argues that we should identify a division "between exploitation and nurture" that are never mutually exclusive in any one individual or community. That is, he sees that these are contradictory internalized tendencies and tensions in all of us as humans, and particularly as humans who have lived within institutionalized logics of domination (Warren, 1998). We are not simply perpetrators or victims of exploitation, but also have the capacity to offer and experience compassion; in general, we all know what it means to care and be cared for. While there are certainly hegemonic experiences among diverse groups, the "division" as he sees it, is "not only between persons, but within persons" (Berry, 1996, p. 7). This is important. We are all interactive products of the culture that we are born into, even those of us who spend our lives struggling against its exploitive structures and tendencies. Recognizing this, Berry implores us not to take ourselves out of that context, but to be vigilant in our reflection on how such oppositional qualities shape us and our work. His own humble recognition of how such tendencies have played out in his own life is instructive. Looking back again at our discussion in the Introduction, he is honest about his own dawning awareness of the ancient presence of Indigenous people on the pathways across his ancestral home.

This is one of the most difficult aspects of Berry's work for some to accept, because again, he refuses either to let any of us off the hook (including himself), or to give up on the fundamental need for, and potential of, love in setting things right. I think this is what makes some of his critics most uncomfortable. He both asks us to confront ourselves (as he confronts himself) as products of a violent and exploitive cultural system, and shows us again and again that the answers to our crises, the essential "reparations" if you will, lie in our capacities to care for each other. To care is to be generous, to exercise restraint, and to be in mutually responsive relationships with all the other living beings upon which we depend for life.

I understand why my colleagues might want to impugn Berry for his personal choice to make his life on stolen land where several generations of his forbears lived as white settlers. It is a mistake, however, to see this personal choice as a simple sign of settler colonial consciousness, or perhaps better, to assume that his interest in returning to farm in Northern Kentucky instead of remaining on the path to academic success signifies a refusal to take account of the lives of those who were removed as his family put down roots. One of the most powerful and even endearing aspects of Berry's work is his capacity for, and commitment to, analyzing his own embeddedness in a culture of violence, his distress, grief, and anger about that reality, and his ability to reflect carefully on his inheritance of a whole long line of mistreatment, mistakes and maladaptation.

I have been asked by members of audiences when I present about Berry's life and work, whether or to what extent he thinks about who lived on the land before him, whether it matters to him personally or shows up in his work. It is true that one would be hard pressed to identify one essay or book where he takes on the task of researching Indigenous knowledge and culture within his home territory of Northern Kentucky. Instead, one finds woven through his work, a deep respect and honoring of that knowledge either via direct statements or in the character of his own beliefs and commitments. Forgive the long passage that follows, but I think it provides a good response to this implicit critique born in part of a misunderstanding, perhaps prejudice, of what it means to commit to the land as a farmer as Berry has done:

> Going day after day about the work of my little farm, I began to have a sense of the thousands of acts, properly honored and understood generation after generation, that are necessary to surround a man with a culture sufficient to his life in a given space.
>
> I became thoughtful of all the work that had been done there on my home ground either by despised men or by men who secretly despised themselves for doing the work of despised men—so many of the necessary acts of my history, neither valued nor understood, wasted in the process of wasting the earth. And I thought back to the time before the brief violent spasm of my people's history there, to the thousands of years when the Shawnees and their forebears lived in the country in its maidenhood, familiar with it as they were with their own bodies, as much at home in it as the plants and animals, wedded to it by an exquisite awareness of its life. They were native as no one has been since. And I began to understand how the racism of my people has been a barrier not just between us and our land but between us and our exemplary predecessors. (2010a, p. 88)

In addition to reflections like this one written in the late 1960s and published later, Berry reports in other essays on what he has learned from particular Indigenous farmers and foresters, specifically the ancient practices employed and the values that guide them. For example, in an essay entitled "Conserving Forest

Communities" (1995), Berry looks to a Menominee tribal forest in northern Wisconsin for affirmation of what he believes to be the means toward a good forest economy. He had read about that forest and went for a visit to see for himself and to talk with the foresters. Recounting the history of territorial loss "as the country was taken up by white settlers" (p. 41) he describes how the Menominee were forced to change their livelihood from hunting and gathering to managing the remaining forest, making timber the major source of their livelihood since the mid-nineteenth century. Praising their foundational principles and traditions that ensure that none of the original ecosystem or the forest's productivity would be harmed, he goes on to describe patterns of management that are technically sophisticated but "still rooted in tradition" (p. 41). With ecological integrity an absolute priority, the Menominee community is able to preserve their tribal identification as forest dwellers. He is careful not to overstate the case, but sees great value in the conservational aspects of keeping the forest productive, far more so than most conventional industrial methods, but also far more than a source of economic value.

> The Menominee forest economy currently employs—in forest management, logging, milling and other work—215 tribe members, or nearly 16 percent of the adult population of the reservation. As the Menominee themselves know, this is not enough; the economy of the forest needs to be more diverse. ... Kentuckians looking for the pattern of a good local forest economy would have to conclude, I think, that the Menominee example is not complex enough, but that in all other ways it is excellent. We have much to learn from it. The paramount lesson undoubtedly is that the Menominee forest economy is as successful as it is because it is not understood primarily as an economy ... the forest is the basis of a culture ... the goal has always been a diverse, old, healthy, beautiful, productive community-supporting forest that is home not only to its wild inhabitants but also to its human community. (Berry, 1995, pp. 43–44)

In another example, Berry learns of the cultivation practices of Andean farmers in Peru. While he does not visit this community, his example of what he terms "a sound pre-industrial agriculture" comes from "the village of Uchucmarca in a valley of northern Peru" where the land farmed is "one of the steepest gradients in the world" (Berry, 1996, quoting Stephen B. Brush, p. 175). His description is of a rich and varied set of agricultural practices that take account of diverse climatic zones, and a range of animal husbandry as well as crops cultivated. He describes the ways the farmers avoid erosion, cope with frost in the higher zones, utilize crop rotation, manage insects and disease using genetic diversity, etc—all ancient traditions developed over centuries of flourishing on the same land using values that sustain their families and honor the importance of the ecosystems they rely on for life.

Settler Colonialism & *The Unsettling of America* **83**

> Nearly all the methods of the Andean farmers are based upon the one prin-
> ciple of diversity. In their understanding and use of the principle, they have
> developed an agriculture much more sophisticated, efficient, and con-
> servative of the soil than our own—and one that is much more likely to
> survive a crisis. (Berry, 1996, p. 177)

And a bit further on, he writes of the use of hedgerows as margins between the
fields where the pollen and seedlings of the cultivars mix with the wild things to
provide new possibilities.

> ... a network of wilderness threading through the fields serves the Andean
> farmer as a college of agriculture and experiment station ... whatever is dis-
> covered there has already been tested in the circumstances of the farm itself,
> and its worth or worthlessness proven. The farmer, in whose mind culture
> and agriculture are wedded, acts both as teacher-researcher and student, both
> extension agent and client. ... It is surely by this means—this graceful,
> practical generosity toward the possible and the unexpected, toward time
> and history—that Andean agriculture has survived for so long, cohering
> even through the severe disturbances of the Spanish Conquest. (Berry,
> 1996, pp. 176–179)

In these passages, Berry acknowledges both the deeply situated knowledge of
the Andean farmers and its persistence in the face of the upheaval of the con-
quistadors. His interest lies in the ancient value system and spirituality guiding
their practices and wisdom, their relationships to each other and to the land. In
fundamental ways, he embraces these practices and relationships as the threads of
love weaving the community together.

Settling as Love: The Body and the Earth

As we've discussed throughout this book, just as he attends to the foundational
violence of European conquest and our current hyper-consumer culture, Berry
always returns to a set of primary principles that define our fundamental
embeddedness within living communities, and our essential responsibilities for
taking care of those communities as a matter of survival, and further as what
makes happiness possible. In the above passages, we read him identifying those
principles in the life-ways and spiritual unity of the Shawnee of his homeland as
well as the current Menominee foresters and Andean farmers. I have traced the
grief he experiences in the face of his own ancestors and others as their greed and
arrogance ravaged the once fertile soil and forests. Berry always comes back to a
deep faith that "people need more than to understand their obligation to one
another and to the earth; they need also the *feeling* of such an obligation" (2010a,
p. 88). The feeling that accompanies such an obligation to others, when

84   Settler Colonialism & *The Unsettling of America*

approached in humility and kindness, is love, the embodied affection, that leads to the desire and active learning to care for one another as a matter of our own happiness and well-being.

Exposing the horrifying mistakes made by his own white European ancestors, Berry seeks to define what it would take to experience such an obligation to one another as we awaken to our dependency with the land and responsibilities to each other. Identifying affection as the glue of relationship and thus of healthy communities, he offers a different understanding of what it means "to settle" that runs entirely counter to the historical strategies and practices of occupation, looking to the Indigenous culture of his native land for guidance.

> From what I have read I gather that the American Indian did not conceive of himself [sic] as a mechanically producing and consuming agent of a political compact, but as the spiritual heir of the life of the Creation. He was the agent and legato of this life, but also a part of it, and his religion was the enactment of his unity with it. (2010a, p. 89)

Laying bare the structures of a cultural and economic system that rationalizes and even demands mobility, separation and fragmentation as a defining quality of "success," he argues that we have never been settlers in the truest, most vital sense. There has never been, among the Europeans who came with the intent to stay a clear recognition of our inherent interdependence with the land or its creatures, human or otherwise, or a lived embodied experience of oneself as wholly engaged in its life and thus responsible for its well-being.

For Berry, "to settle," not just in name or attribution but in full conscious action and commitment, means to recognize and practice a willingness to learn over many generations what a place requires of us. It requires careful protection of embedded and embodied wholeness and attention to life itself in all its complex plurality and mystery. His desire that this obligation define our lives now does not disavow either past or ongoing violence; rather it seeks a remedy in the form of current commitments.

> What we are working for, I think, is an authentic settlement and inhabitation of our country. We would like to see all human work lovingly adapted to the nature of the places where it is done and to the real needs of the people by whom and for whom it is done. We do not believe that any violence to places, to people, or to other creatures is "inevitable." (1996, p. 233)

Berry's plea here that we learn to inhabit the places where we live is not simply "an attempt to relieve settler anxiety and dis-location" (Tuck, McKenzie & McCoy, 2014, p. 17). Again, I recognize the critiques that have been made of approaches that suggest "inhabitation" as a solution to the cultural and ecological crises that we face, especially those that do not critically analyze the specific violence done to possess that land in the first place (Tuck et al., 2014). The descendants and ongoing benefactors of that violence (and here I include myself), can never be neutral in our efforts to reassess how we live in the places we wish to care for. We must acknowledge, analyze, and try to work across these difficult divisions to heal the damages done. That means making authentic relationships and working to expose and challenge the underlying hierarchies.

For Berry, the issue is not simply about claiming the land as a possession, or as a right, and certainly is not inclusive of ignoring the politics and violence of removal. Rather, it is about healing the damages done, by thinking carefully about what needs to be restored if the earth and we with it are to survive. Our bodies, our spirits, our minds are inescapably connected to all the other living creatures on the earth and to the vast cosmos within which our planet is situated, a vast and mysterious network that Berry refers to as Creation. Our endurance as humans on this earth requires that we recognize and support these patterns that connect us to a greater whole, not as a matter of appropriating Indigenous knowledge, but as a matter of recognizing what it takes to support life:

> It becomes clear that the health or wholeness of the body is a vast subject, and that to preserve it calls for a vast enterprise. … All the convergences and dependences of Creation are surely implied. Our bodies are also not distinct from the bodies of other people, on which they depend in a complexity of ways from biological to spiritual. They are not distinct from the bodies of plants and animals, with which we are involved in the cycles of feeding and in the intricate companionships of ecological systems and of the spirit. They are not distinct from the earth, the sun and moon, and the other heavenly bodies. (Berry, 1996, p. 103)

In this sensibility, I find a clear alliance in much of Berry's work with values and wisdom of many Indigenous teachings. For example, traditional teachings from within the Anishinaabe emphasize "living spiritually with respect, relationship, reciprocity and responsibility" (Bell, 2013, p. 89) among people and with the natural world. These values emphasize interconnections and kinship relationships with beings within the animal world and larger cosmos. As Chief Loren Lyons of the Onondaga Nation says, "All living beings are kin." And among Indigenous Hawaiians, "the concept lokahi (unity) conveys the 'nurturing, supportive and harmonious relations' linking land, the gods, humans and the forces of nature" (Posey, 2006, p. 29). Interestingly, Vine Deloria (2008) finds these values alive and well in what might otherwise be considered unexpected places:

> In this sense, Appalachian whites, rural blacks, and Scandinavian farmers are all so much closer to the natural world [than most white people] because they live in it twenty-four hours a day. These groups may not see themselves as a single group yet they are all connected by their oppression by

industrialization, by the destruction of the land bases on which their lives depend, and by their connection to the natural world that teaches them who they are. What's important is not just an abstract connection to an abstract earth, but instead the relationship you have with a particular tree or a particular mountain. (Deloria, 2008, p. 259)

Throughout Berry's work the values of reverence, relationship, reciprocity, and responsibility reign as primary organizing themes and principles that rail against modernist assumptions of individualism, mechanism, anthropocentrism, and "progress." He draws these values from a variety of sources, including the Gospels of the Christian tradition, and other religious sources, as well as ancient scholarly sources within the Western canon. He is firmly unapologetic about the sources of his study. In fact, he has admonished me in personal correspondence not to write off all of Western tradition as evil. Berry looks for their affirmation and development of the principles of the Great Economy (see Chapter 1) and the character traits that support them in whatever traditions they may arise. His friendship with Buddhist scholar and poet Gary Snyder is another example of the breadth of his openness (see the book *Distant Neighbors*, edited by Wriglesworth, 2014). These are principles that Berry asserts as necessary in our efforts to account for our "wayward" culture, and that should influence the sorts of character formations needed to make amends. But such an education can only happen if people stay in place to learn from the land over many generations. This is what it means "to settle" in Berry's estimation, a process fully undermined by industrialization. Supporting Berry's argument, Deloria goes on:

As you live in one place, it becomes so familiar to you that you begin to tear down the defenses you've erected in order to survive in industrial civilization, and you begin to fall into the rhythm of the land. So the first thing is that you begin to have a different sense of the natural. You spontaneously don't have to think of abstract things. You think more in terms of how the land looks, and what it's telling you. I would think many people in Appalachia have this sense already developed. There've been families there now for what, five, six generations? (2008, p. 260)

As we read on in *The Unsettling of America* (1996) we find Berry describing an ideological system that degrades the body as it degrades the earth, a system of education that teaches fragmentation, hierarchized specialization and hyperseparation as fundamentals of a so-called "evolved" civilization, and the source of an essential isolation and loneliness.

Intellectually, we know that these patterns of interdependence exist; we understand them better now perhaps that we ever have before; yet modern social and cultural patterns contradict them and make it difficult or impossible to honor them in practice. ... Healing is impossible in loneliness. It is the opposite of loneliness. Conviviality is healing. (1996, p. 103)

Witness to the ill effects on daily life brought about by a continuous systematized degradation and disconnection, Berry asks us again and again to recognize and revere the power and beauty of Creation both within the possibilities of our own imagination, and in the land itself. "The power of imagination is to see things in their eternal aspect; it is to know the timeless as it 'moves through time,' the eternal presence that is both in and outside time and that comprehends the things we know and remember..." (Berry, 2010b, p. 116).

To Berry, the sacred is everywhere, the very possibility of wholeness and life. But, we live, he says in a time of desecration of most places and all images, the worst perhaps being

the image of humanity itself as "a higher animal"—with the implied permission to be more bewildered, violent, self-deluded, destructive, and self-destructive than any of the animals. From the desecration of that image, the desecration of the world and all its places and creatures inexorably follows. ... We are ruled by whatever unmakes and fragments the world. (Berry, 2010b, p. 117)

Key to the teachings within EcoJustice Education, we recognize that exploitation is the result of any system based on a logic of domination that uses naturalized assertions of superiority to rationalize its excessive extractive actions (Plumwood, 2002; Martusewicz, Edmundson & Lupinacci, 2015). A hierarchized economic system requires that we naturalize violence exercised as part of the right to make decisions about who should live and who should die. For Berry, it would be impossible to argue that the world view or patterns of belief and behavior that came to this continent in the form of white settlers was *not* about exploitation, perhaps not primarily of the people for their labor, but definitely of the land and its creatures. He knows that the white colonists who came here brought such a mindset to the land, and that the "gross misunderstanding" and desecration started with white settlement structured by the ideological and material demands of capitalism (Berry, 2010a, p. 41). He reminds us of this again and again. And he insists that we ourselves—all of us—have inherited the tendencies of such a violent relationship with each other and with the earth. We have been schooled to it. This recognition too is about love, for how can we begin to heal if we do not assess the conditions of the damages perpetrated?

On Education versus the Politics of Knowledge in Academia

The system of institutionalized education, both K-12 and universities, is for Berry at the heart of the problem, part of the colonizing machine that continues to teach us to devalue relationships, to prioritize "making it big" and to engage epistemological assumptions that fragment the world and make "things" out of living beings. That is the ultimate desecration. And yet, he also knows that other tendencies survive alongside it that should be at the heart of how we define what it means to become educated: the possibility to see the evils done, to mourn the harms and deaths, and to work to heal those deep wounds in us and in the land. He asks us, again and again, to step up to such a responsibility, to embrace such a love, and to open ourselves to the teachers around us who can help us to do so.

> If we were lucky enough as children to be surrounded by grown-ups who loved us, then our sense of wholeness is not just the sense of completeness in ourselves but also is the sense of belonging to others and to our place. ... Of course, growing up and growing older as fallen creatures in a fallen world can only instruct us painfully in division and disintegration. That is the stuff of consciousness and experience. But if our culture works in us as it should, then we do not age merely into disintegration and division, *but that experience begins our education*, leading us into knowledge of wholeness and of holiness ... we are led out of our lonely suffering and are made whole. (Berry, 1996, p. 87; emphasis added)

I am quite aware that offering Berry's work in this way may be seen as "a move to innocence," a charge that Tuck and Yang make dismissing white scholarship claiming to be "postcolonial." I make no such claim here and neither does Berry. Rather, I prefer to learn from him (and others) what it could mean to understand the ways that these two tendencies—exploitation and care—operate in us and in our communities (including our academic communities) as a means toward ethical possibilities here and now. Universities and academic relationships are fraught with the normalization of rational analytic approaches and competition for who's work matters most and who will get ahead quickest, be the loudest voice, publish in the most high-status journals, and garner the most power over others. Such positions are created out of hubris, an attitude that can dismiss with ease a writer who asks us to consider love as a form of eternal power providing the needed bonds of survival and regeneration. To identify Wendell Berry as merely "a white settler colonialist" in order to dismiss his work is a pernicious move to blame, rationalizing a certain avoidance that ironically keeps in place any number of hierarchized binaries that reproduce the very violence that we are concerned with.

What Now? A Pedagogy of Responsibility

Defined as I have outlined it here as a process of degradation, dispossession and disavowal, settler colonialism is indeed an ongoing structural and psychological process (Rowe & Tuck, 2017; Calderon, 2016; Tuck & Yang, 2012). To the degree that we do not expose and challenge those processes as part of a program of socio-ecological healing in education and more broadly, we remain complicit in its narratives. As Dolores Calderon (2016) makes clear, "settler colonial knowledge regimes shape social science research" (p. 5) via a "settler colonial metanarrative" that divides and dominates. Concurring with Calderon, I have tried to caution as well, that we in educational research are not so innocent of maintaining those divisions or our own selfish interests. We work in institutions created within that very order.

Berry's work begins with a candid indictment of his own family's blind involvement in the damages perpetrated by a predominant socio-political and economic order that drove many of them to this land in the first place with placeless dreams of progress that led to many of the mistakes he saw etched into the hillside of his own farm, and the lives of his neighbors. To the degree that we in educational institutions accept or do not interrogate our own dreams of individual advancement or power as normal and legitimate practices of success, we too are complicit.

I find in Berry, the courage to argue for love in the face of all that, not as a matter of sentimentality as it may appear to some, and certainly not as a matter of denying all the wrongs that have been inflicted on the people and land and creatures who existed on this continent before our European forebears, but as a means of asking "what now?"

Who are we now, and what is our responsibility to those who came before, to those with whom we share this place currently, and to those yet to come? This is the fundamental task of education defined by the practice of responsibility. How do we reach across ongoing divisions to face, with humility and kindness, the wrongs done to this land and the people who for centuries engaged practices of care as the basis of life and community here and elsewhere? How do we teach our students of all ages to identify and expose the embedded narratives, the "grammars of settler superiority" (Calderon, 2016) and other associated supremacy discourses that they learn in school and all through our day-to-day interactions? For the most part, official knowledge in K-12 curricula denies or mentions only fleetingly the violence done to the Indigenous people of this continent, revises their histories, and ignores other ways of knowing as legitimate and essential. Calderon's work is instructive:

> To do this, I turn to US social studies curriculum an exemplar of colonization, or coloniality in education in relation to Indigenous peoples. Coloniality refers to the manner in which modern systems of colonialism operate epistemically, economically, ontologically, politically, and spatially. ... I use the concept of settler grammars to describe this organizing system of thought and institutional practices. The organizing concept of grammar speaks to the way that settler colonialism is reproduced through narratives, or discourses, in this case curriculum. However, to engage education audiences, concepts of

90 Settler Colonialism & *The Unsettling of America*

> settler grammars and settler colonialism must be augmented theoretically and methodologically because mainstream, and even many critical epistemologies of education, are built upon edifices and lenses that may obscure or distort settler ontology. (Calderon, 2014, pp. 314–316)

These grammars, the discourses of colonialism, have been deeply ingrained in the hearts and minds of ordinary citizens via the ongoing intergenerational violence of erasure perpetuated by our institutions to ensure the ongoing hegemony and governmentality of the corporate state, including and especially via schools. As Tuck and Gaztambide-Fernandez (2013) argue, "Curriculum and its history in the US has invested in settler colonialism, and the permanence of the settler-colonial nation state" (p. 73).

Our teachers and students can learn to expose those narratives by engaging cultural ecological analyses of the discursive structures that support them as normal. This means that teachers and teacher educators have an obligation to introduce conceptual tools that can help make visible the grammars of invisibility that still exist in our school curricula. Imagine for example, using the concepts, "degrade, dispossess, and disavow" as the primary framework for teaching about what happened when Europeans came to this continent. Imagine setting up a series of lessons that ultimately ask students to identify how the process is still at work in our lives and in the land.

Imagine asking them to think about the ways erasure of Indigenous peoples in their own communities works. Community activist and historian Matt Siegfried works in just these ways to awaken residents and students of Ypsilanti, Michigan (our home city) to the ancient and ongoing presence of Indigenous peoples along the shores of the Huron River. Taking a group of teachers and education scholars on a walking tour one summer's day he opened our imaginations to the lifeways of the Huron people, pointing out the way the river bank mounds in such a way at a particular curve to reveal ancient burial grounds, or a lake created by Henry Ford who harnessed the river for one of his automobile plants, in the process destroying fertile fields that were still under cultivation by the local Indigenous people in the early twentieth century. We walked along a path where villages once existed and were transported by Matt's deep knowledge of the violent conflicts among various tribes with white settlers, and military force brought on by European contact during the eighteenth and nineteenth centuries. We talked about who the Huron are today (there unfortunately was no one available to join the tour) where the people of those who refused to be removed live now.

And on a very snowy winter's day, Matt took a group of second through eighth graders on a similar walk asking them too to think about the role of the river in the history of the people who have lived here, the significant differences in how they have thought of and used the river for their day-to-day lives. These Ypsilanti youngsters also learned of removal and replacement of these various lives, observing the now decrepit factory buildings that dot our city along the river's edge. They took that experience back to their art classroom where they worked with their teacher Lisa Voelker and Detroit artist Chazz Miller to contribute to a mural entitled "Learning from the Huron."

That mural project and work with Matt Siegfried led to subsequent discussions with the Indigenous Students Organization on campus, as they began to confront and protest a violent event against one of their community elders, raising consciousness at our university of both the ongoing degradation and their refusal to remain "as ghosts" (Calderon, 2016). They helped us to interrogate the images on the mural, unmasking unconscious implications of a disappeared people that showed up there. There was anger and insistence on changes which were taken on with humility and apologies. Thus, we learn about our own complicity, even as we work to shift both our students' and the public's disavowal of a violent history and the futurity of settler subjectivity.

One other example local to my own region strikes me as important even while we can identify its limitations. A group of students and their teachers joined a local Southeast Michigan organization, the River Raisin Institute, and local Indigenous elders to learn about the cultivation of rice along the shore of Lake Erie. The students learned about the historic and current role of rice in the diets of Indigenous tribes, primarily the Ojibwe, who lived along the shores of the Great Lakes and related tributaries, and the drastic changes as the once marshy land was filled in to become "useful" and productive to European settlers. They studied and learned to plant the rice cultivars and, in the process, were introduced to history, cultural traditions, and current indigenous sciences relative to their local ecosystems.

Critical Indigenous educational scholars raise concerns with environmental education, including critical place-based education that perpetuate a kind of political neutrality that leaves unquestioned current forms of settler colonialism, including understandings of Indigenous peoples as repositories of static forms of cultural knowledge (Tuck, McKenzie & McCoy, 2014). While I do not know the full degree to which these lessons on the shores of Lake Erie took on a critical examination of settler colonial history (I suspect they did not), the opportunity for these students to learn from a local tribal leader about these traditions is a step in the right direction. At the very least, they learned that the Ojibwe are not a past civilization, and that they have much knowledge to share, both ancient and current, about the ecology of the Great Lakes. Still, I want to recognize the limitations of both place-based and environmental education in the absence of deeper more complicated study of the discursive underpinnings of violence undertaken by Europeans on the people and the land, and the particular shape of historical and contemporary Indigenous identification with and claims to the land.

Teachers, with their students, must seek opportunities to hear the painful truths ripped open by settler histories in the places where we live that de-neutralize our relationships to those places. Our responsibility is to provide the provocative descriptions and conceptual framework that lay bare our own unconscious complicity in the systems presented as inevitable and natural. Even young children can be asked to confront the disavowal and degradation into which they have been born and that shape the world view of their families. Students studying to become teachers or working through graduate programs, as well as non-degree students in our communities, can learn to shift their patterns of belief and behavior when asked gently and persistently to engage the ethical implications of these stories, to see them as already forming the land we live on and claim as ours. I thank my friend Richard Kahn for giving me a necessary push, and for the work he obviously does with his students. And I am appreciative of those in my own region who are doing this work.

Reconciliation or reparation is not possible outside the willingness to talk with one another, hear each other's stories, make relationships, and safely ask students to engage "epistemologies of ignorance" (Calderon, 2016; Tuck & Yang, 2012; Tuck & Gaztambide-Fernandez, 2013; Rowe & Tuck, 2017) that many texts and curricula in "whitestream" schools offer. Left unaddressed, curricula in most white-dominated school systems protect the rationalization of the ongoing damages of extractive, dispossessive industrial systems and the socio-ideological processes that support them by simply not addressing these at all or by presenting such systems as superior examples of progress. Even those multicultural curricula that may try to use inclusive, content-based approaches to solve these problems can fall short. Tuck & Gaztambide-Fernandez (2013) warn that:

> When being inclusive, whitestream curriculum begins to absorb and contain, consuming and erasing the other, by always-already positioning the accumulated knowledge as other too, less refined, more subjective and less reliable than the whitestream. The story is just a better story when there are more white people in it. (p. 82)

Canadian scholars Jesse K. Butler, Nicholas Ng-A-Fook, Julie Vaudrin-Charette, and Ferne McFadden write about challenging such erasure via a pedagogy of relationships that invites their students into conversation with Indigenous Elders as their teachers.

> As a team, we envisioned this shift from content-based to relational pedagogy in our everyday practices. Tuning into the TRC's [Truth and Reconciliation Commission's] *Principles of Reconciliation*, we reached out to an Elder to assist us with our planning process. We invited Elders to share stories with our students of the intergenerational impacts of residential schools, language, and broken treaties. These workshops sought to trigger students' curiosity, reflection and desire to foster further relationships between our nations. (Butler, Ng-A-Fook, Vaudrin-Charette & McFadden, 2015, p. 51)

Settler Colonialism & *The Unsettling of America* **93**

This work offers our students the opportunity to engage Indigenous epistemologies as part of living cultures rather than as simply long past historical narratives. Teachers and teacher educators have to take it on ourselves, first by honoring those whose histories tell the story, and by inviting our students into ethical face-to-face dialog with those elders most able to recount these histories (Butler et al., 2015). And, I believe strongly that the first lessons we engage in with our students must confront the truth of the violence and suffering effected by colonization.

If we are serious about relationship-building that reaches across the existing political divides toward reconciliation, this process should include the stories of the perpetrators, offered by those who understand, and can expose, both the historical context and the effects of their ancestors' rationalized violence, the ignorance and mistakes. It might include evidence of what they may have gotten right, what that looks like in today's context but first it means a hard look at ourselves as we have been complicit in the epistemologies of violence. Berry's stories and novels are good examples of both. Learning to be kind in this process, to begin where we are with compassionate hearts may seem impossible especially for those who have suffered most.

Yet, this lesson has been taught to me most powerfully by Annishinaabeg elders Mark and Wendy Phillips from Peterborough, Ontario. As part of their responsibilities as healers and educators, they tell of being given the responsibility by their own teachers to reach out to the white community to teach about the Annishinaabeg people, their knowledge systems, and spiritual traditions. Their teachings are immersed in understanding the land where they have dwelt for centuries, the ancient and complex wisdom of their people about the creatures there, and the stories of disruption and hardship suffered as a result of European contact and colonization. This, they say, is the only way toward healing, and so they offer those who come to learn kindness and openness, along with the strict discipline of their knowledge, as they lay out their teachings. Without sincerity, humility, and fidelity to the integrity of our relationships, we run the risk of staying stuck in the old hierarchies and divisions, when what we need is to acknowledge that "it all turns on affection" (Berry, 2012). Or as my friend the Canadian activist scholar Derek Rasmussen says, these connections must be about more than "alliances;" if we are not creating friendships through this work, what are we doing (Rasmussen, 2013; Akulukjuk et al., forthcoming)? With this recognition, we come back around to Burley Coulter's plea to Wheeler Catlett:

> What is done is done forever. I know that. I'm saying that the ones who have been here have been the way they were, and the ones of us who are here now are the way we are, and to know that is the only chance we've got, dead and living, to be here together. I ain't saying we don't have to know what we ought to have been and ought to be, but we ought'n let that stand between us … we are members of each other. All of us. Everything.

The difference ain't in who is a member and who is not, but in who knows it and who don't. (Berry, 2004, p. 356)

References

Akulukjuk, T., Erkaeva, N., Rasmussen, D., & Martusewicz, R. (forthcoming). Stories of love and loss: Re-committing to each other and the land. In H. Bai & D. Chang (Eds.), *Ecological Virtues*. Regina, SK: University of Regina Press.

Bell, N. (2013). Anishinaabe bimaadiziwin: Living spiritually with respect, relationships and responsibility. In A. Kulnieks, K. Young & D. Longboat (Eds.), *Contemporary studies in environmental and Indigenous pedagogies: A curricula of stories and place* (pp. 89–110). Rotterdam: Sense Publishers.

Berry, W. (1995). *Another turn of the crank*. Washington, DC: Counterpoint.

Berry, W. (1996). *The unsettling of America: Culture and agriculture*. San Francisco, CA: Sierra Club Books.

Berry, W. (2004). The wild birds. In *That distant land: The collected stories*. Berkeley, CA: Counterpoint.

Berry, W. (2010a). *The hidden wound*. Berkeley, CA: Counterpoint.

Berry, W. (2010b). *Imagination in place*. Berkeley, CA: Counterpoint.

Berry, W. (2012). *It all turns on affection: The Jefferson lecture and other essays*. Berkeley, CA: Counterpoint.

Bonds, A., & Inwood, J. (2016). Beyond white privilege: Geographies of white supremacy and settler colonialism. *Progress in Human Geography*, 40(6): 715–733.

Butler, J. K., Ng-A-Fook, N., Vaudrin-Charette, J., & McFadden, F. (2015). Living between truth and reconciliation: Responsibilities, colonial institutions, and settler scholars. *Transnational Curriculum Inquiry*, 12(2): 44–63. http://nitinat.library.ubc.ca/ojs/index.php/tci

Calderon, D. (2014). Uncovering settler grammars in curriculum. *Educational Studies*, 50(4): 313–338.

Calderon, D. (2016). Moving from damage-centered research through unsettling reflexivity. *Anthropology & Education Quarterly*, 47(1): 5–24.

Cronon, W. (1983). *Changes in the land: Indians, colonists, and the ecology of New England*. New York, NY: Hill and Wang.

Deloria, V. (2008). Interview by Derrick Jensen. In D. Jensen, *How Shall I Live My Life? On Liberating the Earth from Civilization* (pp. 243–271). Oakland, CA: PM Press.

Hixon, W. L. (2013). *American settler colonialism*. New York, NY: Palgrave MacMillan.

Isenberg, N. (2016). *White trash: The 400-year untold history of class in America*. New York, NY: Penguin Books.

Linebaugh, P. (2014). *Stop thief: The commons, enclosures and resistance*. Oakland, CA: PM Press (kindle edition). ISBN: 978-1-60486-747-3

Martusewicz, R., Edmundson, J., & Kahn, R. (2012). On membership, humility, and pedagogical responsibilities: A correspondence on the work of Wendell Berry. *Mid-Western Educational Researcher*, 25(3): 44–68.

Martusewicz, R. A., Edmundson, J., & Lupinacci, J. (2015). *EcoJustice education: Toward diverse, democratic and sustainable communities*. New York, NY: Routledge.

Plumwood, V. (2002). *Environmental culture: The ecological crisis of reason*. New York, NY: Routledge.

Polanyi, K. (2001). *The great transformation: The political and economic origins of our time.* Boston, MA: Beacon Press.

Posey, D. (2006). Indigenous ecological knowledge. In J. Mander & V. Tauli-Corpuz (Eds.), *Paradigm wars: Indigenous people's resistance to globalization* (pp. 29–32). San Francisco, CA: Sierra Club Books.

Rasmussen, D. (2013). The priced vs the priceless. In A. Kulnieks, K. Young & D. Roronhiakewen Longboat (Eds.), *Contemporary studies in environmental and Indigenous pedagogies: A curricula of stories and place* (pp.139–170). Rotterdam, Netherlands: Sense Publishers.

Rowe, A. C. & Tuck, E. (2017). Settler colonialism and cultural studies: Ongoing settlement, cultural production and resistance. *Cultural Studies Critical Methodologies,* 17(1): 3–13.

Seawright, G. (2014). Settler traditions of place: Making explicit the epistemological legacy of white supremacy and settler colonialism for place-based education. *Educational Studies: A Journal of the American Educational Studies Association,* 50(6): 554–572.

Tuck, E., & Gaztambide-Fernandez, R. A. (2013). Curriculum, replacement, and settler futurity. *Journal of Curriculum Theorizing,* 29: 72–89.

Tuck, E., & Yang, W. (2012). Decolonization is not a metaphor. *Decolonization: Indigeneity, Education and Society,* 1(1): 1–40.

Tuck, E., McKenzie, M., & McCoy, K. (2014) Land education: Indigenous, post-colonial, and decolonizing perspectives on place and environmental education research. *Environmental Education Research,* 20(1): 1–23.

Veracini, L. (2010). *Settler colonialism: A theoretical overview.* New York, NY: Palgrave MacMillan.

Warren, K. (1998). The power and promise of ecological feminism. In M. E. Zimmerman, J. Baird Callicott, et al. (Eds.), *Environmental philosophy: From animal rights to radical ecology* (pp. 322–342). Upper Saddle River, NH: Prentice Hall.

Wriglesworth, C. (Ed.) (2014). *Distant neighbors: The selected letters of Wendell Berry and Gary Snyder.* Berkeley, CA: Counterpoint.

5

DEGRADED BODIES, DEGRADED EARTH

> And so, I write with the feeling that the truth I may tell will not be definitive, or objective, or even demonstrable, but in the strictest sense subjective, relative to the peculiar self-consciousness of a diseased man struggling toward a cure. (Berry, 2010a, p. 48)

In his book, *The Hidden Wound* (2010a) Berry writes a startlingly blunt self-reflective essay that begins with a deeply personal exploration of his own ancestral family's history as slave owners, its effects and assumptions that were carried forward in the silent complicity of day-to-day life in the border state of Kentucky when he was a child in the 1930s and 1940s. First written in 1968–1969, as the civil rights movement was swirling around him, it is an essay of painful awakening, of coming to terms with his own life within the privilege and violence of white supremacy in particular as it influenced, and continues to influence, his Kentucky home place—the people and the land—but also as an essay critiquing some of the most central attributes of American culture. And it is an essay about love, about his own education at the side of his grandfather's Black hired man, Nick, whom he credits with teaching him many of the foundational values that continue to shape his life and work. And love as connection, care, kindness, generosity and forgiveness, as the only possible redeeming solution to the violence that divides and degrades both humanity and the land.

I write this chapter (and this book) as a white woman thinking about the violence embedded in the very name "white." As I reflect on what this means, I read Berry's essay and I think about three distinct but interrelated scenes where racism is fundamentally at play as the primary force of suffering and resistance. I examine some of my own students' reactions to *The Hidden Wound*, paying particular attention to their anxiety, and exploring what Berry models for us in terms of critical self-examination of his life as it has been shaped by the various strains of white supremacy. I bring his thoughtful critique of his family history to the historical exclusion, violence, and abandonment that has ravaged the lives of people of color both in his homeland of Northern Kentucky, and within deindustrialized cities across our nation. I think carefully about the historic rebellions and resistances in those cities, especially in Detroit as my home region and the metaphoric canary in the mineshaft of American political, economic and ecological crises. I read Ta-Nehisi Coates' piercing reflection on the violence to Black bodies in the letter to his son, *Between the World and Me*. Coates' essay brings to the current urban context Berry's focus on the degradation of bodies, land and our very humanity that is the legacy of slavery, as physical work with the soil was defined by white masters and eventually by Black workers too, as what only inferior others do. To return to love and Berry's insistence on holistic relations as healing relations, I turn to lessons being taught via urban agriculture as a deeply spiritual rebirth and loving reclamation of the land, the body, and work as self-determination and creativity in those same cities.

Finally, this chapter asks what we can learn by threading our way through these contexts as we consider our responsibilities as EcoJustice educators. Specifically, for those of us assigned a white identity, who are we when we claim or simply accept such a naming? What does such an identity demand of us as we face the continuing devastation that is racism in this culture? And, how might "the way of love" help us to understand our ethical responsibilities to each other and to the land? Can we learn to heal these divides? How do we overcome them? What does a pedagogy of responsibility offer us as we face these "hidden wounds"?

On Examining White Supremacy in Ourselves

> A student is responding to Wendell Berry's book, *The Hidden Wound*. Paraphrasing, the response goes something like this: "I struggle with discussing racism. I'm white. What business do I have responding to racism? I cannot possibly understand that experience. So, I often stay silent because I'm not sure I have a right to speak about it." Several classmates, also white, agree that they too feel uncomfortable discussing racism and wonder if Berry should be writing about racism as a white man.[1]

How are we, the white-named and white claiming members of this violence-infused culture to understand our own particular responsibilities in challenging racism? Surely, we have different roles depending on who we are in relation to its damages. I have heard my students of color say to their white colleagues that white people have no right to speak about it, and I have heard others demand that their white professors bring the issue into our courses. I have watched as my white students sit in silence as their Black peers insist that a white author ought not be writing critically about white supremacy. The anger and anxiety

98 Degraded Bodies, Degraded Earth

perpetuate a divide that fundamentally wounds all of us and keeps the violence and suffering wracking our lives, intersecting with and confirming other divides that kill our planet. I read Berry trying to teach us something about his own struggle with this divide, his own deeply entrenched wounded humanity.

Let's begin with some of the most poignant pieces of Berry's analysis. First, the *Hidden Wound* (2010a) begins as a deep examination of himself, his racist ancestral roots and the deeply etched psychological scars of that history on himself and his family within a larger racist and exploitive culture.

> For whatever reasons, good or bad, I have been unwilling until now to open in myself what I have known all along to be a wound—a historical wound, prepared centuries ago to come alive in me at my birth like a hereditary disease, and to be augmented and deepened by my life. (2010a, p. 3)

The wound he references in his title is the wound to all people, that racist violence carves into our souls, whether or not we specifically identify with or practice it intentionally. Of course, the specific brutality of racism is experienced in the Black body, psyche and community in ways those of us assigned to be white cannot imagine. Berry reminds us that we are all damaged by it and must face that truth if there is to be any movement toward healing.

Thus, Berry begins by looking closely at his own place, his own childhood context where Black women and men worked as hired cooks, housekeepers, and farm hands on most of the farms around his own home. He examines his ancestral family history as slave owners in Kentucky, focusing on its lingering mostly unspoken effects on the minds, bodies, and spirit of his community, including the land itself. He tells this story as he knows it, as it was handed down to him in family tellings, and as he experienced it, looking as directly as he can at the historical and psychological forces that shaped his life and language, the deep contradictions, silences, anxieties and complicity in violence among his own people.

> There is a peculiar tension in the casualness of this hereditary knowledge of hereditary evil; once it begins to be released, once you begin to awaken to the realities of what you know, you are subject to staggering recognitions of your complicity in history and in the events of your own life. The truth keeps leaping on you from behind. ... It took me a long time and in fact a good deal of effort, to finally realize that in owning slaves my ancestors assumed limitations and implicated themselves in troubles that have lived on in me. (2010a, p. 6)

Berry approaches the problem of racism as he does with most other parts of his critical work, by refusing stable binary formations. Thus, while exposing the violence in his own family roots, he refuses the easy conclusion that his people were not also damaged psychologically and spiritually, even while they benefitted economically. And, while examining the ingrained tensions and violence shaping the relationships with the Black elders he grew up with, he refuses to accept that love is, or was not, possible therein, even as he looks directly at the most heinous of circumstances in his family history or his own childhood experiences. Telling the story of his relationship with Nick, his grandfather's hired man, he honors the love he experienced and exchanged there, entangled as it was in the silences and particular language practices among his family. And, in particular, he recognizes the way this and other relationships shaped the values he learned to live by, creating his character and his life-long commitments.

I begin with this general overview because it matters to see how Berry works as a cultural theorist, beginning from a problem or question that comes out of his own autobiographical struggles, and working outward to link his own story to the larger cultural forces shaping it. EcoJustice Education asks us to start this way too, with our questions and our stories, examining ourselves as created within powerful relationships and discursive processes that tell us both who we are and who we ought to be. For Berry, these processes are alive in his own family and in himself. He writes of growing up in a community shaped by intersecting logics of domination that degrade bodies, spirits, and the earth. But, there are also important instances of care, and enduring lessons that grew out of, and created an essential love. Berry attends to this love, refusing to banish it, even as he focuses on what he defines with clarity and directness as hereditary evil.

He tells, for example, of deep affection, kindness, and primary ethical socialization that he experienced as a child at the side of his grandfather's Black hired man, Nick, a man he admired and considers a primary teacher. Even as the silence and veil of polite southern society masked the horrors underlying a racist history and enduring system of white supremacy, Berry knew love, and learned about the value of friendship and integrity in his relationship with Nick. As they walked together through the woodlot on the farm, Nick taught him to appreciate the complex life at work there, the importance of silent observation and stillness; he shared laughter, learned animal husbandry and other skills of the farm, and was offered the satisfaction of hard work and good results. He spent the better part of his own birthday party sitting outside talking with him, even as the party (off limits to a Black hired hand) went on inside. Nick taught young Wendell about the value of, and responsibility for the membership, even as Nick himself was fundamentally excluded from it. He served it but he was not of it, not for the adults at least. But for young Wendell, Nick's way with him could only come from the deepest understanding of the absolute power of forgiveness and love, for even as the silence and social mores practiced in the family kept him at a polite and differentiated distance, he was able to be with a young boy as a mentor and loving elder. Without that relationship, I daresay we would not be reading the Wendell Berry we have today. While seeking to unpack the deep wound of racist

100 Degraded Bodies, Degraded Earth

violence, he refuses to ignore what he experienced as abiding affection with Nick and among others around him.

To try to understand the psychological complexity in himself, Berry reflects on his family history, and especially to the stories handed down over generations. He begins by recounting the story of Bart Jenkins, a notorious slave catcher who came in the dark of night to his great grandfather's farm to take possession of a defiant and rebellious slave. In the retelling, Berry invokes and examines the great moral contradiction between his ancestor's economic interests as small farmers who used slaves as labor, their religious commitments as Christians, and their self-identification as good and moral people. The rebellious man was a problem because he refused to be a docile slave. Thus, he was sold. As the family story goes, Bart Jenkins knocked him in the head as he slept, bound him with rope, and led him away.

> The moral complicity of the slave owner in the evil of slavery becomes inescapably clear. In spite of the self-defensive myth of benevolence, it was impossible for the slave owner to secure any limit to the depth or the extent of his complicity. As soon as he found it necessary to deal with the slave as property he was in as deep as he could go. In the commercial and legal aspect of slavery the moral interest is completely crowded out and replaced by the machinery of economics: *to sell a man is to abandon him.* (2010a, p. 7)

Berry tells this story as having come down to him through his family casually among other stories that involved their history as farmers in Kentucky. Having experienced its telling many times and in the context of other stories, Berry is certain that there was grief and shame that stayed in the family, the pain becoming a living thing in the telling. "It is easy for me to imagine a profound sickness of heart permeating the life of the farm for weeks after the sale of the slave and Bart Jenkins' brutality …" (p. 8). This seems odd in some ways, that such a story, if in fact painful, would be retold at all.

Berry explores the ways this telling was complicated both by the relationships of affection that they shared with the men and women who worked with, and for them, and also as its violence was shrouded within a strongly contrived myth of benevolence about who their ancestors had been as people. Even as they "were burdened by a malignant history and a malignant inheritance …" (p. 8), they engaged daily with people they sincerely cared about, and believed themselves and their forebears to be decent, hardworking people. And yet, there it was, the story itself a sign of the immorality and violence of owning another. That contradiction, Berry writes, was never aired or discussed directly either in the telling of the story or in the day-to-day relationships with the Black men and women who worked for their family, but the tensions and anxieties it produced were palpable precisely in the silences that existed among them. Stories of his great-grandfather as a good man and kindly master obscured both the family's participation in, and emotional response to, the horrors of slavery, and their complicity in the day-to-day racism of his community. Hence it also obscured the wound of dehumanization that they all carried.

This myth of benevolence was produced in public discourse in the south and so buoyed his family's and his own early complicity. To understand this Berry reads through the official history of Bart Jenkins, and other historical accounts as a romanticized reflection of the slave owner and slave catchers as "gentlemen and soldiers." While in private, family members knew another harsh truth, one that could not be spoken, public representations allowed for that gap of silence to endure, sheltering them in what they "wish had been true." And so their own misery is held at bay; it could not be spoken.

> All this moral and verbal obfuscation is intentional. Nor do I doubt that its purpose is to shelter us from the moral anguish implicit in our racism—an anguish that began, deep and mute, in the minds of Christian democratic freedom-loving owners of slaves. (2010a, p. 14)

A mythology of paternalistic goodness was further supported by the white community's Christian faith and practices. As his family stories convey, white families, his great grandfather's family included, insisted that the slaves accompany them to church. Reflecting on those practices, Berry uncovers the deep contradiction in the white community's religious faith at the heart of the silence he experienced as a child long after slavery had ended. The silence, this empty space at the heart of his family's language, made it possible to keep the moral obligations and truths from disrupting the economic realities of slavery, and later during Berry's childhood, from implicating the family in the inheritance of racism playing out in the day-to-day interactions on the farm.

How is it possible, he asks, that these ancestors could at once own the bodies of Black men and women, and yet by virtue of having them there in church services, also attest to the immortality of their souls?

> How could he [the master] presume to own the body of a man whose soul he considered as worthy of salvation as his own? To keep this question from articulating itself, he had to perfect an empty space in his mind, a silence, between heavenly concerns and earthly concerns, between body and spirit. (2010a, p. 16)

This contradictory division between the body and the soul had to be maintained by both the preachers and among the entire white community members themselves in order to maintain the institution of slavery as it was premised on debased work. Those they kept as enslaved had to be defined as inferior to maintain them as free labor; thus, their souls would need to be saved, but their bodies were to remain the very definitional site of degenerate existence and rationalized

102 Degraded Bodies, Degraded Earth

degradation. The division between body and soul was part of a whole logic of hierarchized divisions that "disordered the heart of both society as a whole and of every person in the society" (2010a, p. 90). For Berry, as we have been exploring through this book, ours is a fractured society saturated with suffering caused by the violence inherent in stratified divisions

> not only between white people and black people, but between black men and black women, white men and white women. It has come between white people and their work and white people and their land. It has fragmented our society and our minds. (2010a, p. 91)
>
> Divisions of class or race within a society are not superficial, but have a most profound spiritual effect both on the society and on the individuals in it... men [sic] on both sides of these divisions suffer. (2010a, p. 103)

Degraded Bodies, Degraded Work, Degraded Land

This may be Berry's most powerful contribution to an analysis of racism: that at its heart, at the heart of a claimed whiteness, operates a fundamental and intentional desecration of body, spirit, *and earth*, a fiction of superiority created by and through one's relationship to a particular form of work requiring sweat and toil and direct embodied connection with the land. In that lived world, work with one's body upon the earth is assigned to those already defined as inferior beings, and used as a measure of what it means to claim whiteness. These were bodies beset by the worst imaginable brutality, sent to toil in the fields under the whip, with hands and arms and feet in soil already ideologically desecrated by this ugly mindset. African American author Ta-Nehisi Coates (2015), writing to his son in his book, *Between the World and Me*, puts it like this:

> ... the elevation of the belief in being white was not achieved through wine tastings and ice cream socials, but rather through the pillaging of life, liberty, labor and land; through the flaying of backs, the chaining of limbs, the strangling of dissidents, the destruction of families; the rape of mothers, the sale of children and various other acts meant, first and foremost to deny you and me the right to secure and govern our own bodies. (p. 8)

For Berry, this body/work/land triumvirate of degradation and violence forms the basis of ecological and social ruin brought about by a culture and economic system beset by rationalized greed, domination, and violence. As we will explore below, it followed both Blacks and poor whites north to the cities, and it is, ultimately, at the core of social, spiritual, and ecological ruin currently upon all of us. Importantly, Berry examines this division of body from the land as the center of spiritual ruin of those who used slavery to separate themselves. By claiming whiteness, they (we) deny "the elemental experience and the elemental wisdom available only to those in immediate free contact with the earth" (2010a, p. 103).

Viewing the land–body relationship, not as a sacred source of fundamental well-being and happiness, but rather as debased property to be exploited, a resource-machine for individual power and profit, lies at the core of not just this southern economic history, but white supremacist capitalism itself. Work that is exploited, that divides us from one another in order to claim superiority in avoidance with the land or with other creatures as a means of care, is fundamentally destructive of everything. It destroys "the grace of the bonds" made with our fellows as we create what we need to live.

> Men [sic] are whole not only insofar as they make common cause with each other, but also in so far as they make common cause with their native earth, which is to say with the creation as a whole, which is to say with the creator ... no man will ever be whole and dignified and free except in the knowledge that the men around him are whole and dignified and free, and the world itself is free of contempt and misuse. ... The unwillingness, or the inability, to dirty one's hands in one's own service is a serious flaw of character, but in a society that sense of superiority can cut off a whole class or a whole race from its most necessary experience. ... The history of the white man's use of the earth in America is a scandal .... (2010a, pp. 104–105)

When we define hard work—the difficulties, burdens, joys and satisfactions of making a living and a home in a place—as beneath us, as something to escape from via others' labor or by machines, we abstract our relationship to the land, people and creatures into one of ownership, a means of getting someplace in the hierarchy of economic "success."

This degradation of land and people, and ultimately the loss of small farms across the nation, is also at the heart of the tragic errors of post-Civil War reconstruction and what was to follow. "It does not seem unreasonable to say that emancipation was achieved and, almost by the same stroke botched. The slaves were set free only to remain exploited for another hundred years" (2010b, p. 26). Of course, he goes on to say, pragmatically speaking, "a botched emancipation is better than none," and yet, this history requires a true accounting. For Berry, the truth is that the black body was to remain a sign of inferiority and thus as exploitable and vulnerable to harm as ever.

If, for example, the men and women who had been freed from slavery had been truly given their "40 acres and a mule," if there had been an equitable redistribution of existing land among all who inhabited the south (including Indigenous people) and if the former slave holders had recognized their own humanity, their happiness and salvation within a relationship with the soil and the people they once treated as property, perhaps we would not still be suffering under the delusion of division and supremacy.

104 Degraded Bodies, Degraded Earth

Detroit and the Great Migration

Of course, this dream could not come to pass precisely because the psychological and material conditions, that is the culture out of which slavery had been born, did not simply disappear with the end of the Civil War or Reconstruction. Even while some remained to work for white families, and others acquired land, by the early years of the twentieth century, it was clear that work on the land was not valued by or for anyone as the way to livelihood. The promise of success lay in making money and the biggest employers were the burgeoning industries of the north. Between 1920 and 1988 the number of farms owned by Black farmers fell from 916,000 to just 30,000 (Berry, 2010a, p. 117). This was due in part to the unspeakable horrors within the Jim Crow south. Stewart Tolnay (2003) writes that the greatest number of Black migrants came from states and counties with the highest incidence of lynching. The continued violence and degradation of Black bodies, along with ecological and economic crises, made remaining on the land difficult if not impossible for sharecropping families, and land owners alike. By the early years of the twentieth century, Black men and women along with poor whites began to migrate north to cities promising opportunities to "make something of themselves" in the developing industrial economy (Wilkerson, 2010).

As Berry recalls, during his boyhood and young adolescence in the 1930s and into the 1940s, while his grandfather, their hired hands, and neighbors continued to make a living on the land, there was already in dominant white society a move toward urban life as the true location of the American dream. Caught in the very ideology that built slavery, "farming was looked down upon as a hard and generally unremunerative life" (2010a, p. 65). "Reality was defined by the desire for success" in the competitive world of individualized consumerism. The industrial cities, especially in the north, beckoned as the way out of the drudgery and grime of "scratching in the dirt" and toward the dream of advancement in the monetized and commodified world of industry.

> People had begun to live lives of a purely theoretical reality, daydreams based on the economics of success. It was as if they had risen off the earth into the purely hypothetical air of their ambitions and greed. They were rushing around in the clouds, "getting somewhere," while their native ground, the only meaningful destination, if not the only possible one, lay far below them, abandoned and forgotten, colonized by machines. (2010a, p. 66)

By the 1940s with the advent of World War II, the northern factories fully involved in the war effort were beacons of hope and security for millions—Black and white—who had suffered hardship in the south, or who simply dreamt of riches promised by the machines of industry. To go north, especially for the Black community was to escape the stigma of being associated with work on the land. Work in the cites symbolized moving up and out of degradation. "Detroit was known as a city of industry, or more specifically, a city of work" (Kurashige, 2017, p. 16). And yet, even though the mist of white nostalgia offers a different story, the patterns of violence and exploitation that came with that promise are abundantly clear. The work promised did not save the Black body; indeed as Berry would see it, African Americans disconnected themselves from the land and thus from an essential aspect of their own humanity to follow what white and Black workers alike were defining as opportunity and success.

Harriet Arnow's novel, *The Dollmaker* (1954), tells this tragic tale of a white sharecropper family from Kentucky who move to Detroit in search of the promised land. Clovis, the man of the household, a mechanic by trade, a dreamer by nature, goes first and, upon securing a job in one of the factories calls his family to the city. Gertie, his wife, is forced to give up her dream of having her own piece of land and the happiness of self-determination, as she moves her children into a bewildering and violent world of urban industrialism. In Detroit, the family is forced into cramped unsafe tenant housing in a noisy, bigoted neighborhood, and into debt as Clovis insists they buy things on credit as a sign of status among the neighbors and his cronies. Through Gertie's struggles we learn of the development of partnership between banks, the housing industry, and burgeoning corporate power, all tied together in the promise of "making it."

Conditions were even worse for the Black families that migrated to the city. Convinced of the same promise of advancement up the ladder of success and fleeing threats of further violence and degradation in the south, they encountered instead unsafe and crowded housing, the dirtiest and most dangerous jobs, police brutality, and continuous humiliation in the workplace, and on the streets. Scott Kurashige (2017) writes,

> Industrial-era Detroit drew thousands of African Americans fleeing the Jim Crow South. During the 1920s, however, the city's Klu Klux Klan chapter had over 20,000 members, many of whom took root within the Detroit Police Department. The average white citizen did not need to be a Klan-sympathizer to share its goal of confining African Americans to substandard, segregated housing. (p. 17)

While the early American labor movement made living wages possible even for African American workers, Black bodies were still considered the most exploitable. They were offered, for the most part, the lowest paid and most dangerous jobs. Still, white workers resented their presence. In response to "unprecedented fair-employment policies to promote maximum participation in the workforce … thousands of white workers went on 'hate strikes' to protest the notion of working alongside even a handful of African American workers in integrated workplaces" (Kurashige, 2017, p. 17). Work remained for Black men and women who had escaped the south's violence, a degrading and dangerous reality, not to mention its disconnection from the soil.

By the post World War II years, a systematic process of deindustrialization exacerbated the situation. Labor's inroads to control the context of work and provide a decent living for its members began to be undermined as the Big Three Automakers experimented with automation specifically as "a weapon in the employers' antilabor arsenal" (Sugrue, 2005, p. 131). Black workers were of course, the most expendable. While primarily concerned about the effects of mechanization in agricultural contexts, Berry's critique of the devaluation of embodied work via the mechanization of production and his understanding of the ongoing displacement of humans by the requirements of capital is important here:

> The purpose of industrial technology has always been to cheapen work by displacing human workers, thus increasing the flow of wealth from the less wealthy to the more wealthy. We have dealt with the violence always implicit in the substitution by disregarding it, or disguising it by an official, quasi-religious litany of synonyms: *labor-saving, efficiency, progress convenience, speed, comfort*, even *creative destruction* ... obsolescent human workers, characteristically have been both replaced and displaced. The costs of progress have routinely been borne by discarded workers, and often the costs have been exorbitant. (Berry, 2015, p. 106)

In the case of Detroit, as deindustrialization developed, Black families were abandoned to a city in financial crisis leaving many thousands without a livelihood. By the 1950s, the Big Three automakers and subsidiary businesses began to look for cheaper land and labor, first in the suburbs, and later in the south or out of the country completely. White families began to follow "up and out," leaving behind their Black counterparts who were redlined out of suburban neighborhoods by mortgage companies, or who simply could not afford to follow. As the population declined and property was abandoned, the city was left with higher and higher rates of unemployment, a crumbling tax base, blight, toxic land where factories had once stood, a failing school system and infrastructure. "Increasingly," Sugrue (2005) writes, "Detroit became the home for the dispossessed ... as Detroit's population shrank, it became poorer and Blacker" (p. 149). Police brutality continued to rise with unemployment, stoking the fires of racial tension and resentment. Black bodies continued to bear the blame and the brunt of unsettlement and dispossession. Scott Kurashige (2017) writes that in 1967, according to a report put out by the Mayor's office, only 5 percent of the Detroit police force was Black, up from 3 percent in the 1950s and early 1960s. A reportedly bigoted police force

... subjected African Americans to humiliating and unconstitutional stop-and-frisk searches and routinely beat suspects to enact justice through "alley court." Corruption was rampant within the ranks and led to shakedowns that particularly heightened the abuse of black women sex workers. ... Whites lived in an alternate reality ... Roughly 80% of whites in Detroit considered the police to be fair and unbiased. Indeed, Detroit's men in uniform saw themselves as the real victims, regularly claiming that the shooting or beating of African Americans was justified by self-defense or suspects resisting arrest. (p. 19)

In July of 1967, on a hot summer's night, Detroit police raided an after-hours bar in a Black neighborhood, igniting anger, frustration, and resistance that exploded in what Detroiters call the Rebellion of 1967. Considered a "riot" from the point of view of frightened white politicians, residents, and suburbanites, Detroiters on the other hand argue that this was the start of a 50-year rebellion (Kurashige, 2017) where a radical civil rights movement merged with a mostly young Black activist street force fighting back against the brutality their families had been forced to endure since arriving in Detroit.

The 50-year Rebellion and the Neoliberal Response

Fast forward to July 24, 2017, the fiftieth anniversary of the Detroit rebellion. An elderly Black man, sitting in a grassy lot not far from where it started, is interviewed for a local online news outlet, *MLive*. Identified by the publication only as "a looter in the 1967 rebellion," he says of life in Detroit back then:

We were like locked up and closed in and not really able to get out. And then, [the looting] was like taking advantage of the opportunity to get the things you didn't have. ... Right down there where it says Gordon Park now? I think that used to be an after-hours joint, and then the police raid came and when they raided, then it [the rebellion] just started and it just swept the whole city. See, you can only hold a person down for so long, and then after a while, they goin' get tired. Ever since the early fifties, it was brutal man. People were tired. And then all it took was that spark and for someone to throw some gas on it. And it started. And basically, I think we just wanted to own stuff and for people to be a part of the city of Detroit, instead of being a second-class citizen. Little grocery stores and beer and wine stores, we couldn't own that back then. It was all white owned. ... the equality wasn't there. A lot of that has changed. Today, we've come a long way. So, I can't see a lot of that happening again. *Unless*, we get pushed too far back in the corner again ... [He grins and shakes his head.] 'Cause I can see regression even today! But I can't see it going the way it was in the 50s and early 60s. Hopefully! [He grins again.] Trump might do anything!

(Retrieved on July 25, 2017 from www.mlive.com/news/detroit/index.ssf/2017/07/on_this_day_detroit_riot_photo_2.html#incart_target2box_default_#incart_target2box_targeted_)

Hope and Regression

Drive through Detroit today to witness the lasting aftermath of abandonment, dispossession and the 1967 Rebellion. Brownfields and weed-strewn lots dot the city even as wildlife—pheasants, foxes, deer, coyotes—repopulate the land. Boarded up buildings where once busy markets existed; whole neighborhoods gone, returning to fields and scrub vegetation. Yet, amid devastation, in more and more of those abandoned lots, gardens, neighborhood-created playgrounds or parks, and murals appear. Detroit's history in the last 50 years has been one of continued impoverishment and brutality, along with a growing grassroots "revolution" (Boggs, 2011), and a neoliberal counter-revolution (Kurashige, 2017). Hope grows in the form of a strong web of interconnected grassroots organizations, civil rights and environmental activists who have been working since the 1960s to demand more equitable treatment of residents (85 percent African American) and to revitalize their neighborhood commons. In specific places and among hard-working democratically-oriented people, work and wealth is being reimagined beyond the confines of commercialization or even paid labor to include exchanges of care, mutuality and cooperation in the form of community housing and safety, freedom schools, neighborhood bartering, urban art installations, and community-based agriculture (Kurashige, 2017; Lupinacci, 2017; Martusewicz, 2009, 2013; Bowers & Martusewicz, 2006).

But all this is mostly ignored as city and state officials turn toward privatization, market fundamentalism, and corporate power in their vision of a "new Detroit." Using deficit theories to pass the blame for Detroit's economic woes onto the people themselves, a systematic pushout process is underway via illegal foreclosures, water shutoffs, school closings, and anti-democratic emergency management of the city's fiscal policies. Revitalization means attracting middle class consumers as residents and purchasers of sports, theater, and nightlife. City officials backed by large private foundations (for example, Kresge, Broad, and Skillman) have devised a plan to "right size" the city. Neighborhood investment is determined not by the needs of the people who live there, but rather by the performance of real estate values and sales (Pedroni, 2011). Thus, funding of infrastructure repairs like waterlines, street lights, streets, or of schools goes to those neighborhoods deemed to be a good investment. In neighborhoods where market values continue to be low the people are forced to either live with substandard, even non-existing support services, or leave. Thus the city's blatant process of accumulation by dispossession is accomplished via the suffering of its longtime primarily Black residents. This is the strategy by which the revitalization efforts of "Detroit future city" is being produced. Housing projects and business investment in the downtown city center dislocate poor residents and existing small businesses deemed to be in the way of progress. New stadiums, condominiums, bars, restaurants, and a Wholefoods Market are popping up, supported by the idea of bringing back other businesses, and white middle class consumers and workforce as the core of salvation for the city.

The man in the interview above sees hope in the fact that Black ownership of small business has increased since the 1950s and 1960s on the one hand, but on the other, as city leaders and state policy-makers seek upscale businesses for the downtown, Detroit suffers from a crisis of food insecurity as one by one, major grocery stores left the city, and sources of nutritional culturally appropriate food has become hard to access. Some report this situation as evidence that Detroit has become a "food desert" (Gallagher, 2003). Public transportation is practically non-existent as a chronically underfunded and unreliable bus system limps along city streets. Unemployment remains at between 18 and 24 percent. According to the US Census Bureau, the population of the city is down from its peak of 1,849,568 in 1950 to 672,795 in 2016. Where once it was the white residents, now the Black middle class leave the city, forced out by market-based policies for revitalization. The youth leave to look for work, if they are able, and too many, especially young Black men, turn to well-established gang-related drug trafficking as a means of income, status, and power, as well as a means of dealing with their own fears. The Black body remains the target of violence, now not just from powerful white sources—but surely most fiercely legitimated there—but also within the Black community itself.

Violence to the Black Body in the Urban Context

Writing of his boyhood experiences in Baltimore and particularly of historically inscribed fear, Ta-Nehisi Coates reflects on the ways violence to the black body saturates the urban context from police brutality, to neighborhood gang practices, Black family discipline, and schools. Beginning with his experience of street fighting, he remembers:

> When I was your age the only people I knew were black, and all of them were powerfully, adamantly, dangerously afraid. ... I think back on those boys [from the streets and his neighborhood] now and all I see is fear, and all I see is them girding themselves against the ghosts of the bad old days when the Mississippi mob gathered 'round their grandfathers so that the branches of the black body might be torched, then cut away ... I knew that there was a ritual to a street fight, bylaws and codes that, in their very need, attested to all the vulnerability of the black teenage bodies. (Coates, 2015, p. 14)

And then thinking of what seemed to be contradictions between love and violence in his home:

I saw it (fear) in my own father, who loves you, who counsels you, who slipped me money to care for you. My father was so very afraid. I felt it in the sting of his black leather belt, which he applied with more anxiety than anger, my father who beat me as if someone might steal me away ... Everyone was losing a child, somehow, to the streets. Later, I would hear it in Dad's voice—either I can beat him or the police. Maybe that saved me. Maybe it didn't. All I know is, the violence rose from the fear like smoke from a fire ... To be Black in Baltimore of my youth was to be naked before the elements of the world. The nakedness is the predictable upshot of people forced to live for centuries under fear. (2015, pp. 15–16)

Putting Coates' reflection into conversation with Berry's considerations of the violence to the Black body at the heart of white supremacist constructions of identity in the meaning of work and the land, a complex socio-ecological and psychological picture emerges. Toward the end of his essay, Coates makes clear that the violence to the Black body is part of a larger plunder, "not just the body of humans, but the body of the Earth itself" (p. 150). Each has specific and essential lessons confronting the violence of supremacy enactments on Black bodies in relation to a "revolutionary" ravaging of the earth itself, told from very different racialized subjective and geographical locations, but perhaps overlapping conclusions. For Coates, his advice to his son is to "struggle for wisdom," "struggle for the memory of your ancestors, for your grandfather and your grandmother," but "do not pin your hopes on their [white people's] conversion ... [They] will have to learn to struggle themselves, to understand that the field for their Dream, the stage where they have painted themselves white, is the deathbed of us all" (2015, p. 151).

For Berry, too, the answer to the ongoing damages lies in understanding ourselves, our practices, assumptions, and desires—whether we name ourselves white or Black—as subjects caught up within a violent and extractive supremacist dream that ignores, out of greed for mastery and power, the limits of this planet and our lives upon it. Out of the desire for supremacy we ignore the basis for what makes us human:

The root of our racial problem in America is not racism. The root is in our inordinate desire to be superior—not to some inferior or subject people, though this desire leads to the subjection of people—but to our condition. We wish to rise above the sweat and bother of taking care of anything—of ourselves, of each other, or of our country. We did not enslave African blacks because they were black, but because their labor promised to free us of the obligations of stewardship .... (Berry, 2010a, p. 112)

For the Black community, being forced to labor under the yoke of a supposed and rationalized inferiority—whether on the land or in the factories—must ultimately interfere with what may have otherwise been (or perhaps what once was for ancestors on their native African soil) a spiritual wholeness based on intimate knowledge of the land they worked for sustenance. For Berry, this intimacy with work and the land, make them the truest agrarian ancestors (Weibe, 2017). The desire to escape degradation assumed to be born of, and in, the soil itself has led us away from the primary forms of connection, care, and affection needed for life itself. It leads Coates to urge his son not to pin his hopes on the reformation of the white dreamers. Pray for them he says, but don't spend your time trying to make them understand the damages they have caused. In the end, for Coates and many others, staying focused on the needs of his own people is the only solution. For Berry, this is a sad truth, that the answers we seek tend to lead us back to division, the very source of violence. And so my students stay silent and afraid.

On the Land in Detroit: Engaging "The Order of Loving Care"

But let us return to hope.

> A group of teenage boys and their teachers are standing next to a garden plot at D-Town, a seven-acre farm on the northwest side of Detroit. They are joking with each other, antsy as a man speaks to them about this farm, and the work of the Detroit Black Community Food Security Network. A youngster raises his hand, and says, "I thought we left all this behind when slavery ended!" Their elder scratches his beard and looks at the boy. "Well, that's interesting, isn't it! What you don't know is that your ancestors were stolen from their homelands in Africa, and brought here to work in fields in part because of their deep knowledge of how to grow things. They knew that to nurture the body and the spirit was to work with the soil. They knew that their very souls, their humanity was born of that connection to the earth. And now it's our responsibility to bring that ancestral knowledge to you, to our people here in Detroit." The boys are quiet. The lesson continues.[2]

Even while their city is tangled up in neoliberal land grabs and dreams of prosperity based in privatization and extractive profit for corporate gain, the people of the Detroit Black Community Food Security Network (DBCFSN) organize to reclaim their community. They began in 2006 by establishing D-Town farm which started on four acres of a mostly abandoned city park, and now includes seven acres of crop land, growing 30 different varieties of fruits and vegetables, a small orchard, mushroom cultivation, four hoop houses, and bees. In 2008, they wrote a city wide food policy that focuses on access to healthy and culturally relevant food, addresses serious nutrition-related health concerns, environmental justice, and education to establish justice and equity for the people of Detroit (see www.detroitfoodjustice.org/detroit-food-policy/). The policy was

112 Degraded Bodies, Degraded Earth

unanimously adopted by the Detroit City Council on March 15, 2008. The Detroit Food Policy Committee consisting of 21 members, the majority of whom are food activists, representatives from various segments of the food system and environmental justice activists, was established to enact the policy through various key projects. One such project is the Food Warriors project, which works to educate young people, and develop youth leaders through partnerships with schools and religious organizations. Students like the young men in the scene above come to D-Town to learn about agrarian principles organizing the farm, and to experience relationships that are other than the aggressive, competitive and fear based relationships that they may experience in their neighborhoods. They are learning about the specific values that guide their elders' practice.

A central commitment and value is democracy. As Malik Yakini, Executive Director of DBCFSN, puts it in his prestigious Dodge Lecture at Johns Hopkins University in 2013, the goal is for "a people's democracy within our organizations on a grassroots level, how we begin to build organizations where everyone has a voice, how all of the members and all of the supporters help to decide what happens" (Yakini, 2013). As an example, over many months the members of the organization and the Food Policy Council discussed how to address the lack of grocery stores in the city, and more importantly the problem of enclosure and extraction when corporate owned businesses do come to town. Not only do the people served not have a voice in what gets sold there, but the profits leave the community. To address this problem, a food co-op was opened with the specific goals of providing food stuffs needed and desired by the people, and keeping food related dollars circulating within the community rather than extracted via corporate owned businesses with no real investment in the community. Framed by African-centric concepts like Ujima (collective work and responsibility) and Kujichagulia (self-determination), their work is enacted in direct resistance to the city leaders' plans. Intentionally democratic, its members insist that their organization should not be organized in a top-down manner, but rather that the people most effected by decisions should be those centrally involved in making them.[3]

As the food sovereignty movement has spread, neighbors teach each other the old practices of subsistence farming in order to eat and as political action that rails against the anti-democratic ideologies of selfish individualism dominating the city (Martusewicz, 2013; Bowers & Martusewicz, 2006). Organic produce, eggs, honey, and even goat milk and cheese are accessible products shared by farmers and offered in local farmers' markets, soup kitchens, and backyards. This is work that, while often demanding, is first and foremost about love, "the glue that holds all of this together," as Yakini puts it:

> ... a love not only for ourselves as individuals and for our families, but we have a love for humanity, and even going beyond that, we have a love for Creation. We are part of this fabric that makes life on this Earth, and we're part of this fabric that makes life in the universe ... human beings are not the

center of life. We were not put here to dominate the planet, to dominate the animals that we coexist with. We were not put here to dominate the plants … the Earth itself is alive. … From the African and from many Eastern philosophical systems, that … everything is composed of the same thing … everything is spirit. So this love that I'm talking about is love that comes from understanding that "everything is everything" and that we are really part of the whole and we have the responsibility to be good stewards and good guardians of the whole …. (Yakini, 2013)

Thinking about these words, I am reminded of a short conversation with one of the managers of D-Town farm, during a tour he gave to a group of educators and students. A young man in his twenties, he is responsible for developing and managing compost for enriching the soil on the farm. It is physically demanding work. Listening to him describe his daily tasks, I asked what he finds most important in his work at the farm. He described the satisfaction he feels after a hard day's work with his hands in the soil, shoulder to shoulder with others. He spoke of the deep joy and sense of confidence he has gained to be a part of a community working together to enact deep sensible principles. His quiet joyful reflection honored the elders who had invited him into membership with them, teaching him the power of living and working responsibly with his whole spirit and body on this land, in this place. Here again we see the linking of work and affection as a process of building community as a caring collective experience. As Berry writes, work

links us to each other, and it links us to nature. … In taking responsibility for our own lives and work, in unmasking the connections of our labor and nature, in giving up our hopeless fixation on purity, we may ultimately find a way to break the borders that imprison nature as much as ourselves. Work then, is where we should begin. (Berry, quoted in Weibe, 2017, p. 41)

This recognition of the essential connection between work and love didn't just happen out of nowhere in Detroit or in other communities beginning to understand what care of self and others really means. It came from a group of people identifying serious problems in their city and coming together to imagine the sort of community they wanted to create, recognizing the work as part of a spiritual and living whole, making a plan, and creating city-wide policy. Certainly, Berry's incisive critique of an industrialized "global economy—which for five hundred years has plundered the land and exploited, enslaved, or murdered the people of the 'foreign' or 'rural' world" (2017, p. 6) is shared at the heart of this movement for food sovereignty in Detroit as well. With Berry the effects of those globalized structures are identified at home, in this place with its particular history. And this is where work begins.

114 Degraded Bodies, Degraded Earth

Out of this work emerges relationships where young and old are reclaiming what it means to be in membership, and the moral necessity of affection to that process. Urban agriculture in Detroit is embodied work, where physical labor is connected directly to care and community. While in many ways a fierce response to Detroit politics, with Berry, this is work that is first and foremost based on decency, care, kindness, humor and love as the basis of a grounded moral imagination. Their work together demonstrates that such communities are possible and necessary, even in urban places where agrarian values may seem most unlikely. Using imagination to envision what ought to be and then learning together how to create that vision is a way to expose the failure of an extractive economy to care for people and communities. But is a food movement enough to disrupt it?

Yakini has made it clear that their work will not feed the whole city, or even convince all the people that this is the solution to their economic and social problems. But for people who have been so systematically abused by the greed of white supremacist capitalism, it makes no sense at all to expect the leaders of that system to rescue the people they have already brutally harmed. Coming together to feed one another nutritionally and spiritually, to nurture each other and the soil is a primary response to the problems African Americans have faced both historically and currently. And, to go back to Coates' worries, it is a fundamentally different way to experience one's body. The toil and sweat and often back-breaking work yields love among the people, for the land and for themselves as they create the membership. "Everything is everything." As long as those so engaged do not see it as a way of avoiding active resistance to the very real processes of domination still going on, such labor should be understood as a way of collectively growing a powerful political response on their own terms. Of course, there will always be a range of reasons that people get involved and not all members see this as political work. Rebecca Solnit puts the issue this way:

> We are in an era when gardens are front and center for hopes and dreams of a better world or just a better neighborhood, or the fertile space where the two become one. There are farm advocates and food activists, progressive farmers and gardeners, and maybe most particular to this moment, there's a lot of urban agriculture. These city projects hope to overcome the alienation of food, of labor, of embodiment, of land, the conflicts between production and consumption, between pleasure and work, the destructiveness of industrial agriculture, the growing problems of global food scarcity, seed loss. The list of ideals being planted and tended and sometimes harvested is endless, but the question is simple. What crops are you tending? What do you hope to grow? Hope? Community? Health? Pleasure? Justice? Gardens represent the idealism of this moment and its principal pitfall, I think. A garden can be, after all, either the ground you stand on to take on the world or how you retreat from it, and the difference is not always obvious. (Solnit, 2012, p. 1)

Agreed, but for the DBCFSN and other activist groups across the city, this work goes well beyond soaking in the pleasures of a garden, though there is plenty of joy in their work. Using education, organization, and the passed-on wisdom of their ancestors, the Detroiters from whom I have learned are taking a stand against the abuse that they have faced since their forebears came north (and before), by actively caring for each other, and caring for the industrially desecrated earth under their feet. The elders pass on stories of past successes and mistakes, and gently encourage the younger generation into what self-determination means in their neighborhoods. They stand for responsible stewardship of their community, and as such offer an important source of hope for their children. They are creating, in Berry's words, "an order of loving care" (2017, p. 17), not just for the future but as it is needed urgently now. It is precisely in this sense that the relationships they engage model the commitments called for within a pedagogy of responsibility to break through debilitating divisions, even as we name the deep roots of supremacy that implicate us all in a perilous situation.

To work against that destruction as a white educator, is to refuse to turn away from these historically embedded social, economic and psychological systems, to identify them as they shape us, to name them for what they are, for the wounds they have inflicted throughout our culture. This is our central responsibility: to name the violence in our culture, in our lives, and work to take down the systems that perpetrate it. To teach directly against it. To remain silent, or to believe we have nothing to say in the face of racism (or sexism or ecological devastation—all linked divisions), is to continue (however unwittingly) to implicate ourselves. I have been welcomed and I have learned from the most fierce if loving Detroit elders in order to face my own buried fears of those named for me as "Other", even as they made it clear that they are not there for me or my mostly white students. I believe with all my heart in their generosity as a core tenet of this culture's salvation. To engage a pedagogy of responsibility is to learn to dislodge from our *own* unac-knowledged imaginations the foul fiction that is racism. Short of that, we will not recognize our embodiment in, or offer our gratitude for, the gift that is the living holy world.

Notes

1 This scene is reconstructed from several similar interactions I have had with different groups of students.
2 This dialogue is paraphrased from a conversation that was recounted to me by Malik Yakini (2013), Executive Director of the DBCFSN, and a nationally recognized leader of the food sovereignty movement. He recounts it again in the 2013 Dodge Lecture at Johns Hopkins University.
3 For a full list of the organizing values of the DBCFSN see www.detroitblackfoodsecur ity.org

References

Arnow, H. (1954). *The dollmaker*. New York, NY: Simon and Schuster.

Berry, W. (2010a). *The hidden wound*. Berkeley, CA: Counterpoint.

Berry, W. (2010b). *Imagination in place*. Berkeley, CA: Counterpoint.

Berry, W. (2015). *Our only world: Ten essays*. Berkeley, CA: Counterpoint.

Berry, W. (2017). *The art of loading brush*. Berkeley, CA: Counterpoint.

Boggs, G. L. (2011). *The next American revolution: Sustainable activism for the twenty-first century* (with S. Kurashige). Berkeley, CA: University of California Press.

Bowers, C. A., & Martusewicz, R. A. (2006). Revitalizing the commons of the African-American communities in Detroit. In C. A. Bowers, *Revitalizing the commons: Cultural and educational sites of resistance and affirmation* (pp. 47–84). London, UK: Rowman and Littlefield.

Coates, T. (2015). *Between the world and me*. New York, NY: Spiegel and Grau.

Gallagher, M. (2003). *Examining the impact of food deserts on public health in Detroit*. Chicago, IL: Mari Gallagher Research and Consulting Group.

Kurashige, S. (2017). *The fifty-year rebellion. How the US political crisis began in Detroit*. Oakland, CA: University of California Press.

Lupinacci, J. (2017). Resistance wisdom and grassroots urban education: Lessons from Detroit. In W. T. Pink, & G. Noblit (Eds.), *Second international handbook of urban education* (pp. 833–851). Switzerland: Springer International Publishing.

Martusewicz, R. A. (2009). Toward a "collaborative intelligence": Educating for the cultural and ecological commons in Detroit. In M. McKenzie, P. Hart, H. Bai & B. Jigling (Eds.), *Fields of green: Re-storying education* (pp. 251–270). Cresskill, NJ: Hampton Press.

Martusewicz, R. A. (2013). The most unlikely places: Eros and education in the commons. In T. M. Kress & R. Lake (Eds.), *We saved the best for you: Letters of hope, wisdom and imagination to 21st century educators* (pp. 95–98). Rotterdam, Netherlands: Sense Publishers.

Pedroni, T. C. (2011). Urban shrinkage as a performance of whiteness: neoliberal urban restructuring, education, and racial containment in the post-industrial, global niche city. *Discourse: Studies in the Cultural Politics of Education*, 32(2): 203–215. doi:10.1080/01596306.2011.562666

Solnit, R. (2012). Revolutionary plots. *Orion Magazine*, July/August.

Sugrue, T. J. (2005). *The origins of the urban crisis: Race and inequality in postwar Detroit*. Princeton, NJ: Princeton University Press.

Tolnay, S. E. (2003). The African American "Great Migration" and beyond. *Annual Review of Sociology*, 29: 209–232.

Weibe, J. R. (2017). *The place of imagination: Wendell Berry and the poetics of community, affection, and identity*. Waco, TX: Baylor University Press.

Wilkerson, I. (2010). *The warmth of other suns: The epic story of America's Great Migration*. New York, NY: Random House.

Yakini, M. (2013). Dodge Lecture. Johns Hopkins University Bloomberg School of Public Health, April 30, 2013 [video file]. Retrieved on February 19, 2018 from www.youtube.com/watch?v=fNt26eJDkuM

6

STEM EDUCATION AND THE MIRACLE OF LIFE

With Katy Adams

> To suggest that the health of places and communities might be the indispensable standard of economic behavior is finally to ask how a mere human, whose years are like the grass that is cut down in the evening, can justify on his or her own behalf the permanent destruction of anything. (Berry, 1996, p. 234)

As I (Katy) sat down to read *Life is a Miracle* for the first time, the scientifically trained part of me reacted defensively to Berry's scathing indictment of science as steeped in hubris, relying on reductive methods to simplify the world into meaningless abstraction under the misguided presumption that it will lead to absolute understanding and ongoing betterment of humankind. Though I would have been hard pressed to identify a specific part of his critique that I disagreed with, I felt Berry's characterization of science was incomplete. It seemed to me to be an oversimplified portrayal of what I understand to be a rich, diverse, sometimes conflicted, and nuanced discipline of thought and practice.

Oversimplification is not a word one would generally use in association with Berry, who sees the life of his farm as "always emerging beyond expectation or prediction or typicality" (Berry, 2000, p. 45). Careful and wider reading across the body of his work reveals, not surprisingly, a more nuanced interpretation of science, and one which does not necessarily place it at odds with his vision for a healthier world. Berry (2003) explicitly states,

> [Science] would do far better to understand itself as part of a highly diverse effort of human thought, never to be completed, that might actually have the power to make us kinder to one another and to our world. And so I think that science has its proper and necessary place in conversation with all the other disciplines, all being equal members. (p. 189)

118 STEM Education and the Miracle of Life

In this chapter, we trace the techno-scientific world view within our culture that Berry takes issue with, a world view exemplified in the current policies promoting STEM (science, technology, engineering and mathematics) education. At the same time, we explore key qualities that position the discipline and science educators as useful allies for cultivating the kind of humility, inclusiveness, and compassion that Berry calls for as essential "to make something comely and enduring of our life on this earth" (Berry, 1996, p. 234).

STEM has become pervasive in education policy and rhetoric, both within formal schooling and in alternative education settings. The social elevation of STEM has developed within a cultural context where market forces increasingly direct decision-making at the expense of diverse, democratic, and community-minded processes (Wolfmeyer, 2013; Martusewicz, Edmundson, & Lupinacci, 2015). As a result, Cheskey and Wolfmeyer (2015) describe the purpose and content of the national STEM agenda as philosophically grounded in the rationalist, individualistic, mechanistic, anthropocentric discourses that reinforce global market measures of success. This philosophical orientation is evidenced in descriptions of STEM in national policy and as interpreted within local school districts, where it is defined as essential for our youth and our nation to succeed in a competitive, ever progressing, information-based, technologically-advanced society (e.g. YCS website, 2017; NSTA, 2016; NRC, 2012). The goals of science education then become focused on future achievement rather than present work; to gain the skills that will make one competitive in the global job market and flexible in responding to rapid changes in technology.

Berry's prose builds the case for an alternative vision of success which requires a different approach to education. For Berry, success is rooted in how our personal use of the world contributes to its health and therefore our own, a world where we recognize the infinite not as an "enormous quantity" but rather a cycle that renews (Berry, 1996, p. 88), and a world where the "living procession through time in a place *is* the record by which such knowledge survives and is conveyed" (Berry, 2000, p. 153). This world view leads Berry to question fundamental assumptions about the purpose, scope, and value of science and technology as well as our approach to education. He does so largely through his analysis of America's agricultural history in essays and novels (Berry, 2017, 2015, 2008, 2002, 1984). His essay *Life is a Miracle* (2000) and more recently his text *The Art of Loading Brush* (2017), explicitly address Berry's view of scientific thought and practice as contributing to the degradation of nature and our human communities. In *Life is a Miracle*, he sets up an argument to E. O. Wilson's book *Concilience* (1998). Wilson's book describes a theory for unified knowledge through science. Three ideas are essential to Berry's argument with Wilson: (1) Human perspective on the world is limited, science is a human endeavor, therefore science cannot lead to absolute knowledge. (2) Success lies not in progress or our ability to control through technology, but in our capacity to respond appropriately to the real complexities of life in a way that nurtures both natural and human communities. (3) Meaningful knowledge is situated and arises through relationships of affection and action, not the abstract acquisition of more and more information. As we've been noting throughout this book, these themes recur throughout Berry's essays and novels and set-up a framework for critically examining current approaches to education.

Challenging Scientific Orthodoxy

Wendell Berry (2000) uses his critique of *Concilience* as an opportunity to explain and challenge the materialistic, imperialistic, and reductionist aspects of "popular scientific orthodoxy" (p. 24). Reductive explanations, Berry argues, perpetuate the illusion of understanding by oversimplifying the complex, feeding our arrogance and divorcing our knowledge of the world from the places, relations, and affections that might guide and temper how we acquire or use it. Developing or applying knowledge in general terms and without regard to context leads to misunderstanding and knowledge being misapplied, creating greater likelihood that science will impact the world in exploitative ways.

> ... as knowledge expands globally it is being lost locally. This is the paramount truth of the modern history of rural places everywhere in the world. And it is the gravest problem of land use: Modern humans typically are using places whose nature they have never known and whose history they have forgotten; thus ignorant, they almost necessarily abuse what they use. If science has sponsored both an immensity of knowledge and an immensity of violence, what is the gain? (Berry, 2000, pp. 90–91)

Empirical evidence is the basis of scientific knowledge; therefore science is essentially concerned with the material world. Berry sees no inherent problem with this, unless scientific knowledge is characterized as superior or capable of being absolute in its scope, as Wilson does. "Waving aside ignorance and mystery and human limitation as merely illusory or irrelevant, [E. O. Wilson] claims not only all knowledge but all future knowledge and everything unknown as the property of science" (Berry, 2000, p. 30). By default, any other types of knowledge, those not founded on empirical evidence, are stripped of value. Wilson's brand of arrogance "conforms to the values and the psychology of industrialism" (p. 24), justifying the dismissal of other perspectives, other lives, and unwelcome consequences in the name of scientific progress.

Berry further questions the implicit assumptions that science is necessary for progress and progress is good.

> [E. O. Wilson] is in agreement with the apparent majority of the public who now believe that the new inevitably replaces or invalidates the old, because the new, coming from an ever-growing fund of data, is inevitably better than

120 STEM Education and the Miracle of Life

the old ... This is strong, easeful, and reassuring doctrine, so long as one does not count its costs or number its losses. (Berry, 2000, pp 67–68)

An image of the future and science contributing to it in a progressive sense (that is, defining evolution itself as progressive) feeds into individualism and colonial thinking as progress becomes euphemism for justifying the competitive acquisition of ever more without regard to the harm that may cause to living systems. In his novel *Remembering* (2008), Berry's main character, Andy Catlett describes the farmer who has adopted a scientifically-informed, techno-industrial model as "the end of American agriculture—the end of the future. He's successful by way of monstrous debt and a stomach ulcer and insomnia and the disappearance of a neighborhood" (p. 70). Berry offers an alternative model for progress as moving into alignment with the rhythms of the places where we reside, adapting "ourselves, our economies, and our work to the places where we live" (Berry, 2017, p. 101). Doing so requires careful observation, genuine (yet always limited) knowledge of those systems, and an effort to remain always present and attentive to our relationships with them. "In fact, actual work that is actually good requires us to give our minds entirely to the present" (Berry, 2017, p. 100). "Nature readily acknowledges the ceaselessness of change, but she confirms, if not quite clearly, its cyclicality as greater, and as a form, or *the* form, of stability" (Berry, 2017, p. 129).

Putting Science in its Place

Berry describes the value of science and technology in terms of what they can do to help us understand our immediate, lived place and act responsibly. "It seems to me that science is badly corrupted when scientists depart from their responsibly limited and limiting ways of testing or proving comparatively small truths" (Berry, 2017, p. 67). Only by taking local focus, Berry argues, can science avoid becoming "invariably destructive" (Berry, 2000, p. 147) and instead leveraged to restore our landscapes and heal our fragmented souls.

> If local adaptation is important, as I believe it unquestionably is, then we must undertake, in both science and art, the effort of familiarity ... This is the way a locally adapted culture works. Over a long time it learns to conform its artifacts to the local landscape, local circumstances, local needs ... the most resolute and expensive projects of discovery and innovation on the part of science-technology-and-industry cannot take us there. Only a long, patient, loving effort of familiarity can do that. (Berry 2000, pp. 140–142)

Science cannot limit itself to asking "what is possible?" in the abstract, "but what is possible *here*? What will nature permit me to do without damage to herself or to me?" (Berry as quoted in Fisher-Smith, 1993, para. 66). The motivation

STEM Education and the Miracle of Life **121**

to think in responsible rather than exploitative ways about one's relationships lies at the heart of these questions. Therefore, Berry sees science education as a realm that needs to encourage the moral concern within individuals to ask: *What will this do to our community?* before pursuing it as a reasonable course of scientific research or technological development.

> I am not of course proposing an end to science and other intellectual disciplines, but rather a change of standards and goals. The standards of our behavior must be derived, not from the capability of technology, but from the nature of places and communities. We must shift the priority from production to local adaptation, from innovation to familiarity, from power to elegance, from costliness to thrift. We must learn to think about propriety in scale and design, as determined by human and ecological health. By such changes we might again make our work an answer to despair (Berry, 2000, p. 12)

In summary, Berry takes issue (rightly so!) with the belief that:

- all is measurable and knowable through science,
- science can answer any question,
- scientific explanations are only valuable if generalizable,
- science is superior or separate from art,
- science has allowed for progress and growth which are inherently good,
- we should be able to act in the pursuit of understanding without ethical restraint.

This set of beliefs amounts to scientism. But I can be a scientist; I can engage in scientific thought and practice, and not believe any of these things. Such beliefs are *not* essential to the nature of science. Though I cannot deny they are commonly expressed through the actions and priorities of researchers in corporate America and academic institutions.

Is Berry's vision to reorient the standards and goals of our intellectual scientific pursuits at fundamental odds with the nature of science itself? Educational researchers have identified features most scientists would agree are essential to the nature of science (Lederman, 2007; Lederman, Abd-El-Khalick, Bell, & Schwartz, 2002; Meichtry, 1999; Bell, Matkins, & Gansneder, 2011), including: (1) the empirical nature of science; (2) the distinction between observations and inferences; (3) the tentative nature of science; (4) the theory-laden nature of science; (5) the non-linear process of science (not one step-wise scientific method); (6) the socio-cultural nature of science; and (7) the creative and imaginative nature of science. In my (limited) experience, most scientists would acknowledge that the discipline is limited to investigating only certain kinds of questions and offering only specific types of explanations. Most scientists would openly

122 STEM Education and the Miracle of Life

acknowledge the role that funding and politics play in determining the direction of scientific pursuits and the issues that raises. Most would recognize the value of ethical boundaries on science, though disagree about where those boundaries lie.

I (Katy) have been trained as a scientist, or more specifically, an ecologist. I can remember the moment in sixth grade when I realized that those things I enjoyed exploring and thinking about in my free time actually connected to this school subject called science. A few years later, my father handed me copies of Bertrand Russell's and Thoreau's essays. We discussed beliefs about the nature of reality and truth and responsibility. My father, a mathematician and engineer, spoke about scientific truths as tentative and useful. He conveyed to me a sense of science as ultimately humbling, a product of our imagination, and therefore our responsibility. He shared the attitude that it is incumbent upon us to envision and apply our faith in science with integrity and care, and remember its limits. He found the inherent skepticism and expectation of changing dogma within the ideal of science reassuring.

With this foundation, I approached my academic training through deep exploration of what it means for scientific knowledge to be tentative, always incomplete, always a simplification, always refutable, yet useful at least in some circumstances or under certain conditions at particular points in time. I cultivated the perspective that uncertainty is not a weakness but rather a humbling reality, a basis for thoughtful argument (in the best sense of the word), and an inspiration for ongoing curiosity. I have experienced science as practice originating out of an awe and interest in the world and myself as one small part of it.

In principle, scientific inquiry has been heralded as a counter to authoritarian models of knowledge, supporting democratic discourses by placing greater value on an individual's observations about the world than authoritarian doctrines of truth. Within the discipline, explanations for natural phenomena are open to constant revision and a culture of debate is fostered, uncertainty is acknowledged as always present, knowledge always incomplete, explanations always tentative. Scientific training includes practice in questioning one's assumptions, careful attention to detail, and, while predictive, does so while claiming respect for what is different or unexpected or "doesn't go as planned" as educative and interesting rather than a problem or mistake to be corrected. Science can be viewed as a way of thinking and communicating based on the same values that guide democratic governance. Both democracy and science are "founded on open debate, free flow of information, mutual respect, and the critical role of inquiry and evidence" (Branscomb & Rosenberg, 2012). At its best, scientific knowledge is generated through a democratic process, as community members share information and argue the merits of differing interpretations to explain natural phenomena (Bowler & Morus, 2010).

However, science is also culturally embedded, and within an anthropocentric, ethnocentric, materialistic, individualistic society, it should not be a surprise that science plays a significant role in promoting these discourses. In an industrial society

STEM Education and the Miracle of Life   **123**

> blinded by the future … we have to see that Science has become con-glomerated into an allegorical figure, a giant or a god, who supposedly looks all around like a great owl from its highest perch, seeing "objectively" everything involved. But, of course, it does no such thing, and it never has. If we stand outside the sanctuary where its believers have gathered to offer their trust, we see that this Science is a much smaller figure, merely human, humanly capable of being wrong, of directing its efforts toward the most money and the highest bidder, or "proving" and approving the new against the old. (Berry, 2017, pp. 92–93)

Perhaps Berry's greatest critique of Wilson is taking him to task on his role in perpetuating the myth of scientific inquiry and scientific knowledge as somehow operating outside the influence or limits of culture. Science is not a realm that operates free of ethical bounds, but rather reflects the current status of ethics operating within society. This causes harm that goes unaddressed when "our present idea of freedom in science is too often reducible to thoughtlessness of consequence" (Berry, 2000, p. 80). The questions we define as valuable to be asking through science, the type of evidence we accept, which ideas are shared and publicly validated, and the categories that frame scientific knowledge are all reflections of the context within which people are operating. Like democracy itself, science undermines truly inclusive discourse and decision-making when people are excluded through barriers of language or status, or are trained to dis-count their own experience or accept scientific information without questioning it or learning the means to evaluate it (Martusewicz, Edmundson & Lupinacci, 2015). Therefore, the practice and education of science are moral endeavors with ethical implications. Science education has a fundamental role to play in pro-moting or counteracting the appropriation of science out of our communal hands to meet industrial ends.

For better or worse, the majority of science teachers at the K-12 level do not have training as scientists. Many elementary and secondary science teachers are "trusters of Science" (Berry, 2017, p. 93) and hold ideas similar to Berry's portrayal of "popular scientific orthodoxy." When asked, educators describe science as more certain, objective, unemotional, and culturally removed than other forms of knowledge, and requiring greater training, specialization, and intellect than other disciplines (Buaraphan, 2010; Capps & Crawford, 2013; Kaya, 2012; Irez, 2006; Lederman, 2007; Liu & Lederman, 2007). The learning experiences these teachers offer have a profound impact on what youth come to understand as the "nature of science." Embedded within the context of standards-based testing (itself a market-based endeavor) driving current K-12 science, generalizable principles and not ethics are the focus of STEM education. Standards attempt to create a level of uniformity within education. Content remains primarily fact-based, skills are experienced as mechanistic process, and the language of objectivity and generality are taught as tenets of communication within science.

At the same time, the economic health of our industrial society is most commonly cited as the rationale for valuing STEM learning—youth must be prepared to become productive participants in our future. Within STEM education, the underlying nature of our society, its priorities and definitions of success are not discussed in science classrooms, and even more rarely open for debate. The standard for successful education under this model is whether an individual's STEM coursework is preparing the learner for a job or better yet, a career, preferably one with higher earning potential. And, for the most part, such an education encourages the student to leave home in a quest for success, for a place in the professions. And the professions, including Science, Technology, Engineering and Math, become the purview of experts. Thus, Berry argues, we educate our children upon the back of weakened local knowledge, and failing communities.

> The hegemony of professionals and professionalism erects itself on local failure. And from then on the locality exist merely as a market of consumer goods and as a source of "raw material" human and natural. The local schools no longer serve the local community; they serve the government's economy and the economy's government. Unlike the local community, the government and the economy cannot be served with affection, but only the professional zeal or professional boredom. (Berry, 2011, para. 32)

This kind of motivation reinforces individualism and materialism—mindsets focused on meeting personal needs, promoting greed, and not in any way encouraging the development of community, empathy or respect for what we outlined in Chapter 1 as the Great Economy of the living world (Berry, 1984). Youth are thus prepared through the educational system to accept and use scientific inquiry as an agent of industrialism and to compete with one another for a seat at the limited table of status and success.

The current discourse around technology and progress in popular culture and education further reinforces the elevation of STEM as the means to address social and ecological issues without providing due attention to the ways that science and technology have contributed to creating these issues. For example, language within the Next Generation Science Standards calls for students to examine or develop "solutions," methods to "reduce" or "minimize impact," or "protect Earth's resources," but does not explicitly invite critical analysis of the ways existing scientific practices or technologies may be causing harm (NGSS Lead States, 2013). Implicitly STEM standards promote the idea that scientific knowledge and technological development are progressive and positive and the means to our salvation. The impact on attitudes is unmistakable. In our experience, early elementary students readily identify behavior change as a reasonable response to environmental issues (for example, pollution from waste? Let's change our habits so we do not make so much waste), but by middle school, students are much quicker to express their faith in technologies to address such concerns and demonstrate skepticism in our ability to change behavior, especially if such change would be less convenient.

What Needs to Change?

Transforming scientific goals from: *What is possible?* to *What is possible here?* requires a shift in both the content and pedagogy of science education. One cannot counteract "popular scientific orthodoxy" without explicitly addressing its existence and origins, exploring its implications, and imagining alternatives. This kind of critical cultural ecological analysis is the hallmark of an EcoJustice approach to education.

> We cannot speak or act or live out of context. Our life inescapably affects other lives, which inescapably affect our life. We are being measured, in other words, by a standard that we cannot make and cannot destroy. It is by that standard, and only by that standard, that we know we are in a crisis in our relationship to nature. The term "environmental crisis," crude and inexact as it is, acknowledges that we have invoked this standard and have measured ourselves by it. A civilization that is destroying all of its sources in nature has raised starkly the issue of propriety, whether or not it wishes to have done so. Propriety is the antithesis of individualism. To raise the issue of propriety is to deny that any individual's wish is the ultimate measure of the world. (Berry, 2000, pp. 13–14)

STEM education needs to be deeply place-based and convivial, engaging students in investigations of natural history conducted within a specific context as the primary foundation of their scientific experience, rather than theoretically focused on generalized principles. Education needs to allow us to appreciate the history and cycles that sustain and have harmed places. In an interview with Fisher-Smith (1993), Berry observes,

> a farmer's knowledge is usable knowledge; a lot of it comes from experience, and a lot is inherited. The knowledge of most university experts is self-centered— committed to their own advancement in their careers and, therefore, indifferent to the effects of the work they're doing or going to do. And they're usually not committed to any community. (para. 92)

This separation between the researcher and researched is an essential failing of modern science, Berry argues, because it positions us to pursue and use science with callousness. It also creates a false sense of objectivity that fails to acknowledge the extent to which researcher and researched are inescapably bound. Education which reenacts this artificial separation establishes expectations and ethical boundaries in the practice of science that do not honor and support life.

Education expressly designed to develop affection, appreciation, relationships, connection and awareness of dependence—that is, an ethical orientation to the world—is needed to undermine existing assumptions and myths about the ability and value in divorcing researcher from that which is researched, explainer from that which is explained.

We need to refocus science education toward the complex rather than constantly working to reduce our understandings into simple, reductive terms. An important aspect of this is simply creating learning situations that celebrate, appreciate, and respect complexity, difference, and uniqueness of place and time. "If we can't know with final certainty what we are doing, then reason cautions us to be humble and patient, to keep the scale small, to be careful, to go slow" (Berry, 2000, p. 151). Again, this means that our work as scientists or science educators must be oriented to what our communities, human and more than human need in order to flourish. Berry is adamant that we should learn to be good observers of the living creatures with whom we share our places, that they are our best teachers. Imagine reconceiving STEM education toward serving our local economies, as a means of understanding what the land and other creatures require us to learn, rather than as our ticket out into a place in the industrial economy or research institutions that serve it.

However, exposure to these kinds of learning situations may not be sufficient to counteract the systemic and reinforcing impact of mechanistic, progress-oriented, and ethnocentric world views on conceptions about the nature of science. Education that explicitly involves cultural–ecological analysis that critiques the assumptions and priorities of modern industrial culture poises us to consider alternatives. Berry offers examples of the type of priorities that help us to reimagine the goals and practice of science, such as setting for ourselves the goal of kindly use:

> Kindly use is a concept that of necessity broadens, becoming more complex and diverse, as it approaches action. The land is too various in its kinds, climates, conditions, declivities, aspects, and histories to conform to any generalized understanding or to prosper under generalized treatment. ... To treat every field, or every part of every field, with the same consideration is not farming but industry. Kindly use depends upon intimate knowledge, the most sensitive responsiveness and responsibility. (Berry, 1996, p. 35)

Thick Description of Science

Within the context of cultural studies, Geertz (1973) argued that meaningful descriptions include meanings that members of the culture ascribe to their own actions. Geertz (1973) introduced the term "thick description" to define this kind of cultural analysis. Bowers (2008) points out how this kind of "thick description" reveals diversity by drawing out the different ways that individuals within a culture may assign meaning or intent of specific actions. In *Life is a Miracle* (2000), Berry is essentially arguing that science needs to take a "thick description" approach to nature in order to be useful and positive, otherwise it acts destructively. With a few exceptions, Berry does not apply this kind of approach to his analysis of science as it is currently practiced or conceptualized. Perhaps this is because, as he notes, he is not a scientist and does not have the perspective to look closely at the diversity within science. Berry believes in the nature of learning as a holistic endeavor that cannot divorce mind from body or body from place without injury (Berry, 2002, 2015). Such a perspective invites closer investigation of how people actually practice science and teach, learn, and use STEM. A thick description analysis has the potential to uncover ways that individuals and local cultures filter science practice or education to challenge our individualistic, consumer culture and build genuine stewardship. Existing examples of research and education which complement rather than undermine Berry's approach could help those within scientific and educational communities to see themselves as capable of contributing to Berry's vision for a healthier world.

A thick description looks more closely at the place-specific, context-specific, person-specific diversity within the science and education communities. Below we provide a few examples of science practiced and taught with humility, inclusion, empathy, and care.

Example 1

Douglass Smith is the Wolf Project Leader at Yellowstone National Park. Thirty-one wolves were reintroduced to this region in 1995. Smith's research team has been coordinating research efforts to monitor their activities year-round within the park habitat and surrounding areas since that time (Metz, Smith, Vucetich, Stahler & Peterson, 2012; Smith & Ferguson, 2005; Smith, Peterson & Houston, 2003). The behavior of individuals, packs, and ecological interactions are all areas of focus. Although research publications employ statistical analysis and attempt to draw general principles in keeping with the quantitative, abstract model for scientific knowledge, the comparisons that Smith makes in his publications more often serve to highlight the unique and diverse qualities among different places and populations and are grounded in intimate, long-term experience with the wolves and ecosystems he describes. "Often, what is important is subtle and detailed yet can account for the difference between an informed conclusion and one that is not" (Smith, Peterson & Houston, 2003, p. 330).

Example 2

Andrews Bjork is an ice historian at the Natural History Museum of Denmark in Copenhagen with a passionate enthusiasm for the stormy seas and icy fjords of Greenland.

128 STEM Education and the Miracle of Life

What sets Bjork apart, say other scientists, is that he combines the heart of a seafarer with a strong sense of detail and creativity in research. The studies by him and his fellow ice historians are making key contributions to glacial science, says Beata Csatho, a glaciologist at the University of Buffalo in New York. (Schiermeier, 2016, p. 480)

When not on the ice, Bjork spends his time tracking down large caches of aerial photos of Greenland from the 1930s to the 1970s and has discovered about 600 painted images from before film, using these to recreate intricately detailed stories of how Greenland's glaciers have transformed over time.

"Rink and later explorers documented very carefully where they were, and we can trust that what they painted is exactly what they saw," he says. "Their zeal and accuracy is a gift for us"... For Bjork, the historical research goes well beyond science. It also connects him with the pioneering scientists and explorers he grew up admiring. He is grateful that their legacy is finally being dug out from the crypt. "It's part of Nordic history," he says, "and a real gift to modern science". (Schiermeier, 2016, p. 480)

Example 3

Feinsinger et al. (2010) examine case studies of a local farmer, park ranger, and student as examples of researchers who engage in scientific inquiry to explore authentic questions about place. The authors employ a thick description approach by soliciting from participants their interpretation of the role scientific thought and practices are playing in their understanding of the places they live and work. In conclusion, Feinsinger et al. (2010) provide the following summary, which echoes Berry's observations about the dynamic nature of living systems while challenging Berry's characterization of what motivates most academic research, at least among field biologists.

The formal HD [scientific] method is not very relevant to developing a useful understanding of ecological systems where "todo cambia" and local idiosyncrasies intrude but are also prime objects of interest. And it certainly doesn't work for local people focused on questions about their immediate surroundings ... "even if field ecologists and conservation biologists wished to perform strict HD science they couldn't do so ... Why not?" "Todo cambia." So true replication among field studies is impossible even if we yearn for it—*which we don't*. Even given spatial autocorrelation, two places quite close to one another will have unique present-day ecologies that reflect unique biological, geological, biogeographical, and human histories. Successive years in the same place are each unique. Two places or time intervals farther apart are even more distinct, on average. That's the challenge of

STEM Education and the Miracle of Life **129**

conservation of place, because it's dangerous to blindly apply lessons learned at one time in one landscape to decision-making for other landscapes or years. That's also the beauty of ecology of place. A certain landscape attracts field ecologists into returning year after year not as a simple testing ground for universal scientific hypotheses but instead as a unique, fascinating n-dimensional puzzle in which scientific hypotheses may help them to frame the most enticing questions, and possible alternative explanations for the answers they obtain. We suspect that most field ecologists will prefer to think of their years-long or decades long studies as having great intrinsic interest. (Feinsinger et al., 2010, p. 409)

Example 4

In *Braiding Sweetgrass*, Robin Wall Kimmerer (2013) describes her perspective on what it means to be an ethical scientist by weaving together stories of her identity as a botanist, member of the Potawatomi people, daughter, and living being. Kimmerer uses her poetic language and intimate observations of nature, culture, and self to describe how indigenous ways of knowing and cultural traditions not only support, but breathe new life into scientific practice and knowledge. In Berry-like fashion, metaphors of agriculture, spirituality, and family illustrate how it is not simply our knowledge of the world but the stories we use to relate that knowledge which determine whether we live with the world and one another in health. Kimmerer describes surveying university students about their views on the relationship between humans and nature, noting that these students of science have no trouble identifying a number of harmful interactions but reported having no "knowledge of positive interactions between people and land" (p. 16). The problem, Kimmerer asserts, is in our stories because without the stories that help us to imagine reciprocity and sustainability, we cannot move toward such systems.

> For the greater part of human history, and in places in the world today, common resources were the rule. But some invented a different story, a social construct in which everything is to be bought and sold. The market economy story has spread like wildfire, with uneven results for human well-being and devastation for the natural world. But it is just a story we have told ourselves and we are free to tell another, to reclaim the old one. (Kimmerer, 2013, p. 30)
> Patowatomi stories remember that all the plants and animals, including humans, used to speak the same language. We could share with one another what our lives were like. But that gift is gone and we are the poorer for it. Because we can't speak the same language, our work as scientists is to piece the story together as best we can. We can't ask the salmon directly what they need, so we ask them with experiments and listen carefully to their answers. We stay up half the night at the microscope looking at annual rings in the

fish ear ones in order to know how the fish react to water temperature. So we can fix it. We run experiments on the effects of salinity on the growth of invasive grasses. So we can fix it. We measure and record and analyze in ways that might seem lifeless but to us are the conduits to understanding the inscrutable lives of species not our own. Doing science with awe and humility is a powerful act of reciprocity with the more-than-human world. (pp. 251–252)

Example 5

My son Graham and I (Katy) have spent the last two years engaged in the practical side of doing science and learning STEM through an ethical lens of stewardship. As Kindergarten approached, I wrestled with the best course for my son's education, and finally settled on a homeschool approach, which afforded me the opportunity to personalize his learning experiences and creatively consider the design of curricula from an EcoJustice framework. The timing coincided with my father's failing health, giving me new responsibility for a ten-acre area in Southeast Michigan, which has been a part of my family for four generations. This narrow strip of forest, brush, and wetland sitting on the west side of a two-lane highway, bordered by plowed fields, a line of office parking lots, and a few residential backyards has provided a rich cultural, environmental, and emotional context to explore what it means to be a "good steward" of both this place and my son.

Graham and I are both learning from one another and from this place as we spend time in the environment and interacting with members of the community. Our shared and individual understandings of self and membership with this place are affected by the time we spend there. My educational plans for Graham acted as a touchstone but changed as we did. So, contrary to the rigid sequencing or pacing of traditional coursework, I outlined a series of lessons that worked fluidly alongside one another over an extended period of time. We started with a focus on the natural history of plants and animals as a way to build familiarity with the ten acres. We engaged in imaginative play and hands-on exploration to discover the elements that define living beings, traits and qualities of unique individuals and different species, their common and diverse needs and behaviors, and their interactions in this place. We asked whether, and how, our experiences challenged our assumptions. We have interviewed elders and consulted written resources, historical documents, and stories to more deeply understand the significance of the landscape features, vegetation patterns, and family connections. We question the why and how of human activities, and use our observations to predict likely consequences from our choices as stewards. Consistent with research on developmentally appropriate practice with young children, which emphasizes the value in revisiting the same activities multiple times and in various settings, I witness how this approach develops skill and familiarity, allows for comparison and transfer of knowledge, and builds self-esteem (Bransford, 2000). I also witnessed how this approach encouraged the gradual deepening of relationships that are both genuine and nuanced, rather than contrived and superficial. Such relationships have been essential foundations for Graham to develop affection and empathy, and to understand others in this community well enough to act on their behalf in a meaningful way.

Conclusion

It may be argued that these examples are more the exception than the rule, but if Berry advocates for meaningful knowledge about the world being the kind of knowledge that is complex and specific, then following that logic, a closer investigation into the nature and practice of science itself should be valued and pursued. Looking across the body of Berry's work, he unabashedly indicts scientism and elitism within the profession. He calls for a new ethical frame to guide the discipline. He questions the value of much scientific knowledge. But Berry does not turn his back on science. The questions, methods, and knowledge of science have an important role to play.

What Berry fails to celebrate is how much of what he is calling for to change in science may already align with the way that many scientists and members of the public understand or use science, regardless of the dominant discourses that promote a rationalist scientism. In a way, Berry's view of science reveals the same kind of abstraction and generalization that he and others critique about many intellectual pursuits. Such generalization serves a purpose, allowing Berry to identify and challenge patterns of thought and action that cause harm to us socially and ecologically. However, the reality of how individuals may conduct science or STEM education is consistent with Berry's assertion that science and art cannot be separated. Berry notes this with his description of the farmers who are not taught science formally but come to use their natural powers of observation (knowledge) to inform their actions (art) in the world. We would argue that the same is true of the botanist in the field, the microbiologist in the laboratory, or the geologist collaborating with the mathematician to develop a more accurate model of climate. The pursuit of science divorced from emotional attachment or creative action is contrary to how we humans operate. Regardless of the question or context, in real time we are working intimately with our places. Whether farm, forest, or laboratory, we form affections and develop our sense of self and ethical boundaries in dynamic relation with the places where we work, the people we work with, the instruments we use, the skills we acquire, the other living beings we interact with, and the questions we investigate.

Abandoning the fiction of objective and dispassionate science is a critical step toward making science relevant and ethically responsible. For if we pause to consider the places where science is being practiced, it becomes clear that science itself is as diverse as the people practicing it. It becomes clear that some places,

132 STEM Education and the Miracle of Life

some skills, some questions are more likely to foster an ethic of care and appreciation for the systems of dependence than others. Consider, for example, how the conditions experienced by a toxicologist in a sterile lab differ from the environment studied for a marine biologist aboard a working fishing vessel. How differently do these two scientists experience the nature of their work and community role? I think Berry would agree that such differences are not insignificant.

Reductive explanations and associated technologies carelessly or generically applied in the name of scientific progress are pervasive in our lives and their destructive impact cannot be denied. Scientists who perpetuate this kind of vision for science, like E. O. Wilson, need to be challenged. Berry does us all a service in doing so. However, the traditional knowledge passed across generations and among community members, originated, in part, through scientific inquiry, albeit within community-based contexts, not separated realms of expert knowledge. Careful and detailed observing, questioning, testing, and using these personal experiences to inform next steps, or identify more questions is part of our human exploration of the world and our effort to understand it, however imperfect. Some members of the modern scientific community contribute in positive ways to that tradition. Our ability to continue doing so helps us to respond resiliently to cycles and change within our material world. Scientific inquiry has an important role to play.

Conventional content and structure of science education reinforce hegemonic discourses and a Wilson-like image of science. The current STEM reorganization of science education ostensibly claims to step away from that model, but does not genuinely do so and reinforces the politicized and industrialized use of science (NGSS Lead States, 2013; Cheskey & Wolfmeyer, 2015; Wolfmeyer, Lupinacci, & Cheskey, 2017). Berry's ideas about science represent the perspective of someone who is "not at all a scientist" (Berry, 2000, p. 17), but a "conservationist" (p. 24) and one who has, like all members of society, "experienced many of the effects (costs and benefits) of science" (p. 17). In the context of applied sciences that have mechanized farming and established systems of industrial dependence, Berry sees the products of scientific endeavor as abstractions that serve to "come between the mind and its work." (2000, p. 25). When Andy Catlett stands before the room of professionals and agricultural experts in *Remembering* (2008), he challenges the academic researchers with these lines: "This room," he said,

> it's an image of the minds of the professional careerists of agriculture—a room without windows, filled with artificial air, where everything reducible has been reduced to numbers, and the rest ignored. Nothing you are talking about, and influenced by your talk, is present here or can be seen from here. (Berry, 2008, p. 19)

These ways of building and sharing knowledge are harmful realities of science as a discipline and STEM education as a movement. They act as powerful forces within our current culture, but they are not all that science is or all that STEM education may achieve. We have the potential to learn and practice science from a framework of responsibility, humility, and genuine curiosity about the world around and in us.

It is essential that we recognize that some scientists and educators within our communities are already working to explicitly challenge scientism. In the afterword of his latest edition of *The Unsettling of America*, Berry is "encouraged by the knowledge that if this book (and my other books) suddenly disappeared from print and from memory, its advocacy and its hope would continue undiminished" through the work of others, including researchers such as Wes Jackson (Berry, 2015, p. 233). But it is also essential that we recognize the ways that science itself is pursued and learned through lives of personal experience and meaning-making, not abstractions. In doing so, rather than casting science as an enemy, we have the opportunity to enlist its aid and to co-opt the current enthusiasm for STEM to serve this purpose. Thick description shows us examples of how individuals and groups act ethically within the practice and teaching of science despite the context of our dominant modern social paradigms. It is our hope that applying this thick description to science will help to build a more robust counter narrative to scientism and the characterization of STEM education as a panacea for our future. Those within the scientific and education communities have a vital role to play as members of Berry's healthy community—a community built on principles of inclusion, humility, empathy, and care. As Berry reminds us, "the use of the world is finally a personal matter, and the world can be preserved in health only by the forebearance and care of a multitude of persons" (2015, p. 29). We cannot afford to leave anyone out.

References

Bell, R. L., Matkins, J. J., & Gansneder, B. M. (2011). Impacts of contextual and explicit instruction on preservice elementary teachers' understandings of the nature of science. *Journal of Research in Science Teaching*, 48(4): 414–436. doi:10.1002/tea.20402

Berry, W. (1984). Two economies. *Review and Expositor*, 81(2): 209–223. https://doi.org/10.1177/003463738408100204

Berry, W. (1996). *The unsettling of America: Culture and agriculture*. Berkeley, CA: Counterpoint Press.

Berry, W. (2000). *Life is a miracle: An essay against modern superstition*. Berkeley, CA: Counterpoint Press.

Berry, W. (2002). *The art of the commonplace*. Berkeley, CA: Counterpoint Press.

Berry, W. (2003). *Citizenship papers*. Washington, DC: Shoemaker & Hoard.

Berry, W. (2008). *Remembering*. Berkeley, CA: Counterpoint Press.

Berry, W. (2011). The work of local culture. Retrieved October 5, 2017 from https://thecontraryfarmer.wordpress.com/2011/06/10/wendell-berry-the-work-of-local-culture/

Berry, W. (2015). *The unsettling of America: Culture and agriculture*. Berkeley, CA: Counterpoint Press.

Berry, W. (2017). *The art of loading brush: New agrarian writings*. Berkeley, CA: Counterpoint Press.

Bowers, C. A. (2008). Why a critical pedagogy of place is an oxymoron. *Environmental Education Research*, 14(3): 325–335.

Bowler, P. J., & Morus, I. R. (2010). *Making modern science: A historical survey*. Chicago: University of Chicago Press.

Branscomb, L. M., & Rosenberg, A. A. (2012). Science and democracy. *The Scientist*, October 1, 2012. http://the-scientist.com/2012/10/01/science-and-democracy

Bransford, J. (2000). *How people learn: Brain, mind, experience, and school*. Washington, DC: National Academy Press.

Buaraphan, K. (2010). Science teachers' conceptions of the nature of science. *Science Educator*, 19: 35–47. doi:10.1080/90500693.2009.617193

Capps, D. K., & Crawford, B. A. (2013). Inquiry-based professional development: What does it take to support teachers in learning about inquiry and nature of science? *The International Journal of Science Education*, 35(12): 1497–1978. doi:10.1080/09500693.2012.760209

Cheskey, N. Z., & Wolfmeyer, M. R. (2015). *Philosophy of STEM education: A critical investigation*. New York, NY: Palgrave Macmillan. doi:10.1057/9781137535467

Feinsinger, P., Alvarez, S., Carreño-Rocabado, G., Revira, E., Cuéllar, R. L., Noss, A., Daza, F., Figuera, M., Lanz, E., Revira, L. G., Canizares, M., Alegre, A., & Roldan, A. (2010). Local people, scientific inquiry, and the ecology and conservation of place in Latin America. In: I. Billick, & M. V. Price (Eds.), *The Ecology of Place (Chapter 8)*. doi:10.13140/2.1.2150.6562

Fisher-Smith, J. (1993). Field observations: An interview with Wendell Berry. *Orion*. Retrieved on October 21, 2017 from: www.thesunmagazine.org/issues/218/field-ob servations

Geertz, C. (1973). Thick description: Toward an interpretive theory of culture. In *The Interpretation of Cultures Selected Essays*. New York, NY: American Council of Learned Societies.

Irez, S. (2006). Are we prepared?: An assessment of preservice science teacher educators' beliefs about nature of science. *Science Education*, 90: 1113–1143. doi:10.1002/sce.20156

Kaya, S. (2012). An examination of elementary and early childhood pre-service teachers' nature of science views. *Procedia Social and Behavioral Sciences*, 46: 581–585.

Kimmerer, R. W. (2013). *Braiding sweetgrass: Indigenous wisdom, scientific knowledge and the teachings of plants*. New York, NY: Milkweed Editions.

Lederman, N. G. (2007). Nature of science: Past, present and future. In S. K. Abell and N. G. Lederman (Eds.), *Handbook of research on science education* (pp. 31–79). Mahwah, NJ: Erlbaum Publishers.

Lederman, N. G., Abd-El-Khalick, F., Bell, R. L., & Schwartz, R. S. (2002). Views of nature of science questionnaire: Toward valid and meaningful assessment of learners' conceptions of nature of science. *Journal of Research in Science Teaching*, 39(6): 497–521. doi:10.1002/tea.10034

Liu, S. Y., & Lederman, N. G. (2007). Exploring prospective teachers' worldviews and conceptions of nature of science. *International Journal of Science Education*, 29(10): 1281–1307.

Martusewicz, R., Edmundson, J., & Lupinacci, J. (2015). *EcoJustice education: Towards diverse, democratic, and sustainable communities*. New York, NY: Routledge.

Meichtry, Y. J. (1999). The nature of science and scientific knowledge: Implications for a preservice elementary methods course. *Science and Education*, 8(3): 273–286.

Metz, M. C., Smith, D. W., Vucetich, J. A., Stahler, D. R., & Peterson, R. O. (2012). Seasonal patterns of predation for gray wolves in the multi-prey system of Yellowstone

National Park. *Journal of Animal Ecology*, 81: 553–563. doi:10.1111/j.1365-2656.2011.01945.x

National Research Council (NRC) (2012). *A framework for K-12 science education: Practices, crosscutting concepts, and core ideas.* Washington, DC: The National Academies Press. doi:10.17226/13165

National Science Teacher Association (NSTA) (2016). NSTA position statement: Teaching science in the context of societal and personal issues. www.nsta.org/about/positions/societalpersonalissues.aspx

NGSSLeadStates (2013). *Next Generation science standards: For states, by states.* Washington, DC: The National Academies Press.

Schiermeier, Q. (2016). The ice historians: to tell whether Greenland's glacial cap will melt away any time soon, researchers are poring over old photographs and drawings for clues to its past behavior. *Nature Publishing Group*, 535 (7613): 480.

Smith, D., & Feguson, G. (2005). *Decade of the wolf: Returning the wild to Yellowstone.* Guilford, CT: Lyons Press.

Smith, D., Peterson, R., & Houston, D. (2003). Yellowstone after wolves. *BioScience, 53* (4): 330–340. doi:10.1641/0006-3568(2003)053[0330:yaw]2.0.co;2

Wilson, E. O. (1998). *Concilience: The unity of knowledge.* New York, NY: Vintage Books.

Wolfmeyer, M. (2013). STEM meet EcoJustice. *Green Theory & Praxis*, 7(1): 32–46.

Wolfmeyer, M., Lupinacci, J., & Cheskey, N. (2017). EcoJustice mathematics education: An ecocritical (re)consideration for 21st century curricular challenges. *Journal of Curriculum Theorizing*, 32(2): 53–71.

YCS Website (2017). www.ycschools.us/our-schools/high-school/stemm/

7

HEALTH AS HOLISM

With Kristi Wilson

> The grace that is the health of creatures can only be held in common.
> In healing the scattered members come together.
> In health the flesh is graced, the holy enters the world.
> The task of healing is to respect oneself as a creature, no more and no less.
>
> *Wendell Berry (1990a, p. 9)*

People living within hyper-consumerist and technologically developed industrial or post-industrial cultures too often fail to recognize that their own well-being is fully dependent on the health of a larger living system, an ecological community. Or, perhaps more accurately, as a symptom of a more general socialization to individualist ways of thinking, we are taught to think of health as a matter of individual fitness, and not as a condition growing out of a broader network of relationships. In this sense, we live day-to-day generally complicit in a set of hegemonic patterns and practices, identifying ourselves in our specialized professions and our particular expertise, as having a job to do, generally unaware of the ways those practices may wreak havoc upon the larger order of the living world.

Currently nursing as a profession and nursing education more specifically define health as *the absence of disease* within the individual body. This definition limits the practice of nursing to a narrow focus, denying a full understanding of the body immersed and participating in a larger set of living relations with other creatures, and in specific places. Such a definition significantly narrows the scope of examination to the individual body, excluding from concern an ever-widening context of poison and waste generated by the industrial machine of which hospitals, for example, are a part. Hospitals generate 6600 tons of waste per day (Clarke & Butterfield, 2011); yet its dispersal into the very environs that we

Health as Holism **137**

depend upon for life is justified as a necessary side effect to cure humans. Dominating both nursing and the medical field more generally, this definition of health is caught in a long history of individualized, mechanistic, rationalistic, and anthropocentric ways of thinking, powerfully influencing modern institutions and professions driven by an exploitive economic system.

Of course, it is important that we understand the good intentions of nurses who aim to make a difference in people's lives by aiding in the process of healing and caring for their patients. And, knowledge of the human body that medical research has developed over the last century is certainly important to the human condition. We are not disputing these factors. However, nurses along with other medical personnel are embedded within larger socio-political organizations and economic systems that assume knowledge (of healing, for example) to be centralized in professions, and not part of the everyday conditions within communities shared intergenerationally. As we've been arguing throughout this book, these systems create deeply imbedded, mostly unconscious patterns of belief and behavior within a hierarchy of meaning, knowledge, and power that affect how we see ourselves and others, what we accept as "good nursing" and what we prioritize and emphasize in healthcare. Regardless of our good intentions, our practice and identity as professionals with "careers" are produced and limited within these historically embedded discursive and material systems.

As discussed in the introductory chapter, Berry defines the "little economy" (Berry, 2002, p. 222) as consisting of (and prioritizing) human needs for sustenance and the exchange of services, "a narrow circle within which things are manageable by the use of our wits" (2002, p. 222). In contrast, the "Great Economy" is made of up many "little economies" including those subsistence and reproductive relationships and exchanges engaged by other creatures. Every species must find a way to provision itself and it does so via specific species-centric exchanges of the gifts offered within the limits of the Great Economy. Berry warns us that:

> Any little economy that sees itself as unlimited is obviously self-blinded. It does not see its real relation of dependence and obligation to the Great Economy; in fact, it does not see that there is a great economy. Instead, it calls the Great Economy "raw material" or "natural resources" or "nature" and proceeds within the business of putting it "under control." (2002, p. 231)

Berry's insistence that the little economy is a part of a larger network and cycles of life and death—"the slow work of growth and death, gravity and decay which is the chief work of the world" (Berry, 1990b, p. 153)—defines his ideas about health. In contrast to the dominant paradigm perspectives in nursing and medicine, Berry (1996) argues for a definition of health as a condition developing out of an essential interdependence. "While we live, our bodies are moving particles of the earth, joined inextricably both to the soil and to the bodies of other creatures. It is hardly surprising then, that there should be profound resemblances between the treatment of our bodies and of the earth" (1996, p. 97). He begins a critique of our current standards within medical institutions with this clear statement of the problem, a critique of the misapprehension of the idea of health:

> The difficulty probably lies in our narrowed understanding of the word *health*. That there is some connection between how we feel and what we eat, between our bodies and the earth, is acknowledged when we say that we must "eat right to keep fit" or that we should eat "a balanced diet." But by health we mean little more than how we feel. We are healthy, we think, if we do not feel any pain or too much pain, and if we are strong enough to do our work. If we become unhealthy, then we go to a doctor who we hope will "cure" us and restore us to health. By health, in other words, we mean merely the absence of disease. Our health professionals are interested almost exclusively in preventing disease (mainly by destroying germs) and in curing disease (mainly by surgery and by destroying germs). (Berry, 1996, pp. 102–103)

Berry's critique exposes a widely accepted assumption of human nature as autonomous; we have been socialized to think of ourselves primarily in individualized terms, fundamentally isolated from, and in competition with, one another and the larger ecosystems by our very nature. This idea of the solitary individual and his or her independence from the larger world frames our normalized conception of health.

Further, this process, institutionalized in the profession of nursing and medicine more generally, is an analogue of what Berry refers to as the problem of fragmentation in modern society. For Berry, the most critical cultural disease is specialization, the dividing or separating off of worlds of work and the enclosure of care and responsibility into isolated professions, institutions and organization, dividing us from one another as we become dependent on the narrow knowledge and prowess of experts. For Berry, such a system has dismembered communities, cutting off their responsibility for the care of one another and removing important knowledge about what specific communities in specific places need.

> What the specialization of our age suggests in one example after another, is not only that fragmentation is a disease, but that the diseases of the disconnected parts are similar or analogous to one another. Thus, they memorialize their lost unity, their relation persisting in their disconnections. Any severance produces two wounds that are, among other things, the record of how the severed parts once fitted together. (1996, pp. 110–111)

When bodies are isolated and assumed to be autonomous, the generativity produced within relationships is overlooked, its unifying and healing power under-studied, even discarded. And yet, those relationships produce everything that is possible in life, including death which in turn is needed for the growth of new life. Separated into parts in order to be measured and to meet institutionalized "efficiencies," healthcare practices have become standardized sites under the control of "unthinking technicians" (Nancy Johnston, personal interview, 29 May, 2015) who we call nurses.

Yet, as Berry argues, one cannot be healthy unless one is whole. "Healing," he tells us, "complicates the systems by opening and restoring connections among the various parts ..." (1996, p. 110). To be whole is to be nurtured to develop in an orderly, symbiotic and generative connection to other beings that make up existence on this planet. Autonomy is an "illusory condition" (Berry, 1996, p. 111; Plumwood, 2002). We are born into these earthly and cosmological conditions that are always unavoidably relational. "Persons cannot be whole alone" (Berry, 1996, p. 103).

> If the body is healthy then it is whole. But how can it be whole and yet be dependent, as it obviously is, upon other bodies and upon the earth, upon all the rest of Creation, in fact? It becomes clear that the health or wholeness of the body is a vast subject, and that to preserve it calls for a vast enterprise ... all the convergences and dependencies of Creation are surely implied. (1996, p. 103)

The illusion of being separate motivates the desire for selfish accumulation, and apathy for anything other than oneself in the human-made world as if that world was also disconnected. Without the necessary understanding of dependence, we shut ourselves off, or accept systems that encourage, even require isolation. We fail to experience or offer affection which grows out of mutuality and care in membership with others; we do not feel responsible for something that we do not experience as part of us.

The word *health*, Berry writes, has a common origin with the terms "heal, whole, wholesome, hale, hallow, and holy" (1996, p. 103). Humans eat from the soil, digesting and absorbing nutrients deposited there from the bodies of other creatures that also sustained themselves from plants and animals dependent upon the soil. We exist only insofar as we are in relation to a vast and abundant living network of others, the bounty of the earth's gift to us. Thus, Berry ultimately describes health as a condition of this living cyclical network, a condition of wholeness and membership with diverse others that is ultimately generative of life itself and thus must be protected, nurtured, and, in short, loved. The community in its particular place and region on the planet, and not the individual body or an individual body part, is thus the smallest unit of health. Such recognition requires humility and the acknowledgement of sacred limitations and offerings within unavoidable processes of living and dying. This awareness also requires a sense of faith in, and faithfulness to, the larger ecological and communal network which serves and nurtures us.

In a short story entitled "Fidelity," Berry (1992) captures both this complex sensibility about health created as a practice of love among the membership, and his disapproval of the ways modern organizations, captured by the lure of technology, efficiencies, progress, and professional specialization, abstract life from the conditions of its possibility. We share a summary of the story here as a measure of Berry's clarity about, and devotion to, what matters most.

Fidelity

Burley Coulter is dying. All summer his friends, family and neighbors have watched as he slowed down, helping when he could, telling stories as always, but now mostly resting by a post or in his son Danny's truck as others worked nearby. Finally, one day Burley did not respond as Danny tried to wake him. And in a heartbeat, Danny is suddenly conscious of what he had known for months, that Burley was wasting away in his illness. With reticence, he and his uncle and their wives decide "to do something for him" which at the time, and with great uncertainty, meant taking him into Louisville to a hospital. There he is connected to machines and tubes, a respirator keeping him minimally alive. And as he fades, the doctor assures them confidently "with many large words" that they should not worry. The professionals have the situation well in hand.

Eventually, "shaken by a kind of treason," they realize their mistake. So, in the middle of the night Danny decides to go get Burley. He makes some preparations, tells his wife that if anyone asks to tell them he "said something about Indiana." He gets in his truck and drives to Louisville. He enters the hospital, finds a gurney, takes it to Burley's room, disconnects him from the pulsing machines, and leaves the hospital with no one the wiser. He drives back to the farm, to an old barn in the woods where he and Burley had spent many a night out hunting, sheltering and talking as their hounds bayed in the distance. It was here in the woods at Burley's side that Danny had received his most fundamental education about healthy provisioning of his family and his spirit, about devotion and fidelity to the membership. He is here, moved by that same spirit. Under Burley's tutelage, "Danny's first providings on his own to his mother's household were of wild goods … that grew by no human effort but furnished themselves to him in response only to his growing intimacy with the countryside" (1992, p. 118).

While Danny spends the rest of the night in the barn with Burley, Lyda receives a call from the hospital, an official voice telling her that one Burley Coulter has disappeared and that they are doing all they can to locate him. Thus begins a series of decisions, strategies, and conversations among friends and neighbors (in particular their friends Henry and Wheeler Catlett, two lawyers in town) in response to what they know they will need to thoughtfully and carefully face: the legal, regulatory instrument of the hospital, the law, and the rule of experts.

As day breaks, with Burley still alive but unconscious, Danny begins the painstaking process of digging his grave. In the gathering light, "Danny felt a happiness that he knew was not his at all, that did not exist because he felt it but because it was here and he had returned to it" (p. 134). Burley awakens briefly, acknowledges Danny and where they are, and slips away again, eventually into death's embrace.

Meanwhile, a state police investigator shows up at Lyda and Danny's farm, asking for Danny. She tells him "he said something about Indiana" and if he needs to know more he'll need to see their friend Henry Catlett in the nearby town. The investigator goes to the office where first Henry, and then his father Wheeler, proceed to educate him about why his task to locate Danny (who he assumes has kidnapped Burley to ultimately collect an inheritance) is misdirected. With Investigator Bode sitting in his office Henry and the elder Wheeler tell him that they won't cooperate with him. Burley's neighbors, friends and family—the membership—have come to the office and are assembled there as well. And while out in the woods, Danny continues his diligent and careful work with shovel and spade, Wheeler explains the difference between a medical establishment with an economic (that is, money-driven) stake in a patient's "merciful" care, and the duty, responsibility, and nurturance of one's community. It is a matter he says of belonging. The investigator says he's there to serve the law. He aims to bring Danny to justice as it's his job.

> [Wheeler]: "You are wrong about [Danny] insofar as you suspect him of acting out of greed. In the first place he loves Burley, and in the second place, he's not alone and he knows it. There are several of us here who belong to Danny and to whom he belongs, and we'll stand by him, whatever happens ... we are talking about the question of the ownership of people. To whom and to what does Burley Coulter belong?" (1992, p. 174)

Detective Bode says again that all he knows is that the law has been broken and the law is what he is there to serve.

> "But, my dear boy," says Wheeler, "You don't eat or drink the law, or sit in the shade of it or warm yourself by it, or wear it, or have your being in it. The law exists only to serve." [Bode]: "Serve what?" [Wheeler]: "Why all the many things that are about it. Love." (pp. 174–175)

And just there is the central point of Berry's understanding of health. As a matter of wholeness, order and relationship, health is created and maintained only as a condition of the cycles of life, and in the kindness, generosity, nurturance, and attention enacted among those to whom we belong within that cycle. It is not tended (or if it is, only very partially tended and in abstracted and reductionist ways) in the organizations designed to make efficiencies, or in turn to make a

142 Health as Holism

profit from what we must pay to relieve our loved ones' suffering, not from the system that encourages us to consume in wastefulness more than we need. Health is a matter of the relationships and living connections that are made in the particular order of a particular place—among the trees and the soil, and the people's labor and care for one another. It is made in the ongoing unavoidable connection of the body to the earth. As Danny completes his digging, he returns to Burley, now a body, a shell of the man who was his father, carries him to the woodland grave placing him in the earth, among the trees, and soil, and hills which have embraced him his whole life. "Into that great quiet he said aloud, 'Be with him as he has been with us.'" (1992, p. 169).

A Research Project to Reform Nursing Education

As educators, one of us of teachers and the other of nurses, we both became enchanted by this vision of health articulated by Berry, especially as his critique of professionalism and organizations troubled our own righteousness in our work within organizations. For Rebecca, the complexity and beauty of Berry's sensibility, his embrace of the "larger, looser darker order" of love resonates with early childhood experiences that she has off and on tried to put words to (Martusewicz, Edmundson & Lupinacci, 2015; Martusewicz, 2013, 2001). For Kristi, Berry's ideas shake the very foundations of her training as a nurse and nurse practitioner but also touch something deeply lodged in her spirit, an abiding faith in what really matters as we care for others in the world.

Thinking about health professionals in particular, we both wondered whether other nurse educators might have similar doubts about the mainstream medical establishment, with its reductionist definitions of health as the absence of disease in individual human bodies, its machines, techniques, and standardized approaches to nursing education. Grounded in Berry's vision of health as holism and the implied critique of current healthcare education, Kristi undertook a research project to identify and talk with other scholars about her budding sensibility that something needs to change in the education of nurses. Using the EcoJustice framework as her guide, and with Rebecca as mentor, Kristi designed a dissertation project to follow her heart and seek out others whom she hoped might offer insights as to how Berry's vision could help reform nursing and nursing education.

She identified seven nurse educator/scholars including David Allen from The University of Washington at Bothell, Patricia Butterfield from Washington State University, Peggy Chinn from The University of Connecticut, Benny Goodman from The University of Plymouth, UK, Nancy Johnston from York University, Ontario, Dorothy Kleffel, retired from the University of San Diego, and one other nurse scholar who requested anonymity. Having read and identified their work as articulating aspects of this broad ecological vision, Kristi contacted each one and invited them into a conversation. She interviewed them each individually several times. Through these conversations a number of common issues, questions, and critical insights arose that help shape a case against the current mechanistic model of nursing education. With these scholars, Kristi began constructing an alternative approach based on the essential relational nature of our planetary existence, drawing upon and creating a deeper understanding of Berry's definition of health.

Health as More than the Absence of Disease

Within our conversations these nurse scholars described an understanding of health as complex, affected by a larger context of political, cultural, socio-economic, and ecological dynamics that includes our specific values and actions. One scholar, David Allen said, "We need to understand health as a political practice not an individual behavior ..." Patricia Butterfield added, "Environmental health determinants really shape opportunities for health," and another, Nancy Johnston stated that health is, "indivisible with social justice." By contrast, the current definition of health in nursing education (as the absence of disease) supports the notion of health as a commodity, or something that can be fought over at the governmental level, purchased, and coveted by individuals as part of one's privilege. This set of assumptions, as Wheeler Catlett's lecture to the lawman asserts, is not surprising since the practice of healthcare in this society is created within a capitalist industry that stresses efficiency, specialization, and volume for profit. Although most nurses enter into the profession with the impetus to make a difference by helping people, they are taught how to maximize efficiency and speed through triage: patient in, patient out.

Critical of the structures within which they are forced to work and teach, these scholars also alluded to Berry's notion of health as a condition of wholeness. One participant who requested anonymity noted that health represents

> living with alignment, living with integrity, and so the core of health ... has to do with what is it that you see as your guiding principles, and what is it that you see as why you actually were sent to this planet ... I don't think that there are any physiological indicators in and of themselves that you can look at separately from how they're functioning in terms of a person's overall alignment.

In other words, physiological factors that can be measured by nurses or physicians in the health care setting, such as blood pressure, pulse, respirations, temperature, weight, and urinary output do not reflect overall health; rather, living in alignment and in relation with others in ways that offer care without assuming the need to control defines health in a more holistic way.

Benny Goodman described his frustrations with the narrow view of health as defined by The World Health Organization, even as they tried in the late 1940s to define health as more than the absence of disease,

I think it's a great statement of intent. And it's a good starting point. But ... what it doesn't do is ... understand health as collectivity. It doesn't understand health as community. It doesn't understand health as membership. Because ... the writers are steeped in Western philosophy and Western philosophy of dualism. Once you understand dualism, that separation, then, of course, you're going to write it in that way and then therefore, you know ... you can be healthy according to the WHO's definition as an individual. But Wendell Berry keeps saying ... if you live ... with urban deprivation and crumbling infrastructure and poisoned seed, you might be the fittest individual in the world with good mental health but you ain't healthy from that definition.

In contrast, when health is defined as created in diverse holistic relationality, in the holiness of those moving interconnections and in membership with others, healthcare is shifted into a set of principles and commitments with much more eco-ethical intention in nursing education and the work of nurses more generally.

Challenging Discourses of Modernity in Nursing

Anthropocentrism

In their narratives, the scholars challenged the modernist discourse of human supremacy in nursing education, the powerful assumption that human beings are superior to all other species and thus given the right to control or even own them (Martusewicz, Edmundson & Lupinacci, 2015). Dorothy Kleffel answered the question of what keeps her up at night,

> The world is facing its greatest environmental crisis in history, where life as we know it is going to cease to exist. We see this already happening in the changing climate that affects all living things including humans. ... In my opinion the nursing profession has not focused enough in education, research, and practice on these life threatening issues, even though environment is a major multi paradigm of the profession.

By multi paradigm, Kleffel is referring to Jacquelyn Fawcett's metaparadigm for nursing that identifies the core concepts that nursing should focus on during training and practice (i.e., person, environment, nursing, and health). Kleffel challenged the narrowness of Fawcett's category, often used to mean the patient's immediate surroundings within a building or institution, rather than an understanding of our connectedness to a complex set of ecological relations. The result of her rationalized anthropocentric and mechanistic categories is the nurses' inability to place value on the wider living world.

Another scholar challenged the value we hold for human beings over non-human beings in nursing education when noting the importance of "Others." The anonymous scholar described how human beings need to honor a relationship with other species in order to understand living and dying as part of a healthy process,

> I'm real clear that humankind cannot live without the plants and the animals and the earth. ... My spirit actually needed these things. I simply can't imagine a, a world without them. ... When you're in this relationship with plants, you just see the life cycle over and over again. Because it's really helped me as I've thought about what it means to age as a person to see changes in myself uh let alone other people.

Individualism

The modernist discourse of individualism asserts that the individual is autonomous from and valued over the community (Martusewicz, Edmundson & Lupinacci, 2015). The emphasis of health as an outcome situated within an individual human body without consideration of larger connections or context, is a primary concern of these nurse scholars. Thinking about common classroom practices, David Allen pointed out that a common requirement in nursing education is journaling, a process of self-reflection that, as an individualistic activity blocks out any form of acknowledgement of a larger system or structures. "I've always sort of thought of self-reflection as a form of narcissism. You know ... if you reflected on yourself and it's yourself doing the reflection, then you're not really getting outside of your own box." In nursing and hence nursing education, our "own box" is our work with the individual patient's body unto itself as the singular point of our "expert" attention.

Nancy Johnston talked about the philosophy of health and accountability that is valued in nursing education,

> ... it's not like we're, we're radically free and it's all up to us as individuals ... to exert our will on the world. It's, we're, we're already caught up in it. And the world already promotes certain opportunities or denies them to us. ... Or that health is an individual responsibility, and if you have diabetes, well too bad you didn't take care of yourself.

The situations that patients find themselves in are socially and politically, and we should add ecologically, influenced. Johnston questions the assumption of free will that is embedded within the discourse of individualism and victim blaming, mired in the goal of imaginary positive outcomes that include a disease free individual body.

Rationalism/Mechanism

Within institutions like medicine, individualism and anthropocentrism intersect with mechanistic views of the world that call for the rationalization of practice by experts who sell their knowledge and services to the public. For Berry, this form

146 Health as Holism

of enclosure of work and care is a primary cause of the fragmentation and isolation of communities.

> It is absurd to approach the subject of health piecemeal with a departmentalized band of specialists. A medical doctor uninterested in nutrition, in agriculture, in the wholesomeness of mind and spirit is as absurd as a farmer who is uninterested in health. Our fragmentation of the subject cannot be our cure, because it is our disease. The body cannot be whole alone. Persons cannot be whole alone. It is wrong to think that bodily health is compatible with spiritual confusion or cultural disorder, or with polluted air and water or impoverished soil. (Berry, 1996, p. 103)

As we discussed earlier, the modernist discourse of mechanism assumes the world operates like a machine, that the whole can be broken down into parts in order to be fully understood and used most effectively. The discourse of rationalism holds the built-in assumption that the scientific process to study and objectively measure these reduced parts, is the best way to know or understand phenomena (Plumwood, 1993, 2002) and it is the purview of career scientists who will be paid to do that work for us. For instance, in the field of medicine, we use the study of anatomy and physiology to learn about the systems in the body. The body's processes—gastrointestinal, respiratory, musculoskeletal, and so on, are studied for their own specific functions, and each further divided and studied (by specialists) according to particular organ and system function. Disease or malfunction of any part assumed to be created or located within those specific systems or organs is treated separately, often with chemically based pharmaceuticals or with surgery. In contrast, a more holistic approach would include an analysis of how the other systems work in tandem to achieve homeostasis and then scaffolding on how the larger social and ecological systems affect the bodies of humans.

Conclusion: A New Model of Nursing Education

> There is a way of thinking that needs to be cultivated and, and beyond that a way of being that needs to be cultivated. So, you know … if nursing is to be something more than preparing technicians to do technical tasks, what is it? Well, could we begin to think of it as, as a discipline that calls for certain kinds of ways of thinking and ways of being? And, if, if the latter, then it requires nurses to answer the question, well who am I? What are my gifts? How do I come to understand what they are? And how can I use them in, in such a way uh for, for the betterment of patients and, and uh the whole health care system and potentially beyond that too? (interview, Nancy Johnston)

The narratives of the nurse educators/scholars help nurse educators become aware of how such hegemonic discourses and the assumptions created through these discourses have affected nursing as a practice, an identity, and a profession.

Ultimately, these educators/scholars support Berry's notion that "health is membership" (1995, p. 86). Health is a condition of our relationships with others; our bodies are made from cosmological dust, water, and other bodies. We are thus members within the community of life generating relationship, place, and belonging. These principles must become the focus of our care. When we see ourselves as members of a larger living community, we will take care of those relationships and feel responsible for their well-being. Humility grows as we realize our limitations within, and contributions to, the processes of living and dying. Just as soil regenerates through the living and dying of its botanical and animal members, our bodies die and return to the soil where we join with the bodies of other living entities and continue to contribute to the living world. To imagine ourselves superior to or outside this process is to disrupt the essential nature of these living systems, a serious epistemological error now causing a cascading series of social and ecological crises we can barely keep up with. Unique to their profession, the nurse scholars Kristi talked with understand that they too are complicit in these processes as members of industrial capitalism, and a profession that by and large continues to define itself as outside its material and discursive realities.

Together in these conversations, we began to imagine how educators and practitioners might work together to reform the problematic ontological and epistemological foundations in nursing education, even while staying tied to university educational systems. A shift in how we understand our responsibilities as nurse educators is critical. If nurse educators continue to view health as only human-based and located in individual body parts, they will continue to disconnect themselves from the natural world reducing any chance of healthy sustainability for human beings, let alone the natural world around them (Banks, 2014). Obviously, their primary or direct responsibility will be to their human patients, but understanding that we are all part of the Great Economy and its principles should shift how we approach our work together.

To shift our practice, nurse educators will need to be introduced to an analysis of the foundational cultural roots of the social and ecological problems impacting healthy communities, and to see that a shift in what it means to be a nurse is our ethical responsibility. Joining the arguments being made in this book, we thus call for a pedagogy of responsibility, as the basis for a new approach to nursing education. "The approach ... that we address here begins from a fundamental commitment to the recognition that we live together on this planet among all kinds of living creatures, human and non-human, in a fragile but essential interdependence" (Martusewicz & Edmundson, 2005, p. 71). In other words, when nurses become educated, they must first be made aware of the connection of human beings to the natural world via experiences that take them into their communities whether urban or rural, and by learning to critically identify and analyze the cultural roots of the problems they witness there. This requires that the three strands of an EcoJustice approach become the framework for nursing education, in addition to the necessary technical aspects of learning to care for their patients. As Goodman said in his interview,

> If it [the nursing curriculum] doesn't expose nurses to these global issues and allows an insular, first-world, privileged outlook … we have done them a disservice. If at the end of three years, they can, they can understand ECGs, they can … deal with chest drains, they can clean urinary catheters, they know the drugs inside out, they, they can spot deteriorating patients physiologically, they know all about vital signs, but if they're missing that sustainability, the human connectedness part of it, we have done them a disservice.

The following is a sketch of what three courses within a curriculum for undergraduate nursing education might look like. While we will not detail it here for reasons of space, it follows that as nurses continue on in the licensing and academic degree process, they will continue to study in deeper and more detailed ways how these cultural systems work and why recognizing their impacts is essential to a reformed definition of health and health care. We assume that the nurses who go on to study these concerns deeply will become the next generation of eco-ethically informed nurse educators.

Course #1: The History of Nursing – An Ecofeminist Approach

Taken in the first year of the nursing program, generally the sophomore year of a 4-year baccalaureate degree; offered as a 200-level course.

(I) Course Objectives. The course will:

1. explore women's early history as healers with holistic approaches;
2. examine the ways that modern nursing is shaped by dominant discourses that were born out of the Scientific Revolution;
3. trace current nursing language, actions, and behaviors as they are shaped and framed by the history of nursing;
4. examine the cultural foundations of the current definition of health as "the absence of disease" in nursing;
5. analyze how the idea of health as currently defined affects the professional definition of nursing as well as the personal identities of nurses as practitioners;
6. use these critical analyses to explore alternative definitions of health and nursing.

(II) Student Outcomes. Students will:

1. study their own history as holistic healers;
2. learn to define, identify, and trace modernist discourses within the history and professionalization of nursing;
3. write critical analytic essays that engage concepts learned from ecofeminist studies of the history of women and nursing;

Health as Holism   **149**

4.   work collaboratively to design alternative approaches to nursing that take into account the complex systems of life that human communities depend upon and affect.

(III)   Course Outline

1.   Tracing the discursive history of women's work as healers: Witches, midwives and nurses.
2.   Discourses of professionalization: The development of nursing as paid work.
3.   The development of nursing education: intersections in race, class and gender.
4.   Current definitions, identities and practices as created by standards organizations.

(IV)   Suggested Activities

1.   After reading various historical accounts of women's lives as healers and nurses, students write a guided critical analytic essay examining the assumptions and practices within specific eras of the development of the profession and why they are important to understanding the practice of nursing today.
2.   Students engage in critical discussions of the course readings in in-class and online discussions.

(V)   Suggested Texts

1.   D'Antonio, P. (2010). *American nursing: A history of knowledge, authority and the meaning of work.* Baltimore, MD: Johns Hopkins University Press.
2.   Ehrenreich, B., & English, D. (2010). *Witches, midwives and nurses: A history of women healers* (2nd edn). New York, NY: The Feminist Press.
3.   Goodman, B. (2015). Wendell Berry – Health is membership. *Nursing Education Today, 35*(10): 1011–1012.
4.   Griffin, S. (1980). *Woman and nature: The roaring inside her.* New York, NY: Harper and Row.
5.   Kalisch, P. A., & Kalish, B. J. (2004). *American nursing: A history* (4th edn). Philadelphia, PA: Lippincott, Williams & Wilkins.
6.   Kleffel, D. (1991). An ecofeminist analysis of nursing knowledge. *Nursing Forum, 26*(4): 5–18. doi:10.1111/j.1744–6198.1991. tb00890.x
7.   Powers, P. (2001). *The methodology of discourse analysis.* Sudbury, MA: NLN Press, Jones & Bartlett.
8.   Plumwood, V. (1997). *Feminism and the mastery of nature.* New York, NY: Routledge.

150 Health as Holism

9. Sandelowski, M. (2000). *Devices & desires: Gender, technology and American nursing.* Chapel Hill, NC: University of North Carolina Press.

Course #2: Health as Membership

Taken in the second year of the program, generally the junior year of a 4-year baccalaureate degree; offered as a 300-level course.

(I) Course Objectives. This course will:

1. introduce Berry's principle of the Great Economy (Berry, 2010) and the concept of membership as necessary to the condition of health and the responsibilities of nursing;
2. examine the ways conditions within the surrounding ecosystems affect the human condition;
3. explore the implications for health care offered by the idea of membership, as citizens and nurses;
4. examine diverse holistic approaches to health as alternatives to current conceptions and practices in modern industrial cultures.

(II) Student Outcomes. Students will:

1. define and identify examples of membership using Berry's definitions of the principles of the Great Economy;
2. identify and critique barriers to healthy forms of membership inclusive of a larger system of life;
3. compare/contrast assumptions and behaviors in health care that impact the health of both people and the larger living systems they depend upon;
4. examine problems within their local communities, analyze their root causes, and propose solutions relevant to their nursing practice;
5. work collaboratively with peers to study cross-cultural examples of holistic health care practices and present their findings orally to the professor and class.

(III) Course Outline

1. Introduction to "health as holism" and the principles of the Great Economy (Berry).
2. Introduction of the concept "place" and "place-based projects" to study local communities as relevant to health care practices.
3. Field work: Engagement within the community to identify and study problems relevant to health care professionals.
4. Study of cross-cultural examples of holistic approaches to health and nursing.

Health as Holism **151**

    5.   Implications for the reform of nursing and nursing education.

(IV) Suggested Activities

    1.   Students will engage in place-based projects to identify and analyze problems that have health related effects for people and other members in the larger ecological system.

    2.   Students will write critical essays that describe and analyze the cultural foundations of these problems, the economic and political context within which they are created, implications for health care professionals and community members, and ideas for their possible solutions.

    3.   Students will work in groups to study culturally diverse examples of holistic approaches to health and health care, to be presented orally to the class.

(V) Suggested Texts

    1.   Andrews, M. A., & Boyle, J. S. (2015). *Transcultural concepts in nursing care* (7th edn). Philadelphia, PA: Lippincott Williams & Wilkins.

    2.   Berry, W. (1995). Health is membership. In *Another turn of the crank*. Washington, DC: Counterpoint.

    3.   Berry, W. (1996). The body and the earth. In *The unsettling of America*. Berkeley, CA: Counterpoint.

    4.   Berry, W. (2010). Two economies. In *What matters*. Berkeley, CA: Counterpoint.

    5.   Gruenewald, D., & Smith, G. (2008). *Place-based education in the global age: Local diversity*. New York, NY: Routledge.

    6.   McFarland, M. R., & Wehbe-Alamah, H. (2018). *Leininger's transcultural nursing*. New York, NY: McGraw Hill.

Course #3: A Critical Discourse Analysis of Nursing

Taken in the third year of nursing program, or senior year; offered as a 400-level course.

(I) Course Objectives. This course will:

    1.   introduce the theory and methodology of critical discourse analysis as important to the study and reform of nursing;

    2.   introduce the basic methods for performing critical discourse analysis using basic texts and policy documents guiding nursing;

    3.   expose the imbedded value hierarchies and discursive structures by which nursing as a profession is defined, contained, and managed within the organization and institutions of medicine;

152 Health as Holism

4.   identify discourses of care and mutuality that are also at work within the practice of nursing and that offer connections to more holistic approaches to nursing.

(II)   Student Outcomes. Students will:

1.   identify the key theoretical and epistemological foundations within the methodology of critical discourse analysis;
2.   examine the effects of key discourses of modernity on the practice of health care formally and informally;
3.   apply basic methods of discourse analysis to the texts and policy documents defining modern nursing;
4.   consider how their own identities as nurses have been shaped within the discursive processes shaping institutionalized healthcare;
5.   identify alternative discourses in the day-to-day practices and assumptions of nurses that disrupt damaging effects of modernist approaches to nursing.

(III)   Course Outline

1.   Introduction to the theory and methodology of Critical Discourse Analysis (CDA).
2.   Introduction to key modernist discourses and their cultural and ecological effects.
3.   Introduction to the method of Critical Discourse Analysis.
4.   Language, thought, culture, identity: "Becoming nurses".
5.   Identifying an Ethics of Care in the daily practices and discourses of nurses.

(IV)   Suggested Activities

1.   Engage students in an examination and CDA of current policy documents and/or texts that define the primary responsibilities, roles, and standardized practices of professional nursing.
2.   Group project: Students work as teams to interview select nurses about their assumptions, definitions, concerns and day-to-day work as nurses. Students apply CDA to analyze the often-contradictory discourses at work in nurses' understandings and experiences of nursing.

(V)   Suggested Texts

1.   Martusewicz, R. A., Edmundson, J., & Lupinacci, J. (2015). *EcoJustice education: Toward diverse, democratic, and sustainable communities* (2nd edn, especially Chapter 3). New York, NY: Routledge.
2.   Powers, P. (2001). *The methodology of discourse analysis.* Sudbury, MA: NLN Press, Jones & Barlett.

3.   Wodak, R., & Meyer, M. (2016). *Methods of critical discourse studies* (3rd edn). London, UK: Sage.

References

Banks, J. (2014). "And that's going to help black women how?" Storytelling and striving to stay true to the tasks of liberation in the academy. In P. Kagan, M. Smith & P. Chinn (Eds.), *Philosophies and practices of emancipatory nursing: Social justice as praxis* (pp. 188–204). New York, NY: Routledge.

Berry, W. (1990a). Healing. In *What are people for?* Berkeley, CA: Counterpoint.

Berry, W. (1990b). *What are people for?* Berkeley: CA: Counterpoint.

Berry, W. (1992). *Fidelity: Five stories.* New York, NY: Pantheon Books.

Berry, W. (1995). *Another turn of the crank.* Washington, DC: Counterpoint.

Berry, W. (1996). *The unsettling of America.* Berkeley, CA: Counterpoint.

Berry, W. (2002). *The art of the commonplace: The agrarian essays of Wendell Berry.* Berkeley, CA: Counterpoint Press.

Berry, W. (2010). *What matters.* Berkeley, CA: Counterpoint.

Clarke, P. N., & Butterfield, P. (2011). Nursing as if the future matters. *Nursing Science Quarterly, 24*(2): 126–129. doi:10.1177/0894318411399469

Martusewicz, R. A. (2001). *Seeking passage: Post-structuralism, pedagogy, ethics.* New York, NY: Teachers College Press.

Martusewicz, R. A. (2013). Toward an anti-centric ecological culture: Bringing a critical ecofeminist analysis to ecojustice education. In A. Kulnieks, K. Young & D. Longboat (Eds.), *Contemporary studies in environmental and Indigenous pedagogies: A curricula of stories and place.* Rotterdam, Netherlands: Sense Publishers.

Martusewicz, R. A., & Edmundson, J. (2005). Social foundations as pedagogies of responsibility and ecoethical commitment. In D. W. Butin (Ed.), *Teaching social foundations of education: Context, theories, and issues* (pp. 71–91). Mahwah, NJ: Lawrence Erlbaum Associates.

Martusewicz, R. A., Edmundson, J., & Lupinacci, J. (2015) *EcoJustice education: Toward diverse, democratic, and sustainable communities* (2nd edn, especially Chapter 3). New York, NY: Routledge.

Plumwood, V. (1993). *Feminism and the mastery of nature.* New York, NY: Routledge.

Plumwood, V. (2002). *Environmental culture: The ecological crisis of reason.* New York, NY: Routledge.

8

RE-MEMBERING "THE ROOM OF LOVE"

My mind, I think, has started to become, it is close to being, the room of love where the absent are present, the dead are alive, time is eternal, and all the creatures prosperous. The room of love is the love that holds us all, and it is not ours. It goes back before we were born. It goes all the way back. (Berry, 2004, p. 158)

Hannah Coulter, is a novel by Berry (2004) written as a memoir by an old woman looking back over her life as it was lived in "membership" with her husband, children, neighbors and the land they farmed and cared for. More, it is Berry's offering of imagination for what this world could be, what it means to have mutual affection, sensuality, and generosity—love at the center of creativity, security, and community. As expressed in the quote above, Berry uses this novel to explore love as it "holds us all," including the non-human creatures we are in membership with as part of life itself.

In this chapter, I return to an exploration of the creative relational force of love, that eternal connective "something" that is no *thing,* making life possible. In particular, I am interested in the idea of membership and belonging as these maintain love across generations and across creation: "the room of love" as Hannah Coulter says. I see this intergenerational love as embodied and spiritual, that is, as a connective, intimate, and therefore erotic experience, essential to creating what we need for well-being among humans but also beyond us to the larger living world. And, I am interested in the role of education as an ethical endeavor engaged across generations, as a process of becoming responsible for one another, necessary to healthy communities.

This is a story that begins with my mother. Weaving my life with her through Hannah's reflection, I remember her as my first teacher. All relationships hold the possibility for love, but the principles guiding what we *do* in those relationships is what matters for protecting life and flourishing communities. I learned this first from my mother. As we have been exploring throughout this book, this is Berry's ongoing lesson—his insistence that we recognize the essential components of love—generosity, kindness, humility, gratitude, mutual responsibility, and joy—in maintaining healthy life affirming community, and that we learn to expose those cultural, political and economic forces that come to undermine the connective tissue of love that keeps communities healthy and whole.

What does membership mean when we think of love as embodied in work with and for the land and each other? What did my mother teach me about this without ever explicitly saying so, and what is it about our ideological, economic and political systems that breaks apart the belonging that creates membership and stability? I will analyze these connections by looking both at Berry's novel and my own childhood homeland. And, in a direct challenge to the undermining and too often violent effects of modern schooling, I will argue for a way of thinking about education as those relationships that help to develop the eco-ethical consciousness necessary to ensure that we *live on* as careful and protective members of larger communities of living creatures, not as a matter of certainty but as a matter of responsibility, imagination, and love. Love, as we have been discussing throughout this book, is the essential ingredient in, and outcome of, any pedagogy of responsibility.

My First Teacher

As I indicated in the Preface, reading Berry's work, especially his fiction, always brings me face to face, heart to heart with my childhood, the landscape and relationships that filled my life until about age 17, and most especially to lessons given me by my mother. I have been thinking about this for more than 20 years, writing about my mother's influence here and there, recognizing the power of her wisdom and spirit in my life choices and efforts to develop what we could mean by a pedagogy of responsibility strong enough to turn the tide of destruction that we are currently facing (Martusewicz, 2001; Martusewicz & Edmundson, 2005; Edmundson & Martusewicz, 2013).

Then, a few years ago, I spent a final five days with her, learning a whole new set of lessons, final gifts to me as she lay dying. Calling back to her sister and other childhood playmates in the night, she brought generations of elders into the room who mingled with us in memories and intimacy, reminding me that I was born of that community, in communion with those now long-dead members. By calling them to her, literally asking them for their help as she was passing, my mother made real my elders' place in "the room of love," this long line of care and affection, grief and loss, lessons within patterns of membership that had made her life in this place full, and thus the particular contours of my life possible too.

As we moved from these night-time reveries into the daily tasks of care and comfort, I found myself redolent with tenderness and gratitude, even pleasure. A calmness came over me even in the knowledge that I would soon lose her. More than once we nearly collapsed in peels of laughter at the awkward "bear-hug" dance of intimacy required to move her from bed, to chair, to table. We talked about her childhood and mine, of the changes she has seen, and her faith in what she understood to be the real progress made in our country's history. I listened, keeping my own doubts to myself, offering her my thanks for all she had given us over the years.

It is with this memory, this remembering of deeply shared gratitude and affection with my mother that I come to Wendell Berry's *Hannah Coulter* (2004). Writing at the end of her life, Hannah offers to teach us about "the room of love," about the complex intergenerational connections passed on through stories and specific virtue lessons that create membership and the possibility of ethics at the heart of living communities. She is sad at what she witnesses as the dying off of the most important aspects of her place, the land and community. Thus, I read her as I think back on my relationships to my own mother, our life in a small dairy community, as a source of essential knowledge about what a pedagogy of responsibility really requires of us.

Hannah Coulter

As a young woman, Hannah leaves home to begin her life as part of the Port William "membership," a tight-knit group of farmers, business people, and their families; men, women, and children who work together to care for each other and the land that sustains them. In so doing they learn and they teach, each generation offering the next what it means to "live right." Thinking back to her introduction to this community in her early work as a clerk in a local law office where she witnessed the comings and goings of farmers in need of advice, she says: "They were men with long memories who loved farming and whose lives had been given to ideals: good land, good grass, good animals, good crops, good work" (2004, p. 23). And so, with Hannah, we are introduced to the town's characters (and character). The novel opens during the 1940s; it's wartime. Early in the story, we are taken through a whirlwind of love and loss as she meets, falls for, and marries Virgil Feltner who must go off to the battlefields of Europe. Soon he is missing in action, and the overwhelming grief that befalls Hannah and the Feltner family is pierced only by the intense intimacy and support and care they have for one another, and that this community offers them even as others experience similar loss. Berry's prose takes us deeply into the crevices of the heart; he lets us immerse ourselves in the warmth and tragedy that is life in the Feltner household and Port William community. Then, juxtaposed against the horrors of war, greed, and industrialized destruction, Berry shows us the cycles of death, life, and love, created within the connections among land, creatures, community, and place. He introduces us to what it means to belong to a place, the connection and intimacy and care required. Nathan Coulter comes home from the war, and

Re-membering "the Room of Love"   157

eventually through subtle yet seriously intentional courtship, becomes the love and partner of Hannah's life. And, through her telling, we learn about this period just after World War II as one that forever changed the shape and experience of farming in this country.

> He came home to these ridges and hillsides and bottomlands and woods and streams that he had known ever since he was born. And this place, more than all the places he had seen in his absence was what he wanted. It was what he had learned to want in the midst of killing and dying, terror, cruelty, hate, hunger, thirst, blood and fire. Nathan clearly wasn't trying to "make it big" in the postwar world. ... He was where he wanted to be. As I too was by then, he was a member of Port William. Members of Port William aren't trying to *get someplace*. They think they *are someplace*. (2004, p. 67, emphasis in original)

And so this story winds itself around all of the relationships, the bonds, the tragedies, and the wisdom of those who have shared this place as a means of living. And as Hannah, now old and a widow, reflects on her life, she re-members it, bringing back to life in stories all who created the richness that has formed her life, her children's lives, and the lives of those who came before. She brings to life the membership, calls forth the living and the dead to recall the necessary and full intimacy, care and tenderness that was made in the creation of their lives together on that land.

> Watching him and watching myself in my memory now, I know again what I knew before but now I know more than that. Now I know what we were trying to stand for: the possibility that among the world's wars and sufferings two people could love each other for a long time, until death and beyond, and could make a place for each other that would be a part of their love, as their love would be a way of loving their place. This love would be one of the acts of the greater love that holds and cherishes all the world. (2004, pp. 67–68)

When my mother was dying, I became very aware of our lives—hers and mine together—as part of a longer line of people who had been born and learned to be who we are on that North Country land, though too many of us now live elsewhere. As I sat with her I remembered what I inherited from and through her, our connection to this countryside in all its ecological and social complexity, our love of it all even as we watched it change. I am the granddaughter of a small dairy farmer who spent 70 plus years on the same piece of land, raising champion Percheron horses that helped to clear and plow the land early on, and raising Holsteins that provided milk to the region, including our household. We lived just over a mile from where my mother grew up; my siblings and I were raised in

158 Re-membering "the Room of Love"

the fields, streams, and back roads that connected our house to the farm. My family did not have a lot of money, but I lived a charmed childhood so I seldom really thought about that, especially as a young child. I rode horseback from the time I was three or four, played in the woods and fields around our house all year round, and made relationships with all sorts of animals and people, old and young. Of course I didn't understand this then, but I was given a powerful education in what it means to be responsible to a community where the members included were human and more than human. My mother saw to that!

In those last days with her, what was so strong for me was this sudden recognition of our relationship as one small part of a much larger love that was somehow in peril now in our community. We were bound by a storied, erotic connection, rich and sensual with intimacy and care, and full with the memories of time spent together, often in the company of a horse or two: Flashes of sitting on the back of our pinto pony as she taught me to sit properly, hold the reins correctly, communicate to the pony with my legs; the time a young filly took off down a lane in a cornfield with me bareback and barely hanging on, my mother and sister (or perhaps my older brother?) barely able to contain the laughter at the sight. And then too of learning to work to care for the horses, or being present when hay from my grandfather's farm was delivered. I felt those memories, the humor and the tenderness of those moments shared with her deep in my chest, and catching in my throat.

This is what Berry is getting at as well in *Hannah Coulter*: an essential embodied love that holds us but is also bigger than us, generated in the spaces between us, and necessary to life itself. Here, I offer a definition of eros by ecofeminist essayist Terry Tempest Williams: "It means," she tells us, "'in relation.' Erotic is what those deep relations are and can be that engage the whole body—our heart, our mind, our spirit, our flesh. It is that moment of being exquisitely present" (Williams, 2002, p. 311). Present in all sorts of meetings between humans, among humans and other creatures, among creatures themselves, eros is an effect of the connective force created within relationships between everything, dancing along our skin, and down our spines reminding us (if we are willing to notice) that we are alive in inter-being. As I wrote elsewhere, "I am most interested in those embodied experiences that draw us closer, that create connection and pleasure, happiness and well-being, and thus could move us to protect each other and the living systems we depend upon" (Martusewicz, 2005, p. 334). Thinking back and writing this now, I realize that I learned this first from my mother. To hold that memory dear and offer it now is essential.

Our Membership

In the stories my mother shared with me about her life on the farm as a child and later with my father, I came to know who I am, what my commitments should be, and how I would dedicate my life. I tried to thank her during those final moments spent with her, but she would not have it. Still, I recognize that my being is completely tied to that place, to *her* growing up, and to my grandfather and grandmother's love for each other and the farm and their children too.

My grandfather established a farm in the St. Lawrence River valley near Canton, NY. He was encouraged by his mother to leave the family homestead near the Racquette River, because she knew it was losing productivity as the soil, too sandy to support a farm for long, was wearing out. My grandmother Jessie died young, when my mother was just a toddler. Before she married and became a farmer's wife, she was a teacher, my grandfather her student. They fell in love as he courted her from his newly established farm in the second decade of the 1900s. And then, married, they worked together to raise a family of five children and create the farm, raising Holsteins, chickens, horses, and dogs. Jessie died in the spring of 1932 of breast cancer. My grandfather never recovered from the heartbreak of that loss, refusing to talk about her when I would plead to know who she was. All I knew was that she was a teacher, originally from Chicago, sent to live with an aunt in Northern NY in the first decade of the twentieth century. Grandpa loved her like none other, substituting hired women to help raise the children whom Jessie begged him to keep together after her death.

My mother grew up, as she tells it, raised by the horses. Early photos show Mom snuggled up to a German Shepherd named Betty, and given that our house was never without at least one dog, I assume that we could add dogs to those who nannied her. When I asked about her life on the farm, she and my Aunt Mary always responded, "We worked!" They cared for the chickens and gardens, and doing whatever other barn work needed doing. It wasn't all sweetness and light! My mother would say with a shudder, "Oh, I hated taking care of those chickens, and then having to pluck them after they were butchered!" She told me more than once that she knew as a child she would not be a farmer's wife. But she also had plenty of time to herself, usually spent on the back of a horse.

My mother grew up knowing all the backroads as she roamed them on her pony Billy. My father used to say, "Your mother knows these roads like the back of her hand." She was a creature of the North Country, and the love she had for this place and its people even as a motherless child with a heartbroken father, created who she became as a woman, and who I have become too. As I grew up, she taught me what she understood to be the basic knowledge of good land stewardship: crop rotation, manure-fed fields, well-cared for animals, the cycles of planting and harvest. I did not grow up on a farm, but as we lived close by, she was always observing what was happening on the land she knew so well, and would talk about her observations as we visited or passed by in our car: "Ah, look, Uncle Key (her brother) is growing corn in the lower field this year; that field over there is being rested, they'll plant it with some good legume and till it in to feed the soil." The corn grown was used to feed the cows, along with hay grown in another field and baled in summer, some of which got trucked to our little barn to feed our horses. My mother brought that knowledge to our home

160 Re-membering "the Room of Love"

gardens and to the care of our animals, and we lived by much of it, eating what she grew and canned, and learning these home-making skills alongside her as we did chores necessary to the maintenance of our household.

I was taught to work hard, use "elbow grease" and not to leave a job poorly completed. That was the way, the *only* way to be. Work hard, save, create beauty, and care for that for which you are responsible. Be honest, respect your elders, and be a good neighbor. I didn't know it then, but I was learning the basic elements of our particular commons, both the environmental commons (the lay of the land, streams, forest, and creatures we shared this place with) and the cultural commons (the meaning system, principles, and informal rules and relationships of mutual respect and caretaking). As I roamed the same fields, forests, and back roads, and rode my horse along trails or into a nearby stream, I also learned basic values of care and mutuality. Not that I didn't make mistakes along the way, with friends or in my interaction with the animals that we kept. I was always corrected in one way or another and as such, I was being taught to be a good member of this place.

My brothers learned too, albeit via different tasks. They were "invited" to help my uncle and cousins with haying in the summer, for example, a job that as a girl I was never asked to learn. Instead, I learned to fix fence lines, muck out stalls, weed the garden, and "put up" or can in jars what we harvested, all this requiring particular skills instructed and supervised by my mother. I learned to use my body and I became strong although I didn't think about that then. I also developed patience, a certain amount of physical coordination, and the satisfaction that comes by hard work done well, the knowledge that things were clean and put in a certain orderliness. As Berry would put it, I was learning to "live right," respect my parents, and other elders, contribute to the household, and care about the well-being of other creatures. I can't say I was always happy to be doing it; I'm sure I grumbled about a lot of it as many of my friends were off riding bikes, going swimming, or playing games. But as I look back now, I am stunned by the primary lessons that I was given, the knowledge of generations of farmers handed down to my siblings and me as part of our growing up, as part of our belonging. And, I am stunned at what we are losing as communities like mine die.

This is what Hannah Coulter invites us to understand too, as she walks the pathways between her farm and her neighbors' farm, into the hollows, through the meadows remembering her life, and the reciprocities, the learning and responsibilities that made it possible:

> By our work we kept and improved our place, and in return for our work the place gave us back our life. The children knew this. For a long time that was the knowledge they most belonged to. (Berry, 2004, p. 89)
>
> We were four men then, and two women. But in addition to ourselves, a whole company of other people at different times in different combinations

might be at work on our place, or we might be at work on theirs. ... This was our membership. Burley called it that. He loved to call it that. (p. 93)

... he would preach the membership ... "Oh yes, brothers and sisters, we are members one of another. The difference, beloved, ain't in who is and who's not, but in who knows it and who don't. Oh, my friends, there ain't no nonmembers, living nor dead nor yet to come. Do you know it? Or do you don't? A man is a member of a woman and a worm. A woman is a member of a man and a mole. Oh beloved, it's all one piece of work." (p. 97)

It is in membership that we experience and create the power of love, that sensual, connective spirit of humans in mutual relationship with other creatures, the land, and each other. This love is erotic as well as convivial and neighborly: Body, mind and spirit meet and interact with other bodies, minds and spirits in an ongoing process of generating life, and as bodies connect—wind on skin, rain on the land, seed to bird—these meetings create the possibility of meaning and of life. The world touches us sensually, and meaning is made in that connection, not as a universal truth, but as an invitation to reverence and devotion to creation as a unity.

To think of eros in limited terms of sexual exchange is to miss its power, even though we may experience it there most directly. For eros circulates in membership too, in the exchange of sweat and labor and sustenance. It is created in careful connection with others, rippling with laughter or the simple pleasure of sun on the back of one's neck. It is felt in one's arms and back after a long day of work that results in providing sustenance or simply completing a household task that needs doing. This is where relationships among different members, human and more than human, if tended in ethical respect, create joy, wisdom, and the possibility of life. And such care, Berry insists, requires imagination, self-restraint, and fidelity: "It is by imagination, that we cross over the differences between ourselves and other beings and thus learn compassion, forbearance, mercy, forgiveness, sympathy, and love—the virtues without which neither we nor the world can live" (Berry, 1992, p. 143).

Dismembering the Small Farm Community

In 1900, shortly before my grandparents were establishing their farm, around 41 percent of the US labor force worked on small diversified farms. By 1945, when my parents were in high school, that number had dropped to 16 percent, by 1970 when I was growing up, it was at 4 percent, and by the turn of the twenty-first century, only 1.9 percent of our country's labor force worked on farms (Berry, 1996). In grief for what these changes have meant for her community, Hannah reflects that it seems that everyone wants "to get someplace better."

162 Re-membering "the Room of Love"

> Suppose the stories you tell [your children] allow them to believe, when they hear it from other people, that farming people are inferior and need to improve themselves by leaving the farm. Doesn't that finally unmake everything that has been made? (Berry, 2004, p. 114)

My mother once told me of her great relief to have my father "rescue" her from the farm, identifying life there as "backward," in comparison to her "town" friends' lives. Her move began when she went off to college, an "adventure" that was cut short when my father proposed to her, and my grandfather refused to pay her tuition, adamant that if she was going to marry, her husband should take on that responsibility. Her relief at the opportunity to marry my father, and exclamation to me that this was an important move for her came from her experience of, and self-identification within, the class stratification in my hometown between farm families and "town" families: the merchants and professors, and other professionals that made up our small rural college town.

This stratification was part of the growing demise of small farms in the politics of agriculture in post World War II America, which interestingly she taught me about too, albeit without connecting her own feelings or experience to any substantive knowledge of the history of agricultural policy. As Michael Pollan (2006) points out, good agricultural policy takes account of the fact that there will be years when the weather is good and productivity creates an over-supply of food for communities, and bad weather years when there is too little. During the good weather years, too much food makes prices fall condemning farmers who can't sell their crops to lean years and even bankruptcy. This situation is an age-old reality for farmers. As Pollan tells it

> ... going back to the Old Testament, communities have devised various strategies to even out the destructive swings of agricultural production. The Bible's recommended farm policy was to establish a grain reserve. Not only did this ensure that when drought or pestilence ruined a harvest there'll still be food to eat, but it kept farmers whole by taking food off the market when the harvest was bountiful. (2006, p. 49)

By the Great Depression when farmers saw the bottom drop out of the market, there was no such safety net in place. The nation's grain farmers were destroyed. And while in the Northeast there had been cooperatives and other means by which dairy farmers supported each other, they too were hit hard. By 1932, just when my grandmother Jessie lay dying, milk prices dropped to half of what they had been before the crash. It is no wonder she begged my grandfather to keep the family together, knowing the pressures they were under just to survive.

Under the New Deal, farm programs were created to protect farmers and the nation's source of food from such disaster. Based on ancient commons-based principles put in place to protect the community, the government set up price support programs. For the mid-western grain producers, this came in the forms of the "Ever-Normal Granary." For New England and Northern NY dairy producers, the Agricultural Adjustment Act of 1933 offered federal price supports—subsidies for farmers suffering from radical price drops. Such a stabilizing system was about caring for the farmers and their families, as well as insuring stable agricultural production and food for communities across the nation.

However, by the end of World War II, as we discuss in Chapter 2, the introduction of an efficiency discourse was altering the agricultural landscape. Machinery and chemical inputs began to be seen as the modern way to farm. Farmers were encouraged to go into debt to support this new approach.

> Beginning in the 1950s a campaign to dismantle the New Deal farm programs took root. ... Almost from the start, the policy of supporting prices and limiting production had collected powerful enemies: exponents of laissez-faire economics, who didn't see why farming should be treated differently than any other economic sector; food processors and grain exporters, who profited from overproduction and low crop prices; and a collection of political and business leaders who for various reasons thought America had far too many farmers for her (or at least their) own good. (Pollan, 2006, p. 50)

And by the 1970s the policies that had helped protect price fluctuations began to shift. Neoliberal ideologies created policies put in place to initiate a global industrial agricultural system that would increase exports, and radically shift the price of food, while lining the pockets of corporations, banks, mortgage companies, and others, but not farmers. Earl Butz, Nixon's second Secretary of Agriculture supported a "Get Big or Get Out" program that encouraged small farmers to sell out, and move off the land. Part of a burgeoning global market system, federal agriculture policy under Butz dismantled New Deal farm policy, encouraged farmers to put into production as much land as they could (including land that had previously been thought to be marginal), ignore traditional practices of crop rotation and animal husbandry, and grow for the market to "feed the world." In order to accomplish this, a financial system was set up between banks, seed, fertilizer and machinery companies, grain processors, and the transportation sector that forced more and more people off the land while increasing the size of individual farms, and brought increased debt for those farmers as they were forced to borrow more and more money to support modernization. While food prices dropped precipitously via this process, the land, the people and the communities paid a dear and ultimately impossible price.

> Secretary Butz could say with approval in 1974, "only 4 percent of all US farms ... produced almost 50 percent of all farm goods," without acknowledging the human—and indeed, the agricultural penalties. What these men

164 Re-membering "the Room of Love"

> were praising—what such men have been praising for so long that the praise can be uttered without thought—is a disaster that is both agricultural and cultural ... That one American farmer can now feed himself and fifty-six other people may be, within the narrow view of the specialist, a triumph of technology; by no stretch of reason can it be considered a triumph of agriculture or culture. It has been made possible by the substitution of energy for knowledge, of methodology for care, of technology for morality. This "accomplishment" is not primarily the work of farmers—who have been by and large its victims, but of a collaboration of corporations, university specialists, and government agencies. (Berry, 1996, p. 33)

In my home town, the economic crisis brought on by this process grew over a couple decades. In the early to mid-1970s, I remember seeing odd metal corporate-looking signs in my uncle's fields of corn and asking what they meant. Turns out they were from seed and fertilizer companies who required the farmers who purchased their products to post their corporate logos prominently by the roadside. Soon I noticed a difference in the patterns of growth in those fields now planted right up to the ditches, with the corn packed in very tight rows. Crop rotation stopped sometime in the 1980s I think, and by the late 1990s, the cows no longer went out into the fields.

The herd stayed about the same size, but the process by which they lived was now mechanized, making the work of farming more efficient to increase production. My cousin, who had taken over the farm from my uncle before him, proudly showed me the new technology where the cows, standing on concrete floors all day, were moved by electronic shocks from the barn and into machines that extracted the milk automatically. I left the farm that day quite horrified, unable to get the sight of the cows out of my mind. I'm not blaming my cousin; there were intense economic and ideological pressures at play, and very few small farms left in the North Country at that point. By the second decade of the new century in fact the farm was sold and is now used exclusively for crops: corn and soybeans primarily. And now, I can't get the plight of that land out of my mind. I cringe each time I return there and drive by the farm, waiting to see if the woods have been taken to make more room for crops. At the same time, in town, the once-active businesses—grocery stores, clothing stores, barber shops, hardware stores—have almost all disappeared. In spite of the fact that there remain two universities in the town of 5000 people, the village is dying. Big box stores, and "dollar stores" with cheap goods from China have replaced a once-thriving local economy.

These changes were, and are part of, what Berry refers to as the ongoing "unsettling" of America that is at the heart of extractive capitalism and the demise of communities all across the world. While post-colonial theorists correctly analyze the historical and ongoing implications of this process for Indigenous people and land across the world, Berry connects the plight of small farmers and rural

Re-membering "the Room of Love"   165

communities to the same logic. My mother was well aware of increasing debt as farmers bought bigger and bigger machinery. She bemoaned falling milk prices as big factory dairy operations began to undercut small farmers, but she also saw this process as part of "progress," and the inevitability of technological "advancement." Berry and others have traced the demise of small farms and along with it the decline of rural communities to this increased mechanization and specialization, as farms became less and less about feeding families as part of local economies, and more and more about big business.

In Berry's novel, Hannah Coulter too is witness to the destructive results of these changes. Her friends invite her out for a drive but she declines, with this reflection:

> There was a time when Nathan and I would enjoy going for a little drive just in the neighborhood, maybe late in the evening of a hot day, to cool off and see how everybody's crops were doing. Every farm then was farmed by people we knew. But now too many of the old families have died out or gone. Farms have been divided or gathered into bigger farms, or they have been bought by people in the cities who need a place to "get away," and who visit them for a while and then lose interest and sell them again. Such things I would just as soon not see. (2004, p. 174)

And a bit further on in the story, after a visit from a young real estate developer, she takes another walk across her farm, considering it's familiarity, and worrying about the changes she is seeing around her:

> It was as familiar as my old headscarf and coat and shoes, as my body, I have lived from it all these years. ... But I have seen it change. It has changed and it is changing, and it is threatened. The old thrift that once kept us alive has been replaced by extravagance and waste. People are living as if they think they are in a movie. They are all looking toward "a better place" and what they see is no thicker than a screen. ... Port William is becoming a sort of whatnot shelf where, until they can find "a better place" people live and move and have their being. (p. 179)

She sees the membership dwindling as children decide not to continue on the farm and she comes to realize that even her own desires for her children—that they become educated adults—would contribute to the undoing of her community. Hannah reminisces about how her desire with Nathan to give their children a college education seemed natural, how they did it out of love, never anticipating that eventually it would mean that each of their four children would leave and not return. Berry's writing is poignant as Hannah shares the dawning realization that there would be no one to continue to nurture the membership, to maintain the farm, and their caretaking relationship with the fields, woods, and streams.

166 Re-membering "the Room of Love"

My parents did not choose to move away from the town; they were too connected there in too many ways, but they encouraged me and I did leave. Just as my mother identified her life on the farm as stultifying, I remember thinking how I could not wait to leave that small town to see the world, to "make something of myself" by getting a college education. For me, through my parents, there was never a thought of my not going to college. It was expected and inevitable. One generation off the farm, I could never have imagined myself making a life there, a fact of my life that now fills me with regret even as the area is wracked with economic hardship.

Berry uses this novel to present us with a rare critique of the ways that "education" (or actually schooling in both primary/secondary institutions and institutions of higher education) teaches us to participate in the reproduction of ideologies of individualism, technological progress, commodification and careerism, pulling us away from the important give and take necessary to community, especially farming communities, by convincing us that success is about moving out and "up." For Berry, such an "education" is at the heart of the destruction of the small farming communities that once fed this nation, and with them the land they tended. The children of farmers who leave home disconnect from the wisdom of generations in their families who were intimately knowledgeable about the land—at least some were—and the many species of plants and creatures that it supports. We disconnected from the stories passed down about neighbors, and work, and joy and grief, how these all interact to create a particular living system and livelihoods. The stories and the wisdom in them is lost for good. Responsibility to the land and the community it supports is lost as we are taught that a successful future means employment elsewhere with salaries that support what we "need" for the "good life": mortgages, car loans, vacations, and eventually "retirement" (Berry, 1990).

Now an old woman, Hannah cannot bear to see the farmsteads and land in decline or destroyed by developers taking advantage of a transformed agricultural policy marching across the land. Instead, she walks the hollows and woodlands of her farm, dreaming of those who came before, and grateful for those who continue in the membership caring for their acreage and all that it supports, and caring for her.

Pedagogies of Responsibility

What kind of education do we need to revitalize our sense of responsibility to one another and to the earth that supports us? As we name the damage done to communities by a modernist culture and industrialized system seeking profit over life, we recognize our own capture within it. To change the way one sees the world, the way one thinks, is to change the self, and to open oneself to membership in the erotics of place as the beginning of an ethical way of being, and as the beginning of education. How do we help our students and our neighbors expose the harms of a cultural system now so deeply embedded in our psyches as to seem biologically given and thus inevitable? If we interrupt the taken for granted hierarchies that structure this system, "if humans are no longer seen as above nature, one's relationship with the earth, other life forms, ecological processes, and especially with one's own body and mind radically changes" (Griffin, 1995, p. 39).

How do we open the doors to the room of love, and open ourselves to the lively play of erotic meetings among the infinite generative elements offered us by this fantastic and generous planet? Susan Griffin comments:

> An early, still fragile meeting in consciousness between the care for nature and a care for human society offers a glimpse of a possibility redolent with promise. If human consciousness can be rejoined not only with the human body but with the body of earth, what seems incipient in the reunion is the recovery of meaning within existence that will infuse every kind of meeting between self and the universe, even in the most daily acts, with an eros, a palpable love, that is also sacred. (Griffin, 1995, p. 9)

It is precisely upon this sense of the sacred that the work of Berry opens, inviting us into imagination that "thrives on contact," connections and meetings with the more than human world. These are pedagogical meetings too; becoming "educational" only as we bring forward an ethical imperative to discern, to question and challenge that which destroys life (Martusewicz, 2001). This is what it means to educate for eco-ethical consciousness: to connect in trust, generosity, and love. I think of my mother again, in the words of Hannah Coulter: "When you have gone too far … the only mending is to come home" (Berry, 2004, p. 184).

References

Berry, W. (1990). *What are people for?* Berkeley, CA: Counterpoint.

Berry, W. (1992). *Sex, economy, freedom and community.* New York, NY: Pantheon Books.

Berry, W. (1996). *The unsettling of America: Essays on culture and agriculture.* San Francisco, CA: Sierra Club.

Berry, W. (2004). *Hannah Coulter.* Washington, DC: Shoemaker and Hoard.

Edmundson, J., & Martusewicz, R. (2013). "Putting our lives in order": Wendell Berry, ecoJustice, and a pedagogy of responsibility. In A. Kulnieks, K. Young & D. Longboat (Eds.), *Contemporary studies in environmental and indigenous pedagogies: A curricula of stories and place* (pp. 171–184). Rotterdam, Netherlands: Sense Publishers.

Griffin, S. (1995). *The eros of everyday life: Essays on ecology, gender and society.* New York, NY: Doubleday.

Martusewicz, R. A. (2001). *Seeking passage: Post-structuralism, pedagogy, ethics.* New York, NY: Teachers College Press.

Martusewicz, R. A. (2005). Eros in the commons: Educating for eco-ethical consciousness in a poetics of place. *Ethics, Place & Environment: A Journal of Philosophy and Geography,* 8: 331–348.

Martusewicz, R. A., & Edmundson, J. (2005). Social foundations as pedagogies of responsibility and eco-ethical commitment. In D. Butin (Ed.), *Teaching context: A primer for the social foundations of education classroom* (pp. 71–92). Mahwah, NJ: Lawrence Erlbaum Publishers, Inc.

Pollan, M. (2006). *The omnivore's dilemma: A natural history of four meals.* New York, NY: Penguin Books.

Williams, T. T. (2002). Interview with Derrick Jensen. In D. Jensen, *Listening to the land: Conservations about nature, culture and eros* (pp. 310–326). White River Junction: Chelsea Green Publishers.

9

WHAT IS EDUCATION FOR?

The teachers are everywhere. What is wanted is a learner.
In ignorance is hope. If we had known the difficulty, we would not have learned even so little.
Rely on ignorance. It is ignorance the teachers will come to.
They are waiting, as they always have, beyond the edge of the light.

(Wendell Berry, 1990, p. 12)

What is education for? I present all of my students with this question, and almost all of them find themselves in a conundrum as they try to answer. I am not asking them to tell me what education (or schooling) *is*. I am not asking them to describe curriculum, or how a good or effective school should be organized. I am asking them to describe as fully as they can what our work as educators should be aimed at, what are we aiming to create and why? Indeed, as they struggle, I finally have to tell them that what I'm really asking for are the primary values and principles that they hold dear. What sorts of communities should those values create? Who are the individuals that people those communities, who are they as they come together, and how should their membership be engaged? They struggle because most have never been asked to consider that this is in fact the primary task of educators, that we work toward developing individuals who can form the sorts of relationships that ultimately become communities that are happy and healthy in the specific places where they are formed.

Most of them have been asked to consider the problems that face schools, the detrimental social problems that the children they will teach face: poverty, racism, sexism, degradations due to sexual orientation, or the characterizations of their bodies or minds as disabled. And some of them add to this the ecological degradations that we face—primarily climate change as the dominant focus of the current discourse would have it. Some, far fewer, have a sense that there is something connecting social and ecological problems but they are not sure how they know. So, when I ask what deeper values tell them something is going wrong, they balk, unsure what I mean, or unwilling to take the risk of trying to name them or to look closer.

For the most part, they have been conditioned to accept as inevitable the discursive, economic and political systems that we live in, trained to its ideologies of "best practice" and to the expert knowledge they see as belonging to someone else. Most of them see teaching as a job and schools or universities as the location of that job. Some still believe that it will be a job that will allow them to "love kids" while making a salary that will allow them to raise their own families. But, those who have been teaching a while, come to my classes exhausted and depressed from the stresses put on them as corporations and state governments determine what is to be taught and how it is to be evaluated, making schooling and curriculum yet another "market" for text book and testing companies, or a business to be bought and sold, victimizing teachers when test scores don't measure up. So, it is no wonder that they become confused about what I mean when I ask, what is education for?

"Well," I say, "We would not know those are problems if we did not measure the conditions you describe against something that we hold dear. So what is that? What are the principles that tell you those are problems? Look to your hearts for the answer and not just your heads. Look to who and what you love."

And then something shifts. They can hardly believe I am asking them to think about love. But as they begin to go there, they begin to get at very old virtues: honesty, generosity, humility, kindness, respect, trust. Their essays, mostly quite simple and direct, choke me up.

At the heart of the matter is the devaluing of ancient principles that have kept communities safe from harm, values that still operate in our modern culture but mostly in limited ways perhaps in households, perhaps not. This devaluing includes a primary failure to recognize creatureliness as including us. Most of my students don't begin by including creatures other than humans in their definitions of community as important, but as the course and our conversation develop, they begin to see that they are indeed part of a much larger, more complex and mysterious living world than they had ever been asked to consider. More and more of them tell me that they have held these ideas in their hearts, but have never had the words or concepts or encouragement to really say what they have long felt. I bring Berry to them, offered within an EcoJustice framework, in the hopes that his clear and beautiful prose and stories will help to affirm their hearts, and to encourage them toward a pedagogy of responsibility. In what follows, I summarize some of Berry's primary ideas that I've been weaving throughout this book, the virtues and character traits that will be emphasized if we are serious about shifting this violent culture and ourselves toward more humane and sustainable communities. As longtime Detroit activist and educator Charles Simmons told us in a talk at a recent EcoJustice and Activism conference (March 2018), the necessary changes will not happen without love, and must start from the grass-roots, from us. "Ubuntu: I am, because you are."

Back to the Great Economy

In the introductory chapter I laid out five primary principles of the Great Economy that Berry (2010) returns to over and over again throughout his work. Here I want to take them up again as specific aspects of a pedagogy of responsibility, as what can help us to orient our teaching and learning practices toward conviviality and a recognition of holism as the basis of life.

Principle 1: Our place in the membership of Creation: The Great Economy includes everything and every relationship on the planet Earth and in the universe including us. We are all members of this extravagant and mysterious system whether we understand it or not, or whether we desire to be in it or not. This leads to a second principle.

Principle 2: There is an order to this set of relationships, and we are part of that order. Our human capacities and consciousness must be put to work in the preservation of that order, not as a means of subjecting the world to our selfish purposes but rather as part of holding together the sacredness of the order itself. We take our places in it with our particular capacities not as a matter of control or possession, but rather developing relationships that nourish it and help us all to flourish. This is our fundamental responsibility.

For Berry, these two principles lead to "an informed and conscientious submission to nature, or to Nature, and her laws of conservation, frugality, fullness or completeness, and diversity" (2017, p. 8), his second principle of agrarianism. This requires that we cultivate forbearance, within an understanding of natural limits. Of course, this is quite different than what we are taught within consumer culture where an endless stream of commodities flow into our lives promising happiness that never comes, and out again as waste. Within EcoJustice Education we emphasize the question, "What is to be conserved?" as a primary organizing tenet orienting us to identify the particular practices, traditions and relationships that lead to mutual well-being. Such a recognition invites us to turn to nature herself as a primary teacher. She is waiting for us, as Berry says. Recognizing our responsibilities in relation to her laws requires that we use our capacities for curiosity and care together with the discipline of restraint to learn who we need to be within her gifts. Developing an attitude of caution, the necessary related skills, and a will toward nurturance would supplant the need to exploit.

Principle 3: Because we are humans with specific forms of consciousness within limited powers of sense-making generally dependent upon forms of representation, we can never know finally all the complexity that this order entails. The diversity of the world is in constant flux and creation, and because we primarily use language and other symbolic forms to make sense of what we seek to know, there will always be a gap between what we say about it and the world itself. For

172 What is Education For?

Berry this understanding entails an acceptance of a certain level of ignorance, which he embraces as positive. "The way of ignorance" means accepting that there will always be mysteries beyond our reach and once acknowledged leads to necessary humility, even while we seek to define and develop our particular abilities. "The order," he says, "is both greater and more intricate than we can know" (Berry, 2010, p. 116).

Thus, while we must engage curiosity and investigation of the world, asking primary ethical questions about what will lead to the greatest possible "good," we will never reach a final answer. Education holds within itself this primary contradiction: We must use relationships of teaching and learning to pass on wisdom of the good, while accepting that we will never finally know. There will always be more questions, and more possible answers. Errors will surely be made, and thus we must be willing to forgive those who make them, while also demanding an attention to why those errors were made, and working to develop attitudes of care and caution. Again, the first two strands of the EcoJustice framework—a cultural ecological analysis of the roots of our problems, and a willingness to identify the skills of care, mutuality, and collaboration—are always intertwined. Engaging with our students this way, atunes them to the lessons offered by nature herself, asking that they submit themselves to her wisdom, while examining the ways we have historically ignored those lessons and the consequences of such arrogance.

Principle 4: Thus, if we presume to be outside this complex living order—the cycles of life, death and decay—if we endeavor to overcome or control it for our own ends only, we do so at our own peril. We are creatures of this order, fully dependent on it. Recognizing ourselves to be members of an order much larger than but including ourselves, we will act with the requisite care, generosity, gratitude, and humility. We must seek to create via our pedagogical relationships "a persuasion in favor of economic democracy, a preference for *enough* over *too much*," Berry's fourth agrarian principle. Teaching students that "economy" has an ancient set of practices associated with it, that have to do with the protection of one's sources of sustenance in collaboration with others, is essential to their recognition that the economic systems we live within now are not inevitable. For Berry, this leads to a loathing of "waste of every kind … as human folly, an insult to nature, a sin against the given world and its life" (2017, p. 9).

Thrift and practices of conservation are the logical antidotes in a culture of excess, consumerism, and individualism. Thus Berry advocates developing "a preference for saving rather than spending as the basis of the economy of a household or a government" (Berry, 2017, p. 9). Again, to develop these necessary character traits is to engage both a critique of the damages resulting from habits of exploitation and greed created within industrial cultures, and their alternatives within local subsistence economies developed in concert with the requirements and offerings of specific places. Colonization and globalization of market based assumptions have led to willful destruction of the land and of

What is Education For? **173**

human communities. Those processes must be unpacked systematically, their discursive roots identified, named and their effects studied, felt, and challenged. My students report to me that as they are introduced to these critical concepts naming assumptions within modern industrial civilizations, and begin to engage such an analysis, they feel their hearts open. They begin to recognize the pervasiveness of racism as it has been perpetuated and used against both people and the land. And, while their grief comes to the surface they struggle with what to do. Holding them in that experience, we work toward a recognition that such an emotional response, while insufficient on its own, is the first step toward love, affection, and care as shared solutions.

Principle 5: It is not enough to work for the future. We only live in the present, and thus, our imaginations must be put to the task of identifying what is possible today for ourselves and the Earth's living systems. This work to protect the living relationships upon which we depend is our fundamental responsibility. We must accept our responsibility to the places and people where we live now. And again, that responsibility includes a willingness to identify and challenge those systemic forces that impinge upon the well-being of the creatures who dwell in those places as a part of the love that we develop for them and for ourselves. This requires that we recognize the importance of neighbors and neighborliness in creating and attending to mutuality within the membership, Berry's eighth agrarian principle. A pedagogy of responsibility develops "a willingness to *be* a neighbor. This comes from proof by experience that no person or family or place can live alone" (2017, p. 9).

This sensibility can only be developed by engaging students in collaborative experiences whereby they learn to work with and to depend upon one another. The relationships developed must thus engage democracy as a deeply practical way of being together, and diversity as the unavoidable condition of difference energizing the need to attend to each other in fairness, generosity, and coherent forms of discernment. As the teacher steps back from being the sole source of knowledge, students learn to listen carefully to each others' ideas; they learn to articulate their ideas as fully and carefully as possible in order to make careful evaluations together. Using a variety of forms from oral articulation, to writing, art, poetry and media, they learn to express decisions around questions and problems that impact them and their families.

Work, the Body, and the Earth

> What I have been trying to do is to define a pattern of disintegrations that is at once cultural and agricultural. I have been groping for connections—that I think are indissoluble, though obscured by modern ambitions—between the spirit and the body, the body and other bodies, the body and the earth … it is impossible ultimately, to preserve ourselves apart from our willingness to preserve other creatures, or to respect and care for ourselves except as we respect and care for other

> creatures; and, most to the point … it is impossible to care for each other more or differently than we care for the earth. (Berry, 1996, p. 123)

Obviously, engaging the principles of the Great Economy is a circular process that, if done well, should teach us to engage the body with the earth as a process of coming to terms with our own creatureliness. For Berry this means embracing work as an engagement of this essential relationship. As he puts it "Work is the health of love. To last, work must enflesh itself in the materiality of the world—produce food, shelter, warmth or shade, surround itself with careful arts, well made things" (Berry, 1996, p. 132). Thus, work with the soil and the body must be removed from the degradation of hierarchized thinking where it is used to inferiorize and assert a rationalized mastery. A pedagogy of responsibility engages "respect for work and (as self-respect) for good work" (Berry, 2017, p. 9) as a process of interrupting these basic forms of domination, but mostly as an expression of care. For Berry, this implies a sharp critique of the ways our modern industrial institutions reduce work to "a job" that is disconnected from the well-being of one's place, and where someone else's interests are served in the name of having a career that offers monetary income as the primary sign of personal success.

If we begin to offer experiences to students to work with their bodies in ways that connect them to the nourishment and life that arises from the soil itself or that offers mutual support to the membership, they have a chance of learning that the source of happiness and security begins there in those local relationships. This is the foundational meaning of neighborliness. Awareness of this possibility invites us to engage students in the cultivation of gardens, renovation of houses, tidying of neighborhoods, and a myriad of other forms of community projects that require attention to the meaning of work done well as a source of satisfaction. As I wrote in Chapter 5, I learned about the effectiveness of such a pedagogy most directly and deeply from activist educators in Detroit within the food security movement but also throughout a number of grassroots efforts where neighborhoods became active sites of teaching and learning around ancient principles of self-determination, kindness, gratitude and love all generated from the specific needs of that city, its residents, and its land. So as another agrarian principle, Berry calls for "a living sense of the need for continuity of family and community life in place, which is to say the need for the survival of local culture and thus of the safekeeping of local memory and local nature" (2017, p. 9). As I worked side by side with elders in Detroit, they told stories about the successful civil rights strategies they engaged at the grassroots level in the 1950s, '60s, and '70s, including the mistakes made that informed new political and pedagogical strategies. With shovels, rakes, and hoes in hand, these teachers used memory to engage community members in relationships around all sorts of specific community needs, both human and more than human, weaving together a history of suffering with ancient wisdom and principles that recognize the gift of Creation.

Community-based Learning in a Globalized Context

Such learning may be less possible in schools, though as teacher educators, our job is to ask practicing and prospective teachers to examine their assumptions, shift their lenses and world views, and to look for openings in their classrooms and curricula where they can encourage students to do this cultural work. Teachers ask me how they can do such complex work with their students when they are so pressured by state mandates. I do not have easy answers, but I do know this: As we awaken, we become different, and so does our teaching.

Meanwhile, we all live outside schools too, and thus should be engaging with our students, young and old, in practices that address and redress the damages that they find in their own communities. This means recognizing our collective power to make change as an ethics of responsibility. In response to the crises that she spent her life fighting in Detroit, Grace Lee Boggs is clear that "we urgently need to stop thinking of ourselves as victims and to recognize that we must each become part of the solution because we are each a part of the problem" (Boggs, 2011, p. 29).

This is the work that critical place-based educators call for (Gruenewald & Smith, 2008; Lowenstein & Erkaeva, 2016), which can be strengthened through the strands of EcoJustice Education when we include an analysis of the problems we see locally as created in broader cultural, political and economic contexts that have a deep history and powerful psychological (or subjective) consequences. Those consequences, though pervasive, are not set in stone. We will not learn to protect the places where we live if we do not love those places, and we will not love those places fully without first understanding our complicity in the systems that continue to rationalize the damages to those places. Love grows from the compassion that results when we identify and work to alleviate suffering as the effect of violence, not out of guilt necessarily, but rather out of a recognition of the ways culture works to create us as actors in the world. What kind of actors do we need? Or, as Berry asks, "What are People For?" (1990).

This is the question that should energize our teaching and our learning. What do our communities require of us, and how do we prepare our students to have the skills, attitudes and character traits needed to address those needs? As we uncover the intersecting violation to places and creatures resulting from hierarchized divisions, myths of individualism, consumerism, mechanism, and market fundamentalism as the supposed foundations of a more efficient and productive world, we also imagine the possibilities that exist even as those ideas crowd the institutions where we live and work. As we work to expose the narratives that support our extractive exploitive systems, we also open up possibilities for identifying the knowledges and practices of care and mutuality that still exist in the cracks and crevices of our consciousness and communities, and we look to the more-than-human members of our communities as well for what order really means.

The complexity of our present trouble suggests as never before that we need to change our present conception of education. Education is not properly an industry, and its proper use is not to serve industries, either by job-training or by industry-subsidized research. Its proper use is to enable citizens to live lives that are economically, politically, socially and culturally responsible. This cannot be done by gathering or "accessing" what we now call "information"—which is to say facts without context and therefore without priority. A proper education enables young people to put their lives in order, which means knowing what things are more important than other things; it means putting first things first. (Berry, 2003, p. 21)

References

Berry, W. (1990). *What are people for?* Berkeley, CA: Counterpoint.

Berry, W. (1996). *The unsettling of America: Culture and agriculture.* San Francisco, CA: Sierra Club Books.

Berry, W. (2003). *Citizenship papers.* Washington, DC: Shoemaker and Hoard.

Berry, W. (2010). *What matters? Economics for a renewed commonwealth.* Berkeley, CA: Counterpoint.

Berry, W. (2017). *The art of loading brush. New agrarian writings.* Berkeley, CA: Counterpoint.

Boggs, G. L. (2011). *The next American revolution: Sustainable activism for the 21st Century.* Berkeley, CA: University of California Press.

Gruenewald, D., & Smith, G. (Eds). (2008). *Place-based education in the global age: Local diversity.* Mahwah, NJ: Lawrence Erlbaum Press.

Lowenstein, E., & Erkaeva, N. (2016). Developing a language to support healthy partnerships in powerful place-based education: The experience of the Southeast Michigan Stewardship Coalition. In C. A. Bowers (Ed.), *Eco-Justice: Essays on theory and practice in 2016.* Eugene, OR: The Eco-Justice Press.

INDEX

Abram, David 45
abuse 35, 53, 107, 115, 119
academic careerism 36, 166
activist educators 174
Adams, Katy xiv, 117
affection xiii–xiv, 1–2, 43, 45, 60–65, 67, 100, 111, 113–14, 119, 124, 126, 131, 155–56; deep 99; embodied 84; growing 64; identifying 84; mutual 154
affectionate relationships 61
African Americans 102, 105, 107–8
agrarianism xi, 12–13, 25, 171
agriculture xii–xiii, 23–24, 34–36, 38, 63, 83, 120, 129, 132, 146, 162–64
Akulukjuk, T. 72, 93
Allen, David 142–43, 145
American agriculture 23–24, 120
American farms see also farms 36
American nursing see also nursing 149–50
Amyx, Tanya 10–11
ancestors 11, 68, 83, 93, 98, 100–101, 110–11, 115; agrarian 111; white European 84
ancient traditions 16, 82
Andean farmers 82–83
Annishinaabeg people 93
anonymity 142–43
Another Turn of the Crank xi
anthropocentric assumptions 78

anthropocentrism 17, 86; exploitive 78; intersects with mechanistic views of the world 145; nursing 144
anxieties 71, 77, 96–98, 100, 110; and fears associated with their relationships with unknown Others 70; relieving settler 84
Arnow, Harriet 105
art 18, 38, 50, 52–53, 65, 120–21, 131, 173–74; afterschool 63; classrooms 91; installations 108; projects 63, 65
The Art of Loading Brush 25, 38–39, 118
assumptions xiii, 3, 5, 18, 26, 56, 78, 122, 126, 130, 138, 143–46, 149, 152; anthropocentric 78; arrogant 3; critical concepts naming 173; epistemological 88; fundamental 118; implicit 119; modern industrial xiii; modernist 3, 86; primary 5

Baltimore 109–10, 149
banks 31, 105, 163
Barad, Karan 58–59, 64
Bateson, Gregory 6, 15, 44, 50–53, 58–59
Beechum, Jack 36
beliefs 1–5, 7, 14, 17, 20, 67, 71, 76, 81, 87, 92, 102, 121–22, 137
Bell, N. 85, 121
benevolence 100–101
Bennett, Jane 59–60, 64
Bentham, Jeremy 27
Black bodies xiv, 55, 97–98, 103–6, 109–10

178 Index

Black community 104, 109–10
Black families 102, 105–6
Black teenagers 109
Black workers 97, 105–6
bodies xiii–xv, 43–47, 49, 51–57, 59–60,
  85–86, 97–99, 101–2, 110–11, 113–14,
  136–39, 146–47, 160–61, 173–74; Black
  xiv, 55, 97–98, 103–6, 109–10;
  collective 33; fictitious 73; living 14, 57;
  of other living creatures 46, 85, 138–39,
  147; particular 47; sentient 46
Boggs, G. L. 108, 175
Bowers, Chet 3–5, 126
boys 9–10, 35, 37–38, 111, 141; "girding
  themselves against the ghosts of the bad
  old days" 109; good 38
Branch, Danny 36, 37, 75, 140–142
Branch, Lyda 36, 141
brothers 9, 158–61
Brush, Stephen B. 82
brutality 2, 98, 107–8
business cycles 28–29
business people 156
businesses 12, 23, 28–29, 31, 36, 97,
  108–9, 112, 137, 165, 170; large 28–29;
  local 32; small 109
Butler, Jesse K. 92–93
Butterfield, Patricia 142–43
Butz, Earl L. 24, 163

Calderon, Dolores 68–69, 71, 88–92
capacities xiii–xiv, 3, 6–7, 13, 17–18, 43,
  53–54, 65, 80–81, 118, 171;
  autonomous 47; critical xi;
  epistemological 62; ethical 53; forest's
  procreant 45; human 171; productive
  xiii; reasoning 43, 55
capital 30, 106
capitalism 3, 28, 32, 40, 56, 73, 77, 87;
  advanced 55; consumer 63; expansionist
  10, 12; extractive 71, 164; free-market
  29; global 67; industrial 147; regulated
  28, 30; white supremacist 103, 114
care 1–2, 5–7, 9–11, 16–20, 46, 49, 58–61,
  64–65, 110–11, 113–14, 142–43,
  145–47, 155–61, 171–75; earthly 80;
  essential 19; good 16; merciful 141;
  requisite 15, 172
careers 124–25, 137, 174
caretakers 11, 18, 76
caretaking 4, 160; mutual 2; relational 60;
  relationship with the fields, woods, and
  streams 165

caring 20, 39, 76, 113, 115, 137, 163, 166;
  relationships 17–18; ways 43
Catlett, Andy xiii, 27, 35–40, 120, 132
Catlett, Henry 141
Catlett, Wheeler 75, 93, 140,
  143
CDA, see Critical Discourse Analysis
CED see Committee for Economic
  Development
Chatham, Troy xiii, 23, 25, 27
Cheskey, N. Z. 118, 132
childhood 99, 155–56
children 10–11, 19, 24, 37, 46, 102, 105,
  115, 154, 156–57, 159–60, 162, 165–66,
  169; educated upon the back of
  weakened local knowledge, and failing
  communities 124; young 54, 92, 130
Chinn, Peggy 142
Christianity xii, 12–13
Christians 13, 100–101
citizenship 33
claims xiii, 7, 35, 54, 69–70, 72, 88, 91–92,
  97, 119, 132; defining 68; dispelling xiii;
  primary analytic 68
class 3, 78, 102–3, 149, 151
Coates, T. xiii, 109–11, 115
collective responsibility 19
college 35, 37, 83, 162, 166; education
  165–66; town small rural 162
colonialism 72, 78, 89–90
colonies 73
colonization 56, 72, 78, 89, 93,
  172
Committee for Economic Development 29
communities xii–xiii, 4–6, 12–15, 18–19,
  23–40, 47, 82–83, 111–15, 124–26,
  144–47, 154–56, 160–66, 169–70,
  174–75; academic 88; agricultural 30;
  building 113; dismembered 138;
  disrupted 26; ecological 25, 136;
  educational 127; good 18; healthy
  xiii–xiv, 4, 6, 65, 84, 133, 147, 154;
  indigenous 77; land-based 40; living 1,
  13, 18, 83, 156; local xii, 3, 58, 124,
  150; modern scientific 132; orderly 71;
  rural 24–26, 34, 165; small dairy 156;
  strong 19; white 78, 85, 92–93, 97–98,
  101–2, 110
conferences 35, 67–68
connections xiii, xv, 1, 44, 47, 49, 52,
  59–61, 64, 93, 111, 113, 155–58, 161;
  abstract 86; complex intergenerational
  156; essential xiv, 55, 113; family 75,

130; generative 139; larger 145; living 142; restorative 80, 139; sharing 52; transformative 14, 49
conscientious submissions 25, 171
consciousness xiv, 56, 62, 88, 167, 171, 175; eco-ethical 14, 155, 167; human 167; raising 91; settler colonial 81
conservation 25, 128–29, 171–72
consumer culture 127, 171
context 5, 7, 19, 67, 71–72, 80, 93, 97, 100, 106, 119, 123, 125–26, 131–33; historical 28, 93; urban 109
contributions xiii, xv, 18, 102, 147
conversations xi, xiii, 9, 44, 57, 59, 63, 68, 75, 110, 117, 140, 142–43, 147
Coulter, Burley 15, 36, 75, 79, 93, 140, 141, 161
Coulter, Hannah 40, 46, 58, 154, 156, 158, 160, 165, 167
Coulter, Nathan 10, 36, 156
cows 159, 164
creation 2–4, 11, 13–15, 44, 46, 48, 50, 58–59, 84–85, 87, 139, 154, 157, 171; earthly 13; generative 52
creatures xi, 3–6, 12–19, 48–49, 51–54, 56, 58–59, 61–65, 84, 87, 103, 136–39, 158–61, 172–75; dead xi; fallen 88; fellow 65; individual 17; land-based 16; living 14, 16–17, 46, 49, 56, 59, 85, 126, 147, 155; particular 47; prosperous 154
credit (use of) 23, 31, 96, 105
crises xv, 2–3, 76, 80, 84, 97, 104, 147, 175; collective 76; cultural xv; economic 104, 164; financial 106; perpetual 65; social 2
Critical Discourse Analysis 151–52
crop rotation 82, 159, 163–64
crops 82, 114, 162, 164–65
cultural system 46, 53, 80, 167
cultural traditions 5, 91, 129
culture 3, 5–6, 45, 53, 75, 79–82, 97, 102, 104, 115, 118, 122–23, 127, 129; American 96; consumer 127, 171; current hyper-consumer 83, 133; diverse 4–5; dominant white xiv; exploitive 98; indigenous 84; industrial 5, 14, 39, 54, 172; local 26, 174; low 38; modernist 166; post-industrial 136; scientific-industrial 55; violent 97, 170
curriculum xv, 65, 89–90, 148, 169–70; nursing 148; social studies 89; whitestream 92

D-Town (farm) 111–12
damages 4, 12, 36, 76, 85, 87, 89, 97, 111, 120, 166, 172, 175; critical 76; inherited 60; ongoing 92, 110
DBCFSN *see* Detroit Black Community Food Security Network
death xiii, 44, 47, 49, 55, 57, 88, 137, 139, 141, 156–57, 159, 172
debt 23–24, 32, 73, 105, 163; high levels of 31, 120; increasing 163, 165
degradation xiii–xiv, 53, 56, 71, 74, 77–78, 88, 92, 97, 102, 104–5, 118, 169, 174; continuous systematized 87; ecological 169; of land xiv, 103; ongoing 91
Degraded Bodies xiv, 55, 96–115
Degraded Earth xiv, 55, 97–115
Degraded Land 102
deindustrialization 106
Deloria, V. 86
democracy xi–xii, 6, 12–13, 112, 122–23, 173; economic 26, 172; people's 112
dependencies 44, 46, 51, 63, 84–85, 126, 132, 137, 139; absolute 34; embodied xiii; mutual 47, 51–52
Detroit xiv, 97, 104–9, 111, 113–14, 174–75; artists 63, 91; industrial xiv; police force 106–7; politics 114; population of 106; rebellions 107
Detroit Black Community Food Security Network 111–12, 115
devotion 9, 11, 18, 140, 161; indissoluble 9
disasters 5, 39, 162, 164
discipline 117–18, 121–23, 131–32, 146, 171; Black family 109; intellectual 121; strict 93
discourses 3, 17, 52, 89–90, 122, 144–46, 149, 152; alternative 152; analysis 149, 151–52; anthropocentric 118; associated supremacy 89; centric 56; current 124, 169; democratic 122; dominant 131, 148; hegemonic 132, 146; imbedded 3; inclusive 123; individualistic xiv; intersecting 17; modernist 144–46, 152; often-contradictory 152; public 101
disease 62, 82, 138, 145–46; absence of 136, 138, 142–43, 148; critical cultural 138; hereditary 98; prevention of 138
dispossession xiii, 2, 12, 68, 74–76, 78, 88, 106, 108

Eagleton-Pierce, M. 33

180 Index

earth xiii–xv, 8–9, 11–13, 15–19, 43–46,
  48–51, 53–60, 79, 85–87, 102–4,
  110–13, 137–39, 166–67, 173–74;
  abstract 86; desecrated 115; elements xi,
  65; living 14; native 103; particles 60
EcoJustice Education xii, 2–5, 17, 19, 63,
  87, 99, 152, 171, 175
ecological 2, 5, 8, 19, 48, 76, 102, 104,
  157; crises xv, 76, 84, 97, 147; problems
  xi, 170; systems 51, 71, 85, 128, 146
ecology 15, 47, 51, 79, 91, 128–29
economic activity 27, 29, 31–32
economic growth 27–28
economic history 63–64
economic systems xiv, 8, 40, 84, 137, 172;
  exploitive 72, 79, 137; extractive 19;
  hierarchized 87; new 72
economics 36, 100, 104
economy 13, 16, 26, 29, 32, 50, 55, 60, 73,
  82, 120, 124, 151, 172; dominant
  industrialized human 14; extractive 114;
  global 39, 113; good local forest 82;
  government's 124; local 25, 126,
  164–65; national 35; new 54; rural 25;
  subsistence 172
ecosystems 3, 78, 82, 127; large 138; local
  60, 91; surrounding 150
Edmundson, Jeff xi, 5, 67, 118, 152
education xi–xiii, xv, 4, 6–9, 17–19,
  39–40, 43–44, 67–68, 86–90, 118–19,
  123–27, 154–55, 166, 169–76;
  communities 127, 133; current
  healthcare 142; environmental 91;
  institutionalized xi, 87
educational, strategic processes 2
educators 4, 7, 18–19, 93, 113, 123, 133,
  142, 147, 169; activist 174; nurses xiv,
  142, 146–48; science 118, 126;
  sustainability xi; teachers xi, 19, 90, 93,
  175; white 115
elders 92–93, 112–13, 130, 155, 160, 174
elementary students 124
embodied connections 7, 102
embodied work 13, 106, 114
empirical evidence (as the basis of scientific
  knowledge) 119
essays xi–xii, 2, 7–8, 10, 13, 30, 76, 81,
  118–19, 122, 148, 151, 170
Esteva, G. & Prakash, M. S. 21
ethical choices 6
ethics 2, 5, 15, 43, 57–61, 123, 132, 156,
  175; of care 132, 152; ecofeminist 50; of
  responsibility 5, 175

Europe 72–73, 156
European xiv, 56, 64, 69–72, 74–79,
  83–84, 89–91, 93; colonists 56, 64;
  conquests 83; contact and plunder of the
  North American continent xiv; forebears
  89; homelands 77; ideologies 70;
  miscreants 70; settlements 1, 74–75, 79;
  settlers 70, 72, 74, 91; supremacy 70;
  underclasses 70
Europeanization 70, 79
Europeans 69, 78–79, 84, 90–91
evil 98–99
existence xiii, xv, 16, 44–45, 48, 50, 125,
  139, 167; degenerate 101; earthly 43, 47;
  earthly materialist 61; embedded
  embodied xiii; planetary 17, 143;
  unconscious 43
experience 33, 84, 88, 91, 109, 112, 114,
  121, 123, 125, 139, 156–57, 161–62,
  173; collective 113; elemental 103;
  long-term 127; personal 124, 133;
  physical 43; scientific 125; spiritual 6

faith 2, 14, 20, 49, 122, 124, 139, 142, 156;
  earthbound 49; free-market 27; religious
  101; white community's Christian 101
families 23–24, 26, 45, 62, 64, 72, 81–82,
  98–102, 105, 129–30, 140–41, 158–59,
  162–63, 173–74; Black 102, 105–6;
  farming 24, 162; feeding of 165; old
  165; white 101, 104, 106
family connections 75, 130
family histories xiv, 97, 99–100
family stories 101
farmers 9, 23–25, 27, 31–32, 34–36, 49,
  81–83, 100, 112, 120, 146, 156, 160,
  162–66; Andean 82–83; Black 104; dairy
  157, 162; and their families 24, 162;
  financial policies 36; grain 162;
  Indigenous 81; local 112, 128; peasant
  72; progressive 114; settler 68; who
  cannot sell their crops 162; work of 36,
  164; yeoman 33
farms 9–10, 13, 23–25, 35–37, 46, 48,
  74–75, 78–79, 81, 83, 98–101, 104,
  111–14, 158–66; American 36;
  diversified 161; small 34, 103, 162,
  164–65
Fawcett, Jacquelyn 144
fear 8, 35, 70, 109–10, 112; buried 115;
  and contempt of waste 26; inscribed 109
Feinsinger, P. 128–29
Feltner, Margaret 36

Index **181**

fidelity 13, 62, 93, 140, 161
field ecologists 128–29
financial sector 30
food 54, 109, 111–12, 114, 162–63, 174;
activists 112, 114; deserts 109; insecurity
109; items 31; movements 114; policies
111; preparation 54; prices 163;
processors 163; producers 31; scarcity
114; sources 51, 58; sovereignty 113
Food Policy Council 112
Ford, Henry 90
foresters 81–82
forests xi, 12, 17, 20, 34–35, 44–48, 51, 58,
64, 82–83, 130–31, 160
foundations 2, 27, 56, 108, 131, 142,
147–48, 151–52, 175; cultural 2, 148,
151; epistemological 147, 152; essential
131; global capitalism's 56; ideological
27; large private 108; of a more efficient
and productive world 175; of
neoliberalism 27; primary 125; shaky 76
fragmentation 39–40, 84, 86, 138, 146
free-market xii, 27, 29; approach 27, 29;
capitalism 29; faith 27; fundamentalism
xii
freedom schools 108
Friedman, Milton 27
fruit 1, 17, 59–60, 111
Fukuyama, F. 29

gardens 108, 114–15, 159–60,
174
gender 3, 149–50
germs 138
global capitalism 67
global economy 39, 113
globalization 31–32, 172
goals 82, 105, 112, 118, 121, 126, 145;
scientific 125; traditional 10
God 14, 48–50, 54, 56–57, 62, 70, 85
Goodman, Benny 142–43, 147, 149
governments 19, 24, 26, 28–29, 31, 35,
124, 172
grammars 89–90
grandfathers xi, 9, 96, 99, 104, 109–10,
159, 162
grandmothers 37, 110
grandparents 9, 27, 36–37, 161
gratitude 2, 16, 40, 61–62, 115, 155–56,
172, 174
graves 141–42
Great Economy xii, 14–19, 33, 52–53, 58,
61, 65, 86, 124, 137, 147, 150, 171, 174

Great Lakes 91
Greenland 127–28
grief 2, 6, 44, 47, 50, 77, 81, 83, 100,
155–56, 161, 166, 173
Griffin, Susan 59–60, 149, 167
groups 3, 63, 69, 74, 85, 90–91, 111, 113,
151; diverse 80; monolithic 33; single
85; of students 91; tight-knit 156
growth xiv, 30–32, 48, 76, 121, 130, 137,
139, 164; concomitant 31; cultural 79;
economic 27–28

happiness 1, 6, 10, 15, 38, 57, 83–84, 103,
105, 141, 158, 171, 174
harvest 37, 159, 162
healers 93, 148–49
healing 38–40, 85, 87, 93, 98, 136–37, 139;
community 65; necessary xiii; power
138; relations 97; socio-ecological 89
health xiv–xv, 11–12, 47, 63, 85, 114,
117–18, 129–30, 133, 136–53, 174;
bodily 146; definition of 137–39, 143,
148; ecological 121; economic 124;
good 79, 144; idea of 138, 148;
nutrition-related 111; professionals 138,
142
health care 137, 143–44, 148, 150–52;
education system xv; holistic practices
150; institutionalized 152; practices 150;
professionals 150–51; systems 146
"health is membership" (Berry) 147
Henderson, J. 8, 32
hereditary evil 98–99
history 10–12, 26, 64–65, 71, 74, 78–79,
81–83, 89–91, 93, 98, 100, 103, 125–26,
148–49; human 128–29; people's 81
Hixon, Walter 69, 77–78
holiness 59–60, 65, 88, 144
holism xiv–xv, 54, 136–53, 171
holistic approaches 146, 148, 150–52
honor 13, 16–17, 19, 47, 59, 82, 87, 99,
125, 145
horses 158–60
hospitals 24, 136, 140
households 12–13, 26, 32, 44, 54, 105,
157, 160, 170, 172
houses xi, 158–59, 174
Howard, Albert 63
human beings 7, 112, 144–45, 147
human centeredness 17
human communities xiv, 12, 43, 56, 58,
82, 118–19, 149, 173
human culture 5, 58

182 Index

human economy 14, 16, 18–19
human societies 51, 167
human workers 18, 106
humanity xiii, 17, 48, 50, 69, 87, 96–98, 103, 105, 111–12
humility 2, 7, 43, 61–62, 65, 67, 89, 91, 93, 127, 130, 133, 170, 172; and care 18; forbearance, gratitude and generosity 40; and kindness 38; the necessary enactment of 11, 172; and requisite care 15
Huron people 90
Huron River 63, 90
Hursh, D. 8, 32

ice historians 127–28
ideological 26, 39, 47, 58, 63, 73–74, 87, 155; foundations 27; inheritance 60; pressures 164; removal 70; structures 76; struggles 71; system 29, 86
ideologies 3, 19, 26–27, 33, 53, 104, 166, 170
ignorance 7, 39, 93, 119, 169, 172; epistemologies of 92; fundamental 17; the way of 15, 172
imagination 2–5, 9, 18, 46, 62–65, 87, 90, 114–15, 122, 154–55, 161, 167, 173; grounded moral 114; unacknowledged 115
income 28, 30, 109, 174; distribution 28; national 30
Indians 77, 79
indictments on a set of beliefs and practices 76
Indigenous peoples xiii, 56, 62, 67–72, 74, 77–80, 89–91, 103, 164; contemporary 79; dispossessing 12; local 90; removed from ancestral land 68, 74, 76, 78
indissoluble devotion 9
individualism xiv, 1, 27, 30, 33, 61, 86, 120, 124–25, 145, 166, 172, 175
individuals 18, 34, 47, 102, 112, 121, 126–27, 131, 133, 143, 145, 169
industrial capitalism 147
industrial economy 16–17, 38, 126; current globalized 25; developing 104
industrial societies 2, 122, 124
industry 29, 104–5, 126, 176
information xiv, 50–51, 119, 122, 176
information circuits 50–51
institutions xi, 3, 7, 14, 19, 27, 40, 53, 89–90, 138, 144–45, 151, 166, 175; academic 121; educational 89; financial

31; industrial 174; legal 73; medical 138; modern 8, 137; primary/secondary 166; research 126
interpretations xi, 8, 11, 13, 48, 52, 62, 117, 122, 128
interviews 109, 125, 146–47, 152
Isenberg, Nancy 70, 73

Jackson, Wes 16, 63, 133
Jenkins, Bart 100–101
Johnson, Samuel 33
Johnston, Nancy 139, 142–43, 145–46

Kahn, Richard 67
Kant, Immanuel 47
Keith, A. 23–24, 32
Kentucky (USA) 9–10, 79, 98, 105
killings 11, 25, 57, 157
Kimmerer, R. W. 129
kindness 1–2, 7, 11, 38, 40, 61–62, 65, 84, 89, 93, 96, 99, 170, 174; and care on large and small scales 1; and humility 38
Kingdom of God 14, 48–49, 57; *see also* God
Kleffel, Dorothy 142, 144, 149
knowledge 19–20, 53, 61–62, 67–68, 79–81, 87–88, 91–93, 118–20, 122–23, 125, 129, 131, 137–38, 159–60; deep 90, 111; farmer's 125; human 62; intimate 63, 111, 126
Korsybski, Joseph 52
Kotz, D. 28–31
Kurashige, Scott xiv, 105–8

labor 30, 70, 72–73, 87, 100, 102–3, 106, 108, 110, 113–14, 161; costs 31; exploiting of 78; extractive 55; free 101; lifetime's 30; people's 142; physical 55, 114; saving 106; unrest 28
land xiii–xiv, 9–13, 23–25, 31–32, 67–79, 81–93, 96–98, 102–5, 110–11, 113–14, 154–57, 159–61, 163–64, 166; acquired 104; agricultural 31; ancestral xiv; bases 86; cheaper 106; converting 72; crop 111; demands 70; empty 72; exhaustion 26; forested 24; good 156; holders 34; marginal 31; marshy 91; native 84; owners 104; promised 105; stolen 80; toxic 106; use 38, 79, 119; white male farmer occupying 68

landscapes 120, 129, 155; agricultural 163; biological 13; local 120; political 25, 60; scholarly 12; undeveloped wild 71

Landy, B. 30

language 3, 50, 52, 92, 98, 123–24, 129, 152; current nursing 148; family's 101; local 25; practices 99; use of 171

laws 29, 140–41, 171; basic 36; of conservation 25, 171; of property 68

lawyers 9, 140

learning 5–8, 10, 12–13, 17, 19, 37, 39–40, 47, 63, 123, 130, 147, 160, 174–75; nature of xiv, 127; situations 126

Lederman, N. G. 121, 123

lessons 7, 9, 14, 37, 39–40, 82, 90–91, 93, 97, 111, 129–30, 155–56, 172; enduring 99; essential 110; first 93; ongoing 155; primary 13, 160

Life is a Miracle 118

limits 17–19, 33–34, 46–47, 50, 52–53, 56, 61–62, 99, 110, 122–23, 137; definition of 136; natural 171; necessary 56; recognizing 62

Linebaugh, Peter 73

living systems 2, 5, 15, 52, 57, 76, 120, 128, 147, 158, 173; diverse 7, 18; healthy 5; larger 136, 150; protecting 7

living world 4, 14, 50, 56, 58, 65, 124, 136, 144, 147, 170; larger 33, 154; vulnerable 14

Locke, John 27, 69

loneliness 19, 86–87

love xiii–xv, 6–9, 12–13, 38–40, 43–44, 46, 59–62, 64–65, 87–89, 96–97, 99, 112–14, 154–57, 173–75; bonds of xiii, 40, 43–65; complicated 76; deep 10, 17; essential 99, 158; grandmother's 159; intergenerational 154; palpable 167; resonates with early childhood experiences 142; weaving the community together 83

loving care 37, 39, 47, 52, 111, 115; demands 52; an order of 39, 47, 115

Lukacs, John 62

Lupinacci, John 3, 87, 108, 118, 123, 132, 142, 144–45, 152

machinery 31–32, 100, 163, 165

machines 35, 55, 57, 59, 103–4, 140, 142, 146, 164

market economy 72, 129

Martusewicz, Rebecca A. 3, 6, 52, 67, 108, 112, 118, 123, 142, 144–45, 152, 155, 158, 167

Medicare 28

medicines xv, 137–38, 145–46, 151

meetings 10, 36, 57, 60, 124, 158, 161, 167; erotic 167; fragile 167; pedagogical 167

membership xv, 33–35, 37, 39–40, 61, 113–14, 139–41, 144, 149–51, 154–58, 161, 165–66, 169, 173–74; great 49–50

memories xi, 37, 39, 60, 110, 133, 155–58, 174

Menominee forest economy 82

Merchant, Caroline 55

midwives 149

Miller, Chazz 91

Miller, P. 33–34

miracles 57, 117–18, 127

Mirowski, P. 29

mixed family farming systems 31

modernist assumptions 3, 86

money 23–24, 54–55, 73, 104, 110, 123, 158, 163

moral people 71, 100

mothers xi, 44, 63, 102, 154–60, 162, 165–67

Mullen, John 29

mushroom hunting 44

mysteries xii, 13, 15–16, 33, 47, 49, 54, 65, 84, 119, 172

narratives 63, 89–90, 144, 146, 175; embedded 89; historical 93

National Research Council 118

National Science Teacher Association 118

NRC *see* National Research Council

NSTA *see* National Science Teacher Association

nurses xiv, 137, 142–44, 146–50, 152

nursing xv, 136–38, 144–46, 148–52; care 151; education xiv–xv, 136, 142–49, 151; history of 148; practice of 136, 144, 149–50, 152; reform of 151

nursing care, transcultural concepts in 151

order 11, 13, 15, 33, 37–38, 47, 50, 52–53, 58, 61, 65, 76, 171–72, 175–76; complex 15; economic 89; human 48; larger 61, 136; particular 142; political 69; principled 13; world's 17

organizations 7, 29, 39, 72, 112, 115, 138, 141–42, 151; interconnected grassroots

108; larger socio-political 137; local Southeast Michigan 91; modern 140; policy-making 34; religious 112; standards 149

pain 36, 100, 138
parents 23–24, 27, 160–61, 166
Park, Gordon 107
passages 83
patients 58, 120, 126, 137, 141, 143–48
pedagogy xi–xv, 1–20, 24–40, 44–65, 68–94, 97–115, 118–33, 137–53, 155–67, 170–76; critical 5; name 18; practice 25; relational 92; of responsibility 5
Penn, Jack 36
personal choices 32, 80–81
Phillips, Wendy 93
philosophers xi, 7
philosophy 7, 9, 145
Piketty, T. 30
place-based education 151
place-based projects 150–51
planet xiv–xv, 1–4, 7, 12, 14, 19, 25–26, 49, 85, 110, 113, 139, 143, 147
planet Earth 14, 171
plants xi, 25, 44, 47, 51–52, 64, 81, 85, 91, 129–30, 139, 145, 159, 166
Plumwood, V. 56, 87, 139, 146, 149
poems 2, 13, 17, 49–50
poets 2, 48–49
Polanyi, Karl 72–73
policies 8, 25, 53, 111–12, 163
political philosophies 27
politics 36, 85, 87, 122, 162
Pollan, Michael 31, 162–63
Potawatomi people 129
practice science 127, 133
practices 2–6, 13–14, 17–19, 31–32, 34, 39–40, 80–84, 89, 101, 109–10, 136, 149–50, 152, 171–72; healthcare 139; historical 69; scientific 124, 129
Prakash, Madhu Suri ix, 4, 8, 21, 22
principles xi–xii, xv, 13–19, 25, 29–30, 33, 50, 52, 83, 86, 144, 147, 150, 169–74; agrarian 112, 172–74; commons-based 162; ecological 13; first 14; foundational 82; fundamental 7; generalizable 123; generalized 125; guiding 143; necessary 18; primary 27, 83, 171
problems xi–xii, 3, 6–7, 11, 98–100, 112–13, 119, 122, 138, 147, 150–51,

169–70, 172–73, 175; African Americans 114; growing 114; social 114, 169
processes 1, 31, 46–47, 51–52, 61, 74, 77–78, 88–91, 93, 113–14, 137–38, 147, 163–65, 173–74; healthy 145; historic 70, 74, 76; ongoing 18, 69, 71, 161; scientific 146
production 23, 31–33, 55, 70, 72, 106, 114, 121, 163–64; levels 32; limiting of 163
professions 9, 124, 131, 136–38, 143–44, 146–47, 149, 151; isolated 138; medical 7; specialized 136
profitability 31–32, 46
profits xiv, 2, 14, 28, 30, 34, 56–57, 69–70, 77, 103, 112, 142–43, 166; extractive 111; potential 48
progress xiv, 1, 8, 12, 39, 70, 76, 86, 89, 92, 106, 109, 118–21, 124; civilizational 72; profit-based 25; scientific 119, 132; technological 27, 166
provisioning 13, 54

racism xi, xiii–xiv, 55–56, 78, 81, 96–98, 101–2, 110, 115, 169, 173
Raines, Katherine 48
Rasmussen, Derek 5, 93
reality 26, 46, 53, 81, 98, 104, 107, 122, 131–32; cultural 71; dangerous 106; economic 101; embodied 55; humbling 122; psychic 55; spiritual 47; theoretical 104
rebellion 107–8; fifty year xiv, 107; historic 97
relationships 2–8, 12–16, 18, 50–52, 59–60, 64, 69–70, 83–86, 91–93, 99–100, 102–3, 119–21, 154–58, 171; affectionate 61; caring 17–18; educational xi; healthy 6; pedagogical 19, 172; violent 47, 87
research 67, 127–28, 130, 144; historical 128; projects 142
resistance 39, 73, 96–97, 107; avoiding active 114; direct 112
resources 12, 14, 17, 70, 130; common 129; natural 137; on-farm 31; protecting Earth's 124
responsibility xi–xv, 1–20, 24–40, 43–65, 67–94, 97–115, 118–33, 137–53, 155–67, 170–76; central 115; direct 147; essential 83; ethical 58, 97, 147; fundamental 15, 171, 173; individual 145; moral 33; mutual 155; new 130;

paradoxical 6; particular 5, 97; personal 33; primary 152
"Room of Love" xv, 154–67
Rowanberry, Arthur 36–37
Russell, Bertrand 122

Sage, C. 31–32, 153
salaries 30, 166, 170
Schiermeier, Q. 128
Schnakenberg, Gary 23
scholars xi, 7–9, 67–68, 71, 142–44; anonymous 145; ecofeminist 53; educational 8, 90–91; new materialist 52; nursing xv, 142–43, 145, 147
schools xv, 7, 9, 19, 45, 89–90, 108–9, 112, 169–70, 175; freedom 108; high 161; local 124; middle 124; military boarding 9; residential 92; "whitestream" 92
Schreck, Jane 8
science xiv, 7, 34, 52, 117–24, 126–33; educators 118, 126; modern 125, 128; nature of 121, 123, 126; practice of 125–26, 131; teachers 123, 133
scientific knowledge 119, 122–24, 127, 131
Scientific Revolution 56, 148
scientists 34, 39, 120–23, 126–29, 131–33; career 146; ethical 129; pioneering 128
"settler colonial studies" 68
"settler colonialism" xi, xiii, 67–94
"settler grammars" 89–90
settlers 70–72, 74, 77, 79, 84
Siegfried, Matt 91
slave owners 96, 98, 100–101
slavery 100–104, 111
slaves 100–101, 103
small farmers 74, 100, 164–65; see also farmers
Smith, Douglass 127, 151
Smith, Mick 61
Snauwaert, Dale 8
social benefits 28
social problems 114, 169
society 5, 7, 25, 27, 33, 53, 71, 79, 102–3, 123–24, 132, 143; agricultural 54–55; exploitive 2; fractured 102; individualistic 122; modern consumer 44, 48, 138; southern 99; technologically-advanced 118
Solnit, Rebecca 114
space 3, 6, 14, 33, 81, 148, 158; empty 101; relational 51–52
state governments 170

Stegner, Wallace 10
STEM xiv, 117–33
stewardship 34, 110, 115, 127, 130, 159; good land 159; sensible subsistence-based land 34
stories xi, 35–37, 39–40, 44–46, 50–51, 57–58, 74–75, 79–80, 92–93, 98–100, 128–30, 154, 156–58, 165–66; better 92; Patowatomi 129; short 27, 75, 140; telling 140
students xv, 7, 18–19, 63–65, 67–68, 89–93, 96–97, 111–13, 124–25, 128–29, 148–52, 166, 169–70, 172–75; elementary 124; groups of 91; high school 28; non-degree 92; North Dakota 67; outcomes 148, 150, 152; teaching of 172; university 129; white 97, 115
sustainable communities xi, 25, 152, 170
systems 2, 4–5, 14–15, 27, 35–36, 47, 50–53, 56–58, 86–87, 92, 114–15, 132, 137–39, 146; complex 44, 149; educational 124, 147; enduring 99; industrialized 166; larger 145, 150; modern 89; new 73; psychological 47, 115; school 106; stabilizing 163

teachers xi, 3, 7, 19, 39, 63–65, 88, 90–93, 111, 123, 142, 159, 169, 174–75; best 126; as educators xi, 19, 90, 93, 175; first 154–55; primary 99, 171; prospective 175; science 123, 133; victimizing 170
teaching 11, 13, 19, 38–39, 64, 67, 87, 90, 93, 96, 113, 170–71, 175; indigenous 85; and learning 5–6, 8, 13, 47, 172, 174; of students 172; traditional 85
technology xiv, 3, 27, 34, 38, 106, 118, 120–21, 124, 140, 150, 164; ever-expanding 1, 34; industrial 38, 78, 106; new 23, 164
Theobald, Paul 8
Tolnay, Stewart 104
traditions 4–5, 50, 70, 76, 80, 82, 86, 91, 132, 171; ancient 16, 82; cultural 5, 91, 129; disciplinary 50; political 71; spiritual 93
transcultural concepts in nursing care 151
transformative connections 14, 49
trees 18, 20, 23–24, 37, 58–61, 71, 78, 142
trust 13, 28, 34, 39, 123, 128, 167, 170
Tuck, E. 70, 84–85, 88, 90–91

unemployment 106, 109
United States (post-World War II) 32

186 Index

Vaudrin-Charette, Julie 92
Veracini, Lorenzo 67–73
victims 71, 80, 164, 175
violence xiii, 1–2, 7–8, 11–12, 71–72, 74–75, 84–85, 88–89, 93, 96–98, 100, 102, 104–6, 109–11; culture of 8, 81; of displacement 71; of dispossession 68, 75
vision xii–xiii, 8, 47, 55, 108, 114, 117, 132, 142; alternative xiv–xv, 118; sustainable xv

war 33, 38, 156
wealth 20, 30, 38, 55, 60, 72, 76, 106, 108; accumulation 25; created 57; inherited 30; natural 39
white communities 78, 85, 92–93, 97–98, 101–2, 110
white families 101, 104, 106
white settlers 33, 67–68, 81–82, 87, 90
white supremacy 69, 96–97, 99
white workers 105
wholeness 65, 85, 87–88, 139, 141; condition of 139, 143; embodied 84; spiritual 111
The Wild Birds 75

Wilson, Kristi xiv, 118–19, 123, 132, 136
Wolfe, Patrick 69
Wolfmeyer, M. R. 118, 132
women 2, 11, 27, 45, 54–55, 73, 100–101, 103–4, 106, 148–49, 156, 160; black 98, 102; divided 54; healers 149; substituting hired 159; white 55, 102; workers 149
workplaces 105–6
world xiii–xv, 3–6, 14–18, 34–36, 40, 45–47, 52–54, 56–65, 87–88, 117–19, 131–33, 136–39, 144–46, 171–72; active 46; animal 85; biological 53; commodified 104; competitive 104; damaged 39; dangerous 1, 65; ethnocentric 126; extravagant 1; fallen 88; healthier 117, 127; mechanized 55; more-than-human 4–5, 13, 130; natural 5, 85–86, 129, 147; productive 175; rural 113; techno-scientific 118
World Health Organization 143
World War II 25, 28, 104, 157, 163
wounds 17, 40, 76, 98, 101, 115, 138; hidden xiv, 96–98; historical 98

Yakini, Malik 112–14
youth 109–10, 118, 123–24